The
MOFFATT
NEW TESTAMENT COMMENTARY

Based on *The New Translation* by the
REV. PROFESSOR JAMES MOFFATT, D.D. (OXON)
and under his Editorship

THE GENERAL EPISTLES

THE
GENERAL EPISTLES
JAMES, PETER, AND JUDAS

BY

JAMES MOFFATT
D.D. (Oxon), LL.D., D.Litt.
Washburn Professor of Church History
Union Theological Seminary
New York

London: HODDER AND STOUGHTON, Limited

FIRST PRINTED	.	.	.	.	.	.	1928
REPRINTED	.	.	.	.	.	.	1937
REPRINTED	.	.	.	.	.	.	1939
REPRINTED	.	.	.	.	.	.	1942
REPRINTED	.	.	.	.	.	.	1945
REPRINTED	.	.	.	.	.	.	1947

Made and Printed in Great Britain for
Hodder and Stoughton, Limited, London, by
Hazell, Watson & Viney, Ltd., London and Aylesbury

EDITOR'S PREFACE

EVERYMAN'S NEW TESTAMENT COMMENTARY

THE aim of this commentary is to bring out the religious meaning and message of the New Testament writings. To do this, it is needful to explain what they originally meant for the communities to which they were addressed in the first century, and this involves literary and historical criticism ; otherwise, our reading becomes unintelligent. But the New Testament was the literature of the early church, written out of faith and for faith, and no study of it is intelligent unless this aim is kept in mind. It is literature written for a religious purpose. ' These are written that ye might believe that Jesus is the Christ, the Son of God.' That is the real object of the New Testament, that Christians might believe this better, in the light of contemporary life with its intellectual and moral problems. So with any commentary upon it. Everything ought to be subordinated to the aim of elucidating the religious content, of showing how the faith was held in such and such a way by the first Christians, and of making clear what that faith was and is.

The idea of the commentary arose from a repeated demand to have my New Testament translation explained ; which accounts for the fact that this translation has been adopted as a convenient basis for the commentary. But the contri-

v

butors have been left free to take their own way. If they interpret the text differently, they have been at liberty to say so. Only, as a translation is in itself a partial commentary, it has often saved space to print the commentary and start from it.

As everyman has not Greek, the commentary has been written, as far as possible, for the Greekless. But it is based upon a first-hand study of the Greek original, and readers may rest assured that it represents a close reproduction of the original writers' meaning, or at anyrate of what we consider that to have been. Our common aim has been to enable everyman to-day to sit where these first Christians sat, to feel the impetus and inspiration of the Christian faith as it dawned upon the minds of the communities in the first century, and thereby to realize more vividly how new and lasting is the message which prompted these New Testament writings to take shape as they did. Sometimes people inside as well as outside the church make mistakes about the New Testament. They think it means this or that, whereas its words frequently mean something very different from what traditional associations suggest. The saving thing is to let the New Testament speak for itself. This is our desire and plan in the present commentary, to place each writing or group of writings in its original setting and allow their words to come home thus to the imagination and conscience of everyman to-day.

The general form of the commentary is to provide a running comment on the text, instead of one broken up into separate verses. But within these limits, each contributor has been left free. Thus, to comment on a gospel requires a method which is not precisely the same as that necessitated by commenting on an epistle. Still, the variety of treatment ought not to interfere with the uniformity of aim and form. Our principle has been that nothing mattered, so long as the reader could understand what he was reading in the text of the New Testament.

JAMES MOFFATT.

THE EPISTLE OF ST. JAMES

INTRODUCTION

THE epistle of St. James is a pastoral or homily addressed to Christians in general (see on i. 1). The author is a teacher of the church, who writes this tract for the special purpose of recalling Christians to the *agenda* of their faith. But who they were, and who he was, no tradition explains. Neither is there any internal evidence that enables us to place the homily, except within broad limits. It is fairly plain that the writer was acquainted with First Peter, and also with the teaching of the Pauline epistles; it is also more than probable that our tract was known to Hermas, who in the second century composed *The Shepherd*. If it could be shown that Clement of Rome, towards the end of the first century, used James, this would fix the date of James still further, as being not later than about A.D. 90. Provisionally it may be placed between about 70 and 90 (110).

It was addressed to churches which were still governed by presbyters; they and teachers are the only officials mentioned, and the lack of any reference to bishops proves that it was either written prior to the development marked by Ignatius, or composed for communities which were as yet unaffected by the change to a monarchical episcopate. One country which would answer to this is Egypt, and there are some minor indications that point to an Egyptian origin for James, e.g. the use of Alexandrian books like *Sirach* and *Wisdom*, and the fact that the first author to quote it is Origen.

I

Even Origen shows hesitation about citing it as canonical, and down to the fourth century its place in the N.T. canon was both limited and disputed. Thus Eusebius (*Hist. Eccles.* ii. 33) records the opinion that it was composed by James the brother of Jesus, but adds candidly, 'I must observe that it is considered spurious. Certainly not many writers of antiquity have mentioned it.' Evidently there was no tradition linking it to the apostle James ; indeed the western Church seems to have ignored it altogether until the second half of the fourth century. Jerome believed it was the work of the apostle James, but he records another, older view that it was pseudonymous, 'ab alio quodam sub nomine eius edita, licet paulatim tempore procedente obtinuerit auctoritatem.' There are still critics who maintain this theory, although it is not easy to see why a writer who desired to float his tract under the flag of the apostle James did not make more use of the apostolic name and prestige.

The alternative theories are (*a*) that it was really written by the apostle James, either before or after St. Paul, or (*b*) that it was composed by some teacher of the church called James, of whom we know nothing. The latter upon the whole meets the facts of the case adequately; it is no longer needful to discuss the hypothesis that the tract was originally a Jewish document, interpolated by a Christian in i. 1 and ii. 1, etc. The address of the letter, in i. 1, does not claim apostolic authorship, indeed; but as no homily could gain entrance into the canon apart from some claim to apostolic inspiration, it was natural, as it was fortunate, that the church came to read 'James, a servant of God and the Lord Jesus Christ,' as an allusion to James the apostle. In

2

this way the homily won a tardy and partial footing in the canon, which its own merits might not have secured.

And its merits are marked. James, as Zahn remarks, ' is a preacher who speaks like a prophet . . . in language which for forcibleness is without parallel in early Christian literature, excepting the discourses of Jesus.' The style is pithy and terse, often aphoristic ; in 108 verses there are no fewer than 54 imperatives. This corresponds to the spirit of the writer. He has met Christians who—

> In self-belyings, self-deceivings roll,
> And lose in action, passion, talk, the soul.

His arguments and appeals are directed against abuses of popular Christianity as it developed in circles where worldliness was infecting the faith, and where misconceptions of belief were prevalent. There is no problem of Jew and Christian present to his mind ; it is only a misinterpretation of passages like ii. 2 and 21 that has led to the idea that the tract was designed for Jewish Christians of the primitive period. The situation presupposed in the homily is that of oecumenical Christianity, exposed to the ordinary trials and temptations which met the later stages of the apostolic age.

The homily begins with five paragraphs loosely strung upon the thread of trial or temptation (i. 1–16), followed by reflections on the true word and worship (i. 17–27), which open up into a denunciation of some abuses in contemporary worship (ii. 1–13, iv. 11–12). Then comes an indignant refutation of a merely formal faith (ii. 14–26, iv. 17). But excess of words is as fatal as lack of deeds in religion, and James now proceeds to expose the vices of the tongue (iii. 1–12), closing with a passage on the true wisdom of life

3

(iii. 13–18), as opposed to the factiousness and worldliness which are rampant in the church (iv. 1–10). He then censures scheming traders (iv. 13–16) and oppressive landlords (v. 1–6), and exhorts the poor, patient Christians to be of good cheer (v. 7–11). Some scattered counsels (v. 12, 13, 14–18, 19–20) conclude the homily.

The tone of its advice and the very structure of its paragraphs recall the gnomic Hellenistic literature. For it is plain that the writer's mind is steeped in the teaching of *Sirach* and the *Wisdom of Solomon*, two products of Egyptian Judaism, which were much read by primitive Christians. *Sirach* may have been known to Jesus himself ; at anyrate, it was familiar to the authors of the gospels, and perhaps to Paul ; sometimes it even was included among the canonical scriptures. As for the *Wisdom of Solomon*, it was probably known to Paul. In the Muratorian canon of the second century (an Egyptian list of N.T. scriptures) it is 'accepted in the catholic church' along with the epistle of Judas and two of the Johannine epistles. The homily of James shows us on every page how instinctively the writer drew upon these books for his exposition of the Christian wisdom or practical philosophy of life.[1] He knows of course the other books of the Greek Bible, and some current writings which have not come down to us (see on iv. 5–6).

Twice in literature James has been robbed of his due. **Elijah was a man with a nature just like our own.** Pascal cites this in his *Pensées*. Thus ' dit saint Pierre,' he observes, ' pour désabuser les Chrétiens de cette fausse idée qui nous fait rejeter l'exemple des saints, comme disproportionné à

---

[1] See Professor H. A. A. Kennedy's paper in *The Expositor* (8th Series), vol. ii, pp. 39-52.

notre état. " C'étaient des saints, disons-nous, ce n'est pas comme nous." Que se passait-il donc alors ? Saint Athanase était un homme appelé Athanase, accusé de plusieurs crimes, condamné en tel et tel concile, pour tel et tel crime ; tous les évêques y consentaient, et le pape enfin.' Editors correct ' Pierre ' to ' Jacques,' but Pascal wrote ' Pierre ' by some lapse of memory. English literature has a similar instance in Tennyson's *Queen Mary*. Cranmer is on the scaffold, in the fourth act of the drama, and speaks his final words to the people :

> God grant me grace to glorify my God !
> And first I say it is a grievous case,
> Many so dote upon this bubble world,
> Whose colours in a moment break and fly,
> They care for nothing else. What saith St. John :
> ' Love of this world is hatred against God ' ?

But it was James, not St. John, who wrote, **The world's friendship means enmity to God.**

THE EPISTLE OF ST. JAMES

THE salutation or address is shorter than any other in the N.T. letters, closer to the form commonly employed in ordinary correspondence.

1 **James, a servant of God and the Lord Jesus Christ, to the twelve tribes in the Dispersion : greeting.**

Three features in this address are singular. (*a*) Paul calls himself or is called in the addresses of his epistles sometimes ' a servant of Jesus Christ ' (or ' of Christ Jesus '), or ' a servant of God,' while Judas calls himself ' a servant of Jesus Christ,' but **a servant of God and the Lord Jesus Christ** is unique. Any Christian might be termed **a servant of God**, but it was applied to outstanding personalities like prophets. Here **servant** has its general religious sense (see on Judas 1). It corresponded specially to **Lord,** as the Greek term *kurios* meant ' master ' of slaves or servants in ordinary usage. James does not describe God as the Father of Jesus Christ, but the collocation here and the phrase in ii. 1 imply a divine authority for Christ. (*b*) The readers are not described as **exiles of the Dispersion,** though **Dispersion** means what Peter (1 Peter i. 1) and other writers had popularized ; they are **the twelve tribes in the Dispersion,** a figurative term for catholic Christianity as the true Israel, living for the time being in a strange world, far from its true Fatherland. In the second century Hermas (*Similitudes* ix. 17) explains

6

that the twelve mountains in his vision 'are the twelve
tribes who inhabit the whole world, to whom the Son of
God was preached by the apostles'; otherwise the only
parallel to this interesting form of the metaphor is perhaps
the indirect allusion in Revelation vii. 4 f., xiv. 1. Literally
the twelve tribes was a synonym for Israel as a whole, which
could by no means be described as **in the Dispersion.** To
James of course it was a matter of supreme indifference what
had become of the original ten tribes, and he could therefore
coin this bold, double metaphor for the Christian community
throughout the world as the People of God. It is an archaic
metaphor, the first of several equally daring in his homily.
Apart from Peter's earlier usage it would be meaningless,
but unlike Peter he makes no further use of the figure. Nor
does he add a word about the readers' religious position ; he
simply closes (*c*) with a stereotyped epistolary term, **greeting**
(as in Acts xv. 23 and xxiii. 26). An ancient Greek letter
began with the name of the sender, the name of those to
whom the letter was sent, and this word (sends) **greeting** ;
early Christians usually turned it or any equivalent into a
prayer or pious wish, but James adheres to the formal word.

However, by playing on the word, he introduces his first
counsel (2–4) on bearing trials.

Greet it as pure joy, my brothers, when you come across 2
    any sort of trial, sure that the sterling temper of your 3
    faith produces endurance ; only, let your endurance be 4
    a finished product, so that you may be finished and com-
    plete, with never a defect.

Greeting and **greet as** (a reason for) **pure joy** are an attempt 2
to bring out the play on words in the original, where the

courteous *chairein* (greeting) is echoed by *charan* (joy); such a device was not uncommon in letters. The call to joy here is the first of several proofs that he was familiar with the Stoic ethics of the age. Thus Seneca tells Lucilius to avoid hoping (James never speaks of 'hope') and to 'make this your chief business, learn to rejoice. . . . Believe me, real joy is a serious thing' (Epp. xxiii.), for it has to meet experiences like poverty, temptation, trials, and death. James baptizes this moral joy into religion. The opening sentence of his homily resembles the teaching of 1 Peter i. 6–7, where sterling faith exposed to trials is compared to gold being tested by fire, though Peter means the passing trials of persecution, while James thinks of more general hardships. Both go back to what is said in Sirach ii. 1–5: 'My son, if you come forward to serve the Lord God, prepare yourself for trial . . . for gold is tested in fire, and men acceptable to God in the furnace of adversity' (adversity being the same word as James renders in ver. 9 by being lowered).

3 But James strikes an heroic note. He assumes, or rather he calls upon his readers to be sure to realize, that character is the chief concern; it is so for God and it must be so for His People, not outward calm or prosperity, but the inward ripening of the soul, the relationship of man to God. You will then rejoice, with a kind of stern cheerfulness or satisfaction, in whatever forwards that, however trying the dealings and discipline of God may be. For trial advances the interests of the soul, if it be bravely and faithfully undergone. But all depends on how we take it or think of it. James (vers. 13 f.) hastens to repudiate the idea that in trial God is deliberately trying to break down

human faith. The true view of **faith** is that **any sort of trial** (the same words as Peter uses for **various trials**), hardship, or misfortune of any kind or degree, is an opportunity for proving our mettle ; God's meaning in it is our training in courage and patience. Therefore, however unwelcome it may be to flesh and blood, it ought to be actually welcomed as a test and training of our powers.

The divine reward is explained later, in ver. 12 and in **v.** 10-11 ; here James indicates that the ordeal of **faith** brings out **endurance,** the staying power of life. This is not mentioned by Peter, though it had been by Paul in Romans v. 3 (' we triumph even in our troubles, knowing that trouble **produces endurance** ') ; but James uses this cardinal virtue of Jewish and Stoic ethic to rally his **brothers,** i.e. here as always in the homily his fellow-members of the church as a brotherhood (see on 1 Peter ii. 17). Only **trial** can prove what we are made of, whether we possess this supreme quality of stedfastness or constancy to our convictions. And **trial** does attest and ripens this, if we let the discipline attain its end, instead of rendering it incomplete by impatience or repining. It is a moral process which results normally in a **finished and 4 complete** character, faultless and perfect ; there is no immaturity about such constant souls, nothing inadequate or defective. Such is the prospect set before the stedfast Christian by James ; like Wordsworth's Happy Warrior, he is—

> More able to endure
> As more exposed to suffering and distress,

and through his endurance set on the way to be a ripened character, **with never a defect.**

This is the ideal. But in real life some may not always

9

be quite **sure** of themselves, able to maintain this exacting vision of what **trial** means or to carry it out in practical conduct. Besides, it requires a higher power than man's. **The sterling temper of faith** must depend upon God. James recollects teaching like that of Wisdom ix. 6 ('Even if one be a **finished character** in the eyes of men, should the **wisdom** that comes from thee be lacking, he shall be accounted nothing') and viii. 21 (' Perceiving that I could not enjoy **wisdom** unless God gave it, I besought the Lord and prayed to him '), and at once adds a word on prayer to God as one expression of genuine **faith,** during the process of discip·· line and development. ' I understand that you possess a mind blameless and unhesitating in endurance,' says Ignatius to the church at Tralles. This is the temper which James commends and demands in 5–8.

5 Whoever of you is defective in wisdom, let him ask God who
　　 gives to all men without question or reproach, and the
6 　 gift will be his. Only, let him ask in faith, with never
　　 a doubt ; for the doubtful man is like surge of the sea
7 　 whirled and swayed by the wind ; that man need not
8 　 imagine he will get anything from God, double-minded
　　 creature that he is, wavering at every turn.

5 　 **Wisdom** throughout this homily is the insight which enables a Christian to understand and practise and advance the religious life that is in keeping with the law of God. James does not use the term and idea in connexion with God's work in creation and providence, or as a medium of revelation, as the Wisdom literature does ; for him it is purely a human endowment, which comes from God but which operates in human life, i.e. in the common life of the Christian Church

(iii. 13–18). In the Wisdom literature goodness is considered as wisdom rather than as holiness. Under the breath of the Greek spirit it came to mean a life which interpreted the divine law as the rule for faith and morals ; the emphasis fell on moral and spiritual requirements rather than on ritual or dogmatic considerations, and this was what commended it to James, as he expounded the Christian religion. Wisdom denoted an absorbing interest in human relationships and responsibilities, actuated by humble reverence for God's law. This he found in the Wisdom literature, and he carried it over into the vocabulary of the church. Our English term wisdom is almost as inadequate a rendering of the Greek, as the Greek was of the original Hebrew word ; it calls up misleading associations of learning and expert science. But there is no better. What James means by it is the divine endowment of the soul by which the believing man recognizes and realizes that divine rule of life called righteousness (see i. 20, iii. 18), either in intercourse with others or, as here, in the management of his own conduct. Now, while God may inflict trial, He is ever ready to give wisdom, or, as the devout Alexandrian Philo had said, to give anything needful. God is called ' everlasting,' Philo argued, ' as being One who does not bestow favour at one time and withhold it at another, but is ever, uninterruptedly bestowing benefits' ; there is no giver like God, none so prompt and generous. Sirach warns men against the ugly habit of accompanying a gift with some contemptuous remark : ' After making a gift, never reproach the recipient' (xli. 22, also xviii. 15 f., xx. 14 f.) either with his poverty or with the sneer that it is not likely to be repaid in whole or part. God never so taunts our prayers. Nor does He ask questions before He gives **wisdom,** but gives outright. There is nothing ungracious, no thought of self, in His giving; God, as Tindal puts it vigorously, ' casteth no man in the teeth.' He bestows on us what we need without raising embarrassing questions about our deserts, and without a hard word, never harping on the benefit or treating prayer as presumption. There is no jealousy of this mean kind (see on iv. 5), no grudging or reluctance on His part.

6 **The prayer of faith** (see v. 15 f.) on man's part must be equally unhesitating. A **doubtful** or half-hearted **man** prays, but he is secretly not quite sure of God's goodwill and therefore is always **wavering** or fickle in his practical allegiance ; a man who is thus in two minds about the rule of life, now acting on faith and now living as though faith were insufficient, rising and falling constantly like sea-waves between reliance on God and sceptical uncertainty, divided between faith and the world (iii., iv. 4), must not dream of getting any prayer

7 answered. This half-and-half character is familiar in the Wisdom literature, where it is the opposite of **endurance.** Thus in Sirach ii. 12 f., ' Woe to the sinner who goes two ways, woe to the faint heart for it has no faith, woe to you who have lost your **endurance.**'

8 **Wavering** or unstable is often illustrated by a sea-simile. Thus the Greek orator Demosthenes (*De Falsa Legatione* 383) calls democracy **wavering** and compares its shifting, unreliable policy to winds at sea. It is perhaps an undesigned coincidence that the rebuke of Jesus to the disciples, ' Where is your faith ? ' (in Luke viii. 24, 25) comes after the only other use of the Greek word for surge in the N.T. (' he checked the wind and the surf,' or surge). But James (here and **in**

iv. 8) introduced the word **wavering** to the vocabulary of Christianity. It suited his demand for the Christian life being all of a piece. Later, he returns to the reason why prayers are not heard by God; here his point is that the success of prayer depends on personal conduct, and that the one condition of having prayer answered unconditionally lies in single-mindedness.

Up to this point the line of thought is unbroken. Whenever you encounter **trials**, treat them as opportunities. ' Calamity is the occasion for valour,' said Seneca (*De Providentia* 4); ' great souls sometimes rejoice in adversities, much as brave soldiers rejoice in wars.' Christians, says James, always ought to meet troubles in this heroic spirit. But do not, he adds, shut up the lesson-book of **endurance** too soon, as though you had learned all the lessons God meant you to acquire; and recollect that as ' to know God is **complete** righteousness ' (Wisdom xv. 3), so this **wisdom** of true religion will be imparted freely to those who show by their undivided allegiance to God's purpose that they really hold this to be the sole concern in life. What follows (in 9–11) seems abrupt and isolated. But there is a thread of connexion, which is more than verbal, indicated in Sirach, where **wisdom** exalts the poor (' the wisdom of one **in low position raises** his head,' xi. 1), and where the warning, ' approach not the Lord with **double** heart,' is followed by, ' **raise** not yourself up, lest you fall and bring disgrace upon yourself, and the Lord cast you down **in your meeting** ' (same words as in James ii. 2). The paragraph is therefore a pendant loosely attached to what has been said in vers. 2–4, 5–8.

Let a brother of low position exult when he is raised; but let 9 one who is rich exult in being lowered; for the rich will 10

11   pass away *like the flower of the grass*—up comes the sun
with the scorching wind and *withers the grass, its flower
drops off*, and the splendour of it is ruined ; so shall the
rich fade away amid their pursuits.

9   When some man of obscure position, like the **poor man** in
ii. 2 f., not only attended a Christian meeting but received
the gospel, he **was raised** to high rank by his faith ; was he
not one of the pious **poor** whom God had **chosen to be rich in
faith** and heirs of the realm which he has promised to those
who love him ?   Well might he **exult** in his inward elevation,
however mean his social sphere in the world might be.
Though he may belong to the lower classes, **he** is not low in
the sight of God.   Far from it.   Therefore, however little he
may possess in the way of outward comforts and possessions,
let him be proud of what he has received from God.   This is
one way of reckoning the **trials** of life as **pure joy**, instead of
resenting them as though he were badly used by God as well
as by men.

But James has more to say about the opposite case of a
rich man who has become a Christian brother, perhaps
after visiting the church (ii. 2 f.), where at some meeting
he found himself 'wishing himself like to those more rich in
hope.'   The paradox for him is that he is to pride himself
on **being lowered,** i.e. in what from the worldly point of view
seems the humiliating position of membership in a poverty-
stricken brotherhood where wealth is of no account in the
sight of God, and where he has to associate with people the
majority of whom are socially inferior.   **Let him exult** in this,
for thereby he has learned the real values of life.   James does
not say that he loses his wealth, though he may have less as
he makes money honestly, pays better wages to his employees

14

(iv. 13 f., v. 1–6), or parts with much of it in charity (ii. 15 f.) ; the lowering of the rich brother is as inward as the raising of the poor brother. He is lowered from the false consideration and deference paid to him on account of his wealth, even (James indignantly remarks) by some Christians who ought to know better (ii. 2, 3) ; when he comes under the law of the gospel and humbly receives the word that regenerates, he no longer prides himself on his outward possessions.

And he is safer so, James adds. For **the rich** (i.e. the 10 wealthy man who is bound up with his wealth, the unconverted worldly man of property) is to meet a swift, complete doom. In v. 1–6 James describes this fate as applying to rapacious and luxurious landowners, but here he puts the same thought more generally, using a simile from the book of Isaiah (xl. 6) which Peter had employed (1 Peter i. 24) in a different connexion. Syrian peasants knew how shortlived the patches of **grass** 11 were, under the sirocco or **scorching wind** and blazing sun of a summer which made short work of the flowers and herbage. Such **splendour** does not last ; it fades and wilts. So with **the rich** (a generic singular in the original, as in v. 7) **amid their pursuits.** James uses for **pursuits** a term literally meaning 'journeys,' as **turn** in ver. 8 literally means 'way' ; the word denotes the fortunes and occupations of the rich, but it seems as if he were specially thinking of wealthy traders, who made their money by travelling and business (iv. 13–16). In any case he expects a speedy settlement of God with the worldly rich, as in v. 1–6. Let the converted **rich brother** rejoice that he has escaped such a fate, as well as that he has learned how humiliation, the humiliation of becoming a Christian, is no real humiliation but a source of profound joy and pride. Let him be proud to endure the shame of bearing the name of Christian which is reviled by his class, as once by himself perhaps (ii. 7), proud to be less rich than he was, for conscience' sake, proud to undergo the **trial** of enduring sneers and social persecution on account of the unfashionable faith which he now values more highly than any rank or money in the world.

James now adds another pendant, resuming the subject of **trial** (vers. 2 f.), but from another side. Some are depressed by trials, but others are stung by them into a resentment which voices itself in blame of God ; it is to this mood of self-justification that he addresses himself in the following paragraph (12–19*a*).

12 *Blessed* is *he who endures* under trial ; for when he has stood the test, he will gain the crown of life which is promised
13   to all who love Him. Let no one who is tried by temptation say, ' My temptation comes from God ' ; God is incapable
14   of being tempted by evil and he tempts no one. Everyone is tempted as he is beguiled and allured by his own desire ;
15   then Desire conceives and breeds Sin, while Sin matures
16   and gives birth to Death. Make no mistake about this,
17   my beloved brothers : all we are given is good, and all our endowments are faultless, descending from above, from the Father of the heavenly lights, who knows no change of rising and setting, who casts no shadow on the earth.
18   It was his own will that we should be born by the Word of the truth, to be a kind of first fruits among his creatures.
19   Be sure of that, my beloved brothers.

12   Blessed is he who endures is a reminiscence of the beatitude for the latter days in Daniel xii. 12, and is also eschatological ; the strain will soon be over (v. 7 f.), when fortitude is crowned

with life eternal from God. Endurance is a function and
proof of love or devotion to God ; to stand outward trial
loyally, without breaking down under it, is a test that proves
the sterling quality (ver. 3) of the religious life. And after
probation comes reward, as in the similar passage in 1 Peter
i. 6, 7, the reward of real or lasting life. The only other
reference to love for God is in ii. 5, where James speaks of the
pious poor inheriting the realm which God has promised to
those who love him ; both passages recall Wisdom v. 15, 16,
where 'the righteous live for ever, receiving the realm of
splendour' (the word used by James in ver. 11) 'and the
diadem of beauty from the Lord's hand,' the diadem, like
the crown (which is practically an equivalent), being associated
with royal or honourable position.

So much for trial cheerfully and courageously borne. But 13
hardship is apt to start questions in the mind ; it makes some
people think, and think unfairly about God, as if He were to
blame for the temptations to disloyalty stirred by trial. If
trial involves probation, does it mean that God puts temptation deliberately in the way of man, or that He tries him too
severely ? When outward hardship rouses some inward
impulse to give way, a man heavily tried by temptation may
seek to excuse his weakness in yielding by putting the responsibility upon God ; 'this temptation, which is too hard for
me, comes from God.' Paul had met a similar objection in
1 Corinthians x. 13, by arguing that God never makes life
too difficult for genuine faith. But James, as usual, deals
with the question in the world of thought suggested by
Sirach, where (xv. 11 f.) we read : 'Say not, It was owing to
the Lord that I fell away. . . . He deceived me.' Sirach's
reply is that a true view of God's nature rules out such a

complaint (how could God make a man commit sin, when He hates sin ?), and that freewill enables anyone to choose the right course. James also explains (a) that to tempt man would be inconsistent with God's nature, (b) and adds a word on the
13 psychology of temptation and sin. (a) God stands in no relation to temptation, passive or active. James coins a word for incapable of being tempted, which means that the divine nature is utterly unversed in temptation ; no one can tempt another to evil unless he himself has some experience (and, it is implied, enjoyment) in yielding to temptation. Marcus Aurelius put the same truth from the Stoic point of view, when he wrote (vi. 1) : ' The Reason (Logos) which rules the universe has no cause in itself for doing wrong, for it has no malice, nor does it do evil to anything, nor is anything harmed by it.' James, however, feels that he needs to say more about man's responsibility (b) than about God's innocence. He can use popular religious language about resisting the devil (iv. 7), but here he ignores Satan as a source of temptation, and like Sirach concentrates upon a man's **own**
14 desire or lust (as the word is rendered in 2 Peter i. 4). If this inward inclination is indulged, it breeds disastrous consequences, the result of **his own desire,** for which he is therefore responsible himself.

In the *Imitatio Christi* (i. 13) the rise of temptation is thus described : ' First there comes to mind a simple thought, then a strong imagination, afterwards delight and an evil movement and assent.' This corresponds to what James means by illicit desire, the imagination toying with a forbidden
15 idea, and then issuing in a decision of the will. The results of this embrace of evil are depicted graphically (Milton's famous expansion is in *Paradise Lost*, ii. 648 f.). James

18

does not enter into the question, debated in contemporary
rabbinic circles, as to how the evil desire or impulse in man
arose, and how it could be connected with the creation of
man in the likeness of God. As a practical religious teacher
he is content to urge that temptations rise in our own nature,
and that man, not God, is to blame for the presence of evil
desire, sin, and death in the universe. Death is thus the
mature or finished product (ver. 4) of sin. The wiles of evil
desire, that seduce us, are not due to some malign or imperfect
endowment of our being; that notion is a serious mistake, 16
for all we are given is good, and all our endowments are 17
faultless. This reads like a hexameter line, perhaps quoted
from some popular source; our faculties all come from a
God of absolute generosity and goodwill, who bestows nothing
except as a beneficent creator. Perhaps there is a side-
allusion to fatalism in the Father of the heavenly lights, as
the prevalent astrology ascribed the destinies of men to the
influence of the stars; 'we have a God who is the maker of
these luminaries, and our nature is swayed by Him, not by
them.' But any of the readers who had been born and bred
Jews would recollect the praise of God which prefaced the daily
Shema of piety: 'Blessed art Thou, O Lord, creator of the
luminaries.' James knew the traditional title of God as
the Father (i. 27, iii. 9), but he does not use it in describing
the new birth of Christians (ver. 18), and here he takes it as
an equivalent for Creator. However, the main thought is
that of the modern Christian hymn:

> Light of the world! for ever, ever shining,
> There is no change in Thee.
> Light of the world, undimming and unsetting!

James contrasts the periodic changes in luminaries like the

sun and the moon with the changeless God, unvarying in
His light shed on men, from whom **no shadow** of evil ever
falls on the world of human life. The powers He bestows
on us are, like Himself. free from anything low or uncertain
or dark ; no ' light that leads astray ' is ever ' light from
heaven,' and no providence that befalls Christians is designed
to upset or mislead them. Sirach, oddly enough, employs
the idea of the sun's changes to illustrate man's liability to
err, the very point which James is controverting : ' What is
brighter than the sun ? Yet even the sun fails. And how much
more man, with his inclination of flesh and blood ? ' (xvii. 31, i.e.
why wonder that poor man has sometimes darkened phases of
conduct ?). But the conception of James was familiar in Jewish
and ethnic circles. Thus the devout Philo (in his *Legum Allegor.*,
ii. 22) remarks that the only way in which one can believe
God is to learn that ' while all things change, He alone is
unchangeable.' Epictetus (i. 14. 10) observes : ' If the sun
can illuminate so large a part of the universe, leaving only
unilluminated what the earth's shadow covers, cannot He
who made the sun itself and causes it to revolve, perceive all
things ? ' The Greek words for **change** and casting a **shadow**
are both semi-astronomical terms, employed in a popular
sense to suggest the irregularities and defects of the **heavenly
lights,** as compared with their Maker. Whatever goes wrong
on earth, He is not to be blamed, as though He failed to
afford sufficient and undeviating light to men. Philo, in the
treatise just quoted (ii. 19), praises the true penitence involved
in the confession of Numbers xxi. 7 (' We have sinned,
because we have spoken against the Lord '), since usually,
' whenever the mind has sinned and departed from goodness,
it throws the blame upon things divine, attributing its own

change to God.' This is what James has in mind here. Any deviations in human conduct are due to man himself, not to some imperfection in the life we owe to Him or in the providence under which our ordeal is set. Changing the metaphor, to 18 prove that man is neither unfairly handicapped nor left to his unaided powers, he reiterates that the very object of our being is to reproduce God's nature. Doubt God? Why, He deliberately willed to make us His own choice offspring ; surely His high purpose in regenerating us proves that our faculties must be pure and perfect, as they are meant to contribute to this end? The **Word of the truth** as the regenerating medium had been already mentioned in 1 Peter i. 22 f., where Christians owe their faith or re-birth to the gospel message or revelation (see the note there). **The Word,** not the Wisdom, of God is for James the vital expression of His real purpose and life, as we have already seen. This preference for **the Word,** which is shared by the author of the Fourth Gospel, is deliberate ; for him it was rendered more easy by the fact that already in the Hellenistic theology of Egypt there had been a vague effort to think of some creative Word of God at work in the world of men, revealing and redeeming. At anyrate, this is James's equivalent for Paul's doctrine of ' grace,' a technical term which James never uses (see on iv. 6). When he wishes to emphasize the Christian truth of life beginning with God alone, of God's will underlying faith and fellowship, instead of speaking as Paul did about the Spirit (which again he never mentions), he chooses the language of birth into God's own life. Philo had sadly reflected (in his treatise *De Mutatione Nominum* 24), ' There are few whose ears are open to receive the divine words that teach us that it belongs to God alone to sow

21

and give birth to what is good.' James puts a deeper content into this doctrine of regeneration, as bound up with our faith in the Lord Jesus Christ (ii. 1), though he implies it instead of stating it. To God we owe our new, true life, to God's set purpose and to that alone; and—this is the implication which leads him to mention it—so He would be undoing His own work and defeating His own aim, were He to send temptation to us. Whenever man's lower desire is in question, there is a grim, ugly Birth (ver. 15); when God acts, there is a very different Birth and Breeding.

We have been **born** anew, James concludes, **to be a kind of first fruits among his creatures.** The Greek term *aparchê* might mean ' gift ' or ' sacrifice,' but not here; it is an archaic biblical phrase for ' the pick of creation,' Christians being the choicest product of the divine creative purpose in the world. Philo could speak of the Jews as being ' set apart from the entire human race as a kind of first fruits to their Maker and Father' (*De Spec. Leg.*, iv. 6), and James takes over the honour for Christians as the real ' twelve tribes ' of the Lord, in whom the divine purpose was to be realized in its choicest form. There is no allusion here to these Christians being the first of many to follow; it is the supreme honour of their position, the superlative rank of their relationship to God, not any primacy in order of succession, which is implied in **first fruits.** James does imply, of course, that they must live up to their exalted destiny **from above ;** he is about to urge this in his next paragraph. Here he mentions their privilege in order to prove the lofty character of the God to whom some were being tempted to do less than justice as they felt their own weakness under the trials of life. Judge His Fatherly character from His purpose **as** shown in His work, and you will recognize it is good. **Be sure of that,** my beloved brothers. And with this crisp, emphatic word he shuts the question up.

But the regenerating Word requires our co-operation : we have a duty towards the Word (19*b*–25), and our religion is not to be a religion of mere ' words ' (26, 27). This is the sum of the next paragraph.

Let everyone be quick to listen, slow to talk, slow to be angry— 19
    for human anger does not promote divine righteousness ; 20
    so clear away all the foul rank growth of malice, and make 21
    a soil of modesty for the Word which roots itself inwardly
    with power to save your souls. Act on the Word, instead 22
    of merely listening to it and deluding yourselves. For 23
    whoever listens and does nothing, is like a man who
    glances at his natural face in a mirror ; he glances at 24
    himself, goes off, and at once forgets what he was like.
    Whereas he who gazes into the faultless law of freedom 25
    and remains in that position, proving himself to be no
    forgetful listener but an active agent, he will be blessed in
    his activity. Whoever considers he is religious, and does 26
    not bridle his tongue, but deceives his own heart, his
    religion is futile. Pure, unsoiled religion in the judgment 27
    of God the Father means this : to care for orphans and
    widows in their trouble, and to keep oneself from the stain
    of the world.

The three opening counsels are common in ancient social 19 ethics, and the following sentences are strung more or less closely upon them. Anger or bad temper is the theme of 20, 21 ; to listen and do nothing more is the danger marked in 22–25 ; and talk suggests the final admonition of 26, 27.

23

The transition from the previous paragraph is through the double sense of the **Word** as seed, which is put clearly in I Peter i. 23–ii. I, a passage parallel to this. When James, like Peter, hastens to urge the moral and spiritual activities of Christians, he passes from the idea of the regenerating **Word** to the conception of the **Word** as seed which has to be cared for, if it is to thrive ; indeed, he develops the

20 metaphor more definitely than Peter. Give the divine seed **a clean soil.**

21 **Clear away** is the same word as that rendered in Peter **off with,** and both writers denounce virulent **malice,** though James does not contrast it with Christian love. **Human anger,** he begins, a man's animosity or irritation against his fellow-Christians, **does not promote** either in himself or in other people **divine righteousness, i.e.** the divine goodness and character, the devout life as lived under the scrutiny and standards of God, in fact the high purpose spoken of in ver. 18. He may be referring to the general sin of hot temper or sullen anger, which is so markedly branded in N.T. ethics, the sin of those who, like Pope's lady, are ' for ever in a passion or a prayer.' But he probably includes (as in iii. 14) sarcasm and angry argument on the part of earnest Christians, the anger which tried to justify itself as righteous indignation against offenders in the community, the mixture of personal animosity and religious zeal which discredits the faith, hasty wrath against those who differ from us in opinion, and so forth. ' All other hatred of sin which does not fill the heart with the softest, tenderest affections towards persons miserable in it, is the servant of sin, at the same time that it seems to be hating it,' says William Law in his *Serious Call.* This

24

is the foul rank growth of malice (see on 1 Peter ii. 1) which gives no chance to the saving, vital power of the Word. The soil for **the Word is modesty,** i.e. submissiveness to God and at the same time gentle consideration for one's fellow-men. The Greek term had acquired this range of meaning in the Wisdom literature, where it is synonymous with docile 'humility,' that is, with a religious attitude of receptivity towards God which manifests itself, in human relationships, ' in self-restraint and patience of temper, in thoughtful consideration in the presence of men, or, in matters of importance, in slowness to speak' (A. B. Davidson, *Biblical and Literary Essays,* p. 52). What James had said about human nature did not mean that it was faultless ; only as the divine **Word** was received humbly and allowed to **root itself** in good soil, cleansed from spitefulness and arrogance, could the saving work be accomplished, and Christians be **first fruits** for God.

The Greek term rendered 'engrafted' in the A.V. originally meant 'innate,' but this meaning is impossible here ; an innate or inborn Word cannot be received. James gave it the sense of 'engrafted' or **which roots itself inwardly,** that being the property of the divine revelation. There was an affinity between God's saving truth and the human nature ; the seed suited the soil. But the seed was not innate in the soil ; it entered into the soil, and had to be inwrought, as it were, or developed by a moral process. Here, as in ver. 18, James stresses the vital activity of the Word, even as he recalls the need for human activity, and this explains his application of the Greek term in an unusual sense.

Be quick to listen was a common ethical maxim which

applied to life in general; thus, to listen patiently to both sides of a case was better than to put in one's word hastily. But it specially denoted good listening to advice and instruction. James urged this, but he knew the danger of listening to the Word and doing no more. Jesus had put the warning against this peril in a parable of ancient house-building (Matthew vii. 24–27); here (22–25) the figure is different.

22 Merely to listen to the preaching and teaching of the gospel is self-delusion; it seems reverent, it makes one feel comfortable and safe; but you must act on the Word, James insists, otherwise your eager attention is a form of self-deception. A teacher or preacher may give an eloquent address on the gospel, or explain ably some O.T. prophecy about Christ, but when the sermon is done, it is not done; something remains to be done by the hearers in life, and if they content themselves with sentimental admiration or with enjoying the emotional or mental treat, they need not imagine that this is religion. It does not lead to any lasting benefit of real self-knowledge. The attention to the Word which does not make a man act upon it by doing something to his life, altering his real self in obedience to what he has heard, is no equivalent for religion, whatever people may think.

23 This is the point of the mirror-simile. Natural face is literally 'the face of his birth,' i.e. the face a man is born with. James uses the phrase to bring out the casual, superficial character of such religion. He is not necessarily censuring the man. A busy man cannot be thinking of his personal appearance; unless he is idle and conceited, he had better

24 forget what he looked like when he caught a casual glimpse of himself in a mirror, unless indeed he ought to have noticed some sign of disease or a mark of dirt on his face.

26

James may be merely taking a common illustration of how a passing glance or casual impression in life leads to no permanent or practical result. But his simile was not unfamiliar to ethics, though it was ethnic rather than Jewish. Moralists had actually advocated the use of a metal mirror as a means of self-discipline. Thus Socrates told young men to look at themselves in the mirror; if they were handsome, it would remind them that an ugly life was out of keeping with good looks; and if they were plain-looking, they might remind themselves that handsome actions did much to counteract any impression of facial ugliness. This is quoted sophistically by Apuleius (*Apologia* 14), as he defends himself against alleged conceit and magical predilections in his use of a mirror. Seneca (*Nat. Quaest.*, i. **17**. 4) similarly declares that mirrors were invented to enable men to know themselves, not simply their outward appearance but their moral needs; and that a bad life left ugly traces on the face, the sight of which in a mirror ought to be a warning. So James may well be hinting that the moral use of a mirror resembles the true, thoughtful use of listening to the Word.

> We see time's furrows in another's brow,
> And death entrenched, preparing his assault,
> How few themselves in that just mirror see!

Whereas in closely examining the divine Word—a more ' just **25** mirror ' than that which ought to reveal to us any physical change and decay in our own natures, we win eternal profit. He who gazes with concentrated attention on this Mirror of the Word and remains in that position perseveringly, thereby proves himself to be no forgetful hearer but an active agent (literally ' a doer of work '). How? The figure of the mirror is not quite adequate here; the truth is too large for the illustration. The best of men cannot always remain in front of a mirror, scrutinizing their defects. But the obvious point is that such attention is no mere superficial interest ; the man does something with what he has learned of his real self and duty, and acts upon the knowledge which he has thereby taken time and pains to acquire of the **law** imposed by the Word upon true hearers. Through his close care, as he keeps on looking at God's will for life, a moral obligation comes to bear upon his practical conduct, and in obedience to these deep and abiding impressions of the **law** he is **blessed.**

This is the second beatitude of James. The first was pronounced on the passive mood of life (ver. 12), but this is on the active. **The faultless** or perfect **law of freedom** means that the gospel revelation as a rule for life is, like all the endowments of God, **faultless** (ver. 17) ; there is none better ; it meets all the needs of life, and (this is the fine paradox) **it is a law of freedom,** by obeying which men are truly free, emancipated from their passions (see 2 Peter ii. 19 and 1 Peter ii. 16). Stoic moralists pled that only the wise man was free, obeying God, and devout Jews had claimed that the only real freedom was through obedience to the Mosaic law ; James claims all this for the moral and spiritual law as fulfilled and embodied in the Christian gospel (ii. 8 f.). What is in his mind as he speaks of **the law of freedom** becomes plain in ii. 12, where the expression is again used deliberately in connexion with lovingkindness. Here, too, this context is implied (see vers. 20–21 and 26–27) ; the gospel revelation of the Word binds us to a service of practical **love,** which is at once an impulse and an obligation. It is

28

in order to emphasize the truth that this service is both binding and spontaneous that he coins the striking phrase a law of freedom. 'Law' suggests something statutory and external; but, as a contemporary put it, 'the new law of our Lord Jesus Christ is free from any yoke of compulsion' (Barnabas ii. 6). The ethical hope of the age, in all quarters, was in the obedience of the inward life to the law of divine duty, expressed in some form or another, and James here puts this in terms of the Christian religion, as Jewish rabbis and Stoic teachers were trying to do in their own way around him.

Slow to talk suggests another form of self-deception, that **26** of the religious worshipper who **considers he is religious** because he attends service and listens to the Word, and yet **does not bridle his tongue.** This was a flagrant temptation of teachers in the church, and James returns to it in iii. 2 f. But it was not confined to teachers. He is not referring to the habit of using pious phrases as a substitute for real religion, as in ii. 15, 16. Nor does he merely mean talking about religion to excess, though the talkative person is liable to become self-confident and arrogant in pouring out his opinions. To **bridle the tongue** is to curb the impulse to express **malice** (ver. 21) or contempt in words. James is thinking of people in the religious world who let their tongues run away with them in spiteful and hasty criticism of their neighbours, or in acrimonious discussion. It may sound and seem very **religious** to denounce the errors and failings of fellow-Christians, and to let oneself go in indignation against those whose views or conduct may appear unsatisfactory. So, people think, they are serving God (see ver. 20). But such so-called **religion** is futile, it makes no appeal **to God the Father,** whose **judgment** of religion is very different. James employs a term for **religion** (as for **religious**) which commonly suggests the expression of religious faith in reverence and worship. He does not deny the place of public worship (see ii. **2**, v. **14**) or of religious observances, but he explains that in God's sight a **pure, unsoiled religion** expresses itself

27 in acts of charity and in chastity—the two features of early Christian ethics which impressed the contemporary world.

In Psalm lxviii. 5 God is called ' the father of orphans and the champion of widows,' but James need not be recalling this special allusion ; **orphans and widows** in ancient society were the typical and outstanding instances of those who needed aid. No provision was made for them. Hence private charity was called out on their behalf, and Jewish as well as early Christian writers repeatedly urge their claims. ' Be as a father to orphans and as a husband to their mother, and so shalt thou be a son of the Most High,' says Sirach (iv. **10**). To **care for** means to visit, i.e. to give personal service, and the thought is that expressed more fully in the trenchant passage on practical religion in Isaiah lviii. **2–12**, or in Matthew xxv. **34–40**, where the verb **care for** is rendered **visit**. In the *Apocalypse of Peter* (**15**) there is a Dantesque vision of the punishment in hell reserved for ' those who were rich and trusted in their riches and had no pity on orphans and widows, but neglected the commands of God ' ; but James does not confine the duty to the rich.

The second expression of true religion is personal purity, **the world** being used as in iv. **4** and 2 Peter i. **4**, ii. **20**, for the corrupting life of pagan society ; the term for ' unstained ' recurs in 2 Peter iii. **14** as **unspotted** ' from the contagion of the world's slow stain.' Perhaps James included the thought that to mix with the outside world, even in doing charitable actions, exposed one to the risk of moral contamination (the idea of Judas 23). In any case he implies that personal purity was not to be sought or gained by a selfish withdrawal from the common, kindly tasks of life. ' A white bird, she [his mother] told him once, looking at him gravely, a bird which he must carry in his bosom across a crowded public place—his own soul was like that ' (Pater, *Marius the Epicurean*, ch. 11). This suggests a fastidious, dainty avoidance of human contact. A twofold sensitiveness, to the need and suffering of others and to personal purity amid the contaminating risks of the age, both coarse and refined—such is the moral ideal of James for anyone who claims to be devout.

The thought of religion as worship, indeed as public worship, now suggests a word against another danger of religious services (ii. 1-4).

ii.

My brothers, as you believe in the Lord Jesus Christ, who is 1 the Glory, pay no servile regard to people. Suppose 2 there comes into your meeting a man who wears gold rings and handsome clothes, and also a poor man in dirty clothes ; if you attend to the wearer of the handsome 3 clothes and say to him, ' Sit here, this is a good place,' and tell the poor man, ' You can stand,' or ' Sit there at 4 my feet,' are you not drawing distinctions in your own minds and proving that you judge people with partiality ?

The Christian religion has hitherto been called **The Word** or **The Word** of truth or **The** faultless law of freedom ; here it is more explicitly belief in the Lord Jesus Christ, who is the divine Glory—a striking term for Christ as the full manifestation of the divine presence and majesty. The Jews called this the *shekinah* ; thus one contemporary rabbi (quoted in *Pirke Aboth* iii. 3) said that ' when two sit together and are occupied with the words of the Torah, the shekinah is among them.'

Belief in Christ is incompatible with any social favouritism. Yet it is combined with such **servile regard to** certain persons in public worship as James proceeds to describe in vivid words. As Christians had no church-buildings at this period,

2 their place of **meeting** was usually some large room in the house of a wealthy member or a hall hired for the purpose (Acts xix. 9), where outsiders were free to attend the ordinary services, that is, pagans or Jews who were interested in the new faith (1 Corinthians xiv. 16, 23–25). They were to be welcomed, but welcomed without any servility or snobbery. No unseemly deference or obsequious politeness to a rich

3 stranger at the expense of a shabbily dressed visitor ! **There** goes better with **sit at my feet** than with **you can stand,** in the direction for the poorer worshipper. The thought of such bad behaviour in a congregation rouses James to the first of his indignant questions. Does not this outward

4 behaviour prove that **you are drawing** invidious **distinctions** between people **in your own** minds and **that you judge people with partiality**—literally, that you use wrong criteria of judgment ? Favouritism was a characteristic vice of Oriental judges (e.g. Deuteronomy i. 17).

Instead of arguing that this is out of keeping with the character of God, who is ' no respecter of persons,' James declares that this truckling to the wealthy is contrary to the estimate of God (5–6*a*) ; besides, it is futile—you gain nothing by it (6*b*–7). Finally, it is a fatal breach of the Christian law (8–13, iv. 11–12). The two former arguments hold together closely.

Listen, my beloved brothers ; has not **God chosen the poor of** 5
this world to be rich in faith and to inherit the realm
which he has promised to those who love him ? Now 6
you insult the poor. Is it not the rich who lord it over
you and drag you to court ? Is it **not they who** scoff 7
at the noble Name you bear ?

Poor people have a rich calling from God. James, for 5
whom, as for some of the psalmists, ' poor ' is practically
synonymous with ' pious ' and ' rich ' with ' impious,' insists
that they are far more likely to become Christians than
the rich visitors to the congregational worship ; possibly he
recalled, though he does not quote, the beatitude of Jesus
on the poor, or a word like that preserved in Luke xii. 21.
Their inheritance in the next world is sure and ample (i. 12),
for these poor, shabbily dressed people, to whom you behave
so shabbily, belong to a class to which God has opened up
rich prospects ; you would do better to devote yourselves to
them than to wealthy, elegant outsiders who repay your
attentions by haling you **to court.** James knew cases like 6
those which occur in modern India, where rich Hindus will
bully and prosecute unjustly the poor pariahs who join the
Christian church. He was speaking of and to communities
which apparently were in the main composed of humbler-
class members, labourers or tenants, perhaps in debt to wealthy
pagans or Jews. **Lord it over you** seems to exclude the idea that
the hardships were due to religious persecution ; they were social
in origin, and justice in the East was apt to be in favour of
the rich, if they chose to take advantage of their influence
with legal authorities. Some might come to Christian
worship, but as a rule they derided the **Name of Christian,** 7

noble as it was. This may be an allusion to prosecution of Christians on the ground of their religion (as in 1 Peter ii. 12), but it includes more. Scurrilous abuse of Christians on account of their religious beliefs and practices went on, apart from direct interference with them ; indeed the persecutions at this period usually started from the mob, not from the upper classes.

The next paragraph is addressed to an objection which James anticipates (8 f.). ' Are you not making too much of this ? Is such social deference so very serious ? After all, it is only a single offence.' It is a sin, he replies ; indeed it is *the* sin of sins, for God's supreme Law is the law of brotherly love (8–13, iv. 11, 12).

8   If you really fufil the royal law laid down by scripture, *You*
9   *must love your neighbour as yourself,* well and good ; but if you pay servile regard to people, you commit a sin,
10   and the Law convicts you of transgression. For whoever obeys the whole of the Law and only makes a single slip,
11   is guilty of everything. He who said, *Do not commit adultery,* also said, *Do not kill.* Now if you do not commit adultery but if you kill, you have transgressed the Law.
12   Speak, act, as those who are to be judged by the law of
13   freedom ; for the judgment will be merciless to the man who has shown no mercy—whereas the merciful life will
iv.   triumph in the face of judgment. Do not defame one
11   another, brothers ; he who defames or judges his brother defames and judges the Law ; and if you judge the Law,
12   you pass sentence on it instead of obeying it. One alone is the legislator, who passes sentence ; it is He who is able to save and to destroy ; who are you, to judge your neighbour ?

34

Like Paul (Romans xiii. 8–10), James held that love to 8
fellow-Christians was the essence and summary of the moral
Law ; you cannot really fulfil it, if you behave as you are
doing. **As laid down by scripture** refers to Leviticus xix. 18,
i.e. in the Greek Bible used by Christians. He calls it **the
royal** or supreme **law,** as it was the law for the royal **realm**
(ver. 5), which the subjects of the King were to **obey** (see
iv. 11). Any **servile regard** paid to the rich, which involved 9
an unloving attitude towards the poor, is pronounced a
breach of this law. ' You shall not be partial to a poor
man, nor defer to a powerful man ' (Leviticus xix. 15), is the
strict injunction which precedes the Royal Law.

But James is now passing away from the special case of
invidious partiality with which he started, and dealing with
the general question of harshness inside the Christian community. The illustration of callous conduct towards a poor
visitor to the service is now dropped ; he takes broader
ground in attacking the unmerciful spirit, the censoriousness
and hard temper, of which such conduct is one expression.
' A sin perhaps, but only one breach of the Law,' is the plea 10
met (in vers. 10 and 11) by the argument that the Law is a
unity ; **a single slip** (the term rendered stumble in Romans
xi. 11, and slip in 2 Peter i. 10) or deliberate lapse makes
the offender **guilty of everything ;** you cannot pick and choose
in the requirements of the Law. People may desire to—

> Compound for sins they are inclined to,
> By damning those they have no mind to,

but by more than damning such offences ; they may com-
placently point to their freedom from one sin as condoning
some lapse in another direction, or hold that obedience to
certain primary laws is as good as obedience to the whole.

11 James selects as examples of this two precepts of the decalogue singled out by Jesus (in Matthew v. 21 f., 25 f.), and it would lend force to his argument if we could suppose that he had in mind Christ's interpretation of the sixth commandment, where the angry, unforgiving spirit is reckoned the essence of murder. If he was conscious of this, however, or of any other view (see on v. 6), he does not put it into words, though the next sentences show that for him the Law was the embodiment of the divine will summed up in the supreme ethical principle of love to one's neighbour ; the moral law of the O.T. runs up into this cardinal obligation as stated by Jesus, i.e. God's law as working inwardly on
12 the conscience of Christians, the law of freedom (as in i. 25), not an external code of statutes. Specific commands rise out of the central unity of the law of brotherly love, to which Christians owe obedience and by which at the end they shall be judged.

Two considerations are put forward. (*a*) The law of freedom is not laxity but a strict ethical rule of God, and we shall be judged by our adherence to its supreme principle of brotherly love or mercy, i.e. compassion for the sins and sufferings of our fellows. This had been already urged, in i. 20, 21 and 27. Jesus had demanded it from his followers ; one of his favourite quotations from the prophets had been, ' I care for mercy, not for sacrifice,' and he had made the cold, inhuman spirit that would not forgive or that ignored human need, the damning sin. James puts this truth dramati-
13 cally ; the judgment at the end will be merciless to the man who has shown no mercy. Which sums up the teaching of parables like those of Matthew xviii. 21–35 and Luke xvi. 19 f., or of Sirach xxviii. 1–7. In the positive encouragement, the

36

merciful life will triumph in the face of judgment, he personifies as usual ; it is a daring expression of the thought expressed elsewhere, e.g. in v. 20 and I John iv. 17–21, that much will be forgiven to a loving spirit. **Mercy** or (as in 1 Peter iv. 8) **love hides a host of** sins ; the life of brotherly love need not fear the judgment of God, for it has been true to the spirit and standards of Him who judges human life. This does not contradict what James has said about the unity of the Law, for brotherly love or mercy constitutes the essence of the Law ; in fulfilling it, James implies, all other offences such as immorality and murder are avoided.

The second consideration (*b*) is that the unbrotherly spirit is a piece of arrogant presumption towards the Law of God. At some early period the passage was misplaced ; its proper and original position is here, not in iv. 11, 12. It is terse and epigrammatic rather than lucid, but James seems to be developing his charge that the unbrotherly and censorious dare to judge people at all (ver. 4). The Greek verb *krinein* iv. could mean not only judge in the widest sense, but pass sentence 11 on, and James avails himself of this to demand that harsh, irresponsible judgments on one's fellow-Christians (such as Jesus forbade in Luke vi. 37) must be stopped, as being implicitly a criticism of the Law itself and (12) an infringement of God's prerogative.

The latter is plain, the former is not so clear at first. To defame one another is the sin of slander denounced in 1 Peter ii. 1, malicious insinuations and backbiting in the community ; but James associates it with censoriousness, the sharp, critical temper which dares to mount the tribunal and lay down the law for others, generally in a hard spirit and often hastily, without pausing to make allowances or to be generous. **The**

37

difficulty is to see how **he who** thus **defames or judges his brother defames or judges the Law,** unless it means either that such irresponsible fault-finding implies that the Law has to be supplemented by our verdicts (which would be a slander on it, an overt criticism of its adequacy), or that such a severe, unbrotherly attitude shows that we have misinterpreted the Law and so may be said to have **defamed** or slandered it, by failing to recognize that its fundamental truth for us is brotherly love. The former seems to underlie the charge, **you pass sentence on it,** by assuming this superiority to its rule. In any case, James holds that to **judge** the faults and defects of a neighbour or fellow-Christian censoriously is to insult the Law of God. Similarly in the *Testament of Gad* (iv. 1–3) we read, ' Beware of hatred, for it works lawlessness even against the Lord himself ; it will not listen to the words of His commands upon love to one's neighbour, and it sins against God. For, if a brother stumble, it is immediately eager to proclaim it to all men, and is eager for him to be judged and punished and put to death.' James declares that this temper reverses our true attitude towards the divine Law ; to act thus is to **pass sentence on it** (probably by taking matters into your own hands, as though it were not severe enough), whereas our one duty is to obey it (implying perhaps that this will occupy all our time and attention). Besides, 12 it is impertinent. Ours only to obey ; God's unshared prerogative is to pass sentence on human life. **Legislator** is used only here in the N.T. ; **able to save** recalls i. 21 ; **able to destroy** may be an echo of the warning of Jesus (preserved in Matthew x. 28), ' fear Him who is able to destroy both soul and body.'

> Who made the heart, 'tis He alone
> Decidedly can try us.

Who are you (the stern question comes, to which there **is**
no answer), **to judge your neighbour** and encroach thus **on**
the function of his God and yours ?

The next paragraph (ii. 14–26, iv. 17) is an equally pungent
criticism of the religious belief which failed to fulfil itself **in**
practical service and obedience. James states his thesis
(14–17), replies to an objection (18–20), clinches his argument
by proofs from scripture (21–25), and concludes by a couple
of general statements about the vital importance of practical
religion (26, iv. 17).   ii.

My brothers, what is the use of anyone declaring he has faith, 14
if he has no deeds to show ? Can his faith save him ? 15
Suppose some brother or sister is ill-clad and short of
daily food ; if any of you says to them, 'Depart in 16
peace ! Get warm, get food,' without supplying their
bodily needs, what use is that ? So faith, unless it has 17
deeds, is dead in itself.

Act on the Word, be an active agent, speak, act. James 14
has already touched this string ; he now strikes some resonant
chords from it. **Faith** for him is religious belief in the Christian
revelation, in the unity of God (ver. 19), in the divine Law **or**
Word, and in Jesus Christ (ii. 1). **What is the use of such a**
profession of faith, if it is belief and no more ? If a man
has no deeds to show, no moral character and conduct corresponding to his religious belief, **can his faith save him** before
the judgment of a God who is **merciless to the man who has**
shown no mercy in his life ?

> In deeds, in deeds He takes delight.

No pious sentiments or talk avail.

15 In 1 John iii. 17, 18 a similar vignette of heartless conduct
is drawn, but the sketch of James is more sharply etched.
If you coolly dismiss a shivering, starving fellow-Christian by
16 saying, '**Depart in peace** (good-bye), you had better get
warm and **get** some **food**,' what **use is that** kind of faith?
The truth that fine words need fine deeds to back them was
common. Thus one character in a play of Plautus (*Trinummus*
ii. 4. 38 f.) says, 'You have his good wishes'; whereupon
another observes sarcastically, '"Good wishes" is an empty
phrase unless the speaker does good deeds.' Movement and
action are the proof of life; thus any religious belief not
attended by **deeds**, by the practical action for which God
17 means it to be a vital impulse, is **dead** matter, **dead in itself,**
dead, as we might say, at the very root and heart of it, no
matter how voluble and orthodox it may be; it is inert, not
simply because it is hindered, but because it lacks power and
vitality. Epictetus (iii. 23. 27, 28) observes that a true philosopher like himself tells his hearers frankly their moral defects
and requirements; 'if the philosopher's address does not drive
this truth home, both speaker and speech are dead'—the
point being that an ethical address, however cultured and
finely phrased, is a dead thing, unless it produces a vital
change in character and conduct. This illustrates the use
of **dead** here. As high-sounding words and pious wishes
are unavailing, apart from practical beneficence, so is religious
belief apart from **deeds**. James uses **deeds** deliberately, as
their range is wider than beneficence; the two examples he
is going to cite from the O.T. were of actions inspired by
faith which had no direct relation to the important **duty**
of charity.

He now meets curtly an objection to his view (**18-20**).

Someone will object, 'And you claim to have faith!' Yes, 18
and I claim to have deeds as well; you show me your
faith without any deeds, and I will show you by my deeds
what faith is. You believe in one God? Well and good. 19
So do the devils, and they shudder. But will you under- 20
stand, you senseless fellow, that faith without deeds is
dead?

James overhears an objector retorting, 'And you claim to 18
have faith, you who talk so highly of deeds! What do you
know of religious belief?' The reply is that the two are a
unity; Yes, James answers his critic, 'I do claim to have
faith and I claim to have deeds as well—which is more than
you can do! I can show you by my deeds what faith is, the
genuine religious belief which always comes out in living
obedience to the will of God. (This is the equivalent in
James for Paul's word on faith active in love; both writers
are agreed that the first thing to do with faith is to live by
it.) But can you show me your faith without any deeds?
You cannot, he implies. All you can produce is a declaration or profession of faith, a mere statement. Let me cross-
examine you on it: You believe in one God? Well and 19
good; it is the fundamental article of the creed, this mono-
theism; but such religious belief, devoid of any deeds, lifts
you no higher than the devils or daemons. They believe in
one God too, James ironically adds (recalling an old Orphic
phrase, see on iii. 6), and they shudder; their faith is shown
by their terror, an emotion of self-interest, but that does not
save them!'

He does not pursue the subject further; with a touch of
scorn for the senseless, empty-headed defender of a purely 20
formal religious belief, he turns to show him two classical

examples of the **deeds** which demonstrate **what faith is.** The next paragraph (21–25) is a scriptural proof of the challenge just maintained.

21 When our father *Abraham offered his son Isaac on the altar,*
22   was he not justified by what he did? In his case, you see, faith co-operated with deeds, faith was completed by
23   deeds, and the scripture was fulfilled : *Abraham believed God, and this was counted to him as righteousness*—he
24   was called *God's friend.* You observe it is by what he does that a man is justified, not simply by what he believes.
25   So too with Rahab the harlot. Was she not justified by what she did, when she entertained the scouts and got them away by a different road?

21   Abraham is our father, the ancestor of all true Christians ; real believers are sons of Abraham. Paul had said this in a different connexion already (Galatians iii. 6, 7) : ' the real sons of Abraham are those who rely on faith,' for Abraham ' had faith in God, *and this was counted to him as righteousness,'* i.e. it was counted to his credit by God, as ground of acceptance ; in technical language, he was justified or saved by his faith. James draws another inference from the famous phrase in Genesis xv. 6. It had long ago been connected with the incident of the sacrifice of Isaac (Genesis xxii. 1–12) ; thus in 1 Maccabees ii. 52 the devout are bidden ' remember the deeds of our fathers. . . . Was not Abraham found faithful in temptation [i.e. in the trying ordeal of having to sacrifice or be ready to sacrifice Isaac] and it was counted to him as righteousness ? ' Clement of Rome (xxxi.) also cites the sacrifice of Isaac, as he asks, ' Why was our father Abraham blessed ? Was it not because he wrought righteous-

ness and truth through faith ? ' James also takes this as
the supreme manifestation of Abraham's faith. And note,
he urges, it was a deed. Abraham acted on his faith. Was
he not justified by what he did, not by a mere assertion
or profession of his belief in God ?   A telling proof that faith 22
and deeds are a unity. In his case—and James regards it
as typical and decisive—faith co-operated with deeds, faith
was completed by deeds, ripening in the exercise of obedience
to God.

In some early manuscripts of Genesis xviii. 17, God called 23
Abraham ' my friend ' ; at least the text is so quoted by
Philo, and to this tradition, rather than to the title as used
in Isaiah xli. 8 or 2 Chronicles xx. 7, James alludes, when he
adds, he was called God's friend.   This is by the way, however,
for James continues passionately to drive home his teaching ;
you observe (he is speaking now to his hearers in general, no 24
longer, as in ver. 22, to the supposed objector) it is by what
he does that a man is justified, not simply by what he believes.
Paul had argued that Abraham was justified by faith, not by
obedience to the Law ; but James knew nothing of deeds or
' works of the Law,' i.e. observance of the ritual and ceremonial
Law as constituting a claim for merit before God. The
notion that religious belief justified by itself arose out of a
misapprehension of Paul's antithesis between faith and works.
Whether James's readers were familiar with what Paul said,
or not, James himself is attacking either some ultra-Paulinists
or certain people who appealed to Paul's teaching about faith
as justifying a religious belief which did not need moral exercise.
Living and real faith, says Archdeacon Julius Hare (*Victory
of Faith*, p. 26), ' is a practical power ; nay, of all principles,
of all powers, by which man can be actuated, the most

practical ; so that when it does not show forth its life by good works, we may reasonably conclude that it is dead ; just as we infer that a body is dead, when it has ceased to move. Not that the works constitute the life of faith . . . any more than motion constitutes or imparts the life of the body. . . . On the contrary, it is from the living principle of faith that they must receive their life.' This is the idea of James (see vers. 17 and 26) ; it is also the idea of Paul, though he would have put it differently ; he would have called, indeed he did call, such moral actions **fruits of the Spirit** rather than **deeds,** even while he would have agreed heartily with James that no mere assent to religious truth had any saving power. But for James the expression of faith in deeds is also spontaneous. Deeds do not reinforce faith, they are or ought to be the outcome of that relation to the regenerating Word which implies submission of life to the royal law of love (ii. 8 f.). This is bound up with true faith in Jesus Christ. The argument of i. 17 f. was that Christians must let their divine nature or birth have free play within them, and the present argument puts the same truth from another side. For James the exercise of obedience to God or of brotherly love, which is the unforced fulfilment of the law of the Lord, springs out of a vital relation to that Law or Word—that is, out of faith rightly conceived. Or, as he puts it here, **what a man does** verifies and completes, as nothing else can do, **what he believes ;** his obedience to God is not the discharge of some additional obligation by means of which he makes up for something that mere faith in God has left undone, but the natural issue of what faith involved.

25   Like the author of Hebrews (xi. 17–19, 31), James cites

Rahab, a woman and a pagan, after Abraham ; harlot as she was, before her conversion, from his point of view, her conduct was another proof of religious belief prompting active effort. **She entertained the scouts** (in the tale of Joshua ii. 1-21). One early Christian writer observed that ' Rahab the harlot was saved on account of her faith and hospitality ' (Clem. Rom. xii.), but James is content to cite her actions as a proof that **she was justified by what she did ;** she believed in God, and evinced her faith by the trouble she took in receiving the scouts and assisting them to escape, at the risk of her own life. No mere belief, this ! You need not appeal to Abraham or Rahab in defence of your theory and practice of mere **faith as** enough !

Two final applications follow, one in ver. 26, which really is a sequel to ver. 24 (ver. 25 being a sort of afterthought), the other in iv. 17, which originally lay here.

For as the body without the breath of life is dead, so faith 26 is dead without deeds. Whoever, then, knows to do iv. what is right to do and does not do it, that is a sin for 17 him. ii.

Again, as in the previous paragraphs (17, 20), James 26 strikes at a dead faith, a religious belief which never gets beyond intellectual assent or emotions or talk. This has been explained on ver. 24. The second sentence clinches the whole argument of 14-26. Then, in view of what I have iv. urged, you cannot plead ignorance ; I have shown you **what 17 is right to do** with your faith, and any failure is therefore **a sin.** Sins of omission are not venial. ' Often he who does not do a certain thing does wrong, not simply he who actually does something ' (Marcus Aurelius, ix. 5). It is another

45

terse maxim of James, a warning winged against religious
knowledge that is satisfied with itself.

Sins of speech: the might and mischief of the human
tongue; this is the theme of iii. 1–5a, 5b–8, 9–12. James
had already mentioned the peril of talkativeness and un-
bridled speech (i. 19, 26), but he now deals vividly with the
general temptations of the tongue in social life. He believed,
as Sirach had said (v. 13), that 'a man's tongue is [responsible
for] his fall.' Words may be a substitute for true religion
(as in ii. 14), but here they are studied as explosions of bad
temper and passion.

iii.

1 My brothers, do not swell the ranks of the teachers; remember,
2   we teachers will be judged with special strictness. We
    all make many a slip, but whoever avoids slips of speech
    is a perfect man; he can bridle the whole of the body
3   as well as the tongue. We put bridles into the mouths
    of horses to make them obey us, and so, you see, we can
4   move the whole of their bodies. Look at ships, too;
    for all their size and speed under stiff winds, they are
    turned by a tiny rudder wherever the mind of the steersman
5a   chooses. So the tongue is a small member of the body,
    but it can boast of great exploits.

1 The churches addressed by James had teachers, of
whom he was one, as well as presbyters (v. 14). It was a
position of repute and prestige in the early church, and
evidently many felt called to this vocation, in which they
could exercise above all their powers of rhetoric and culture,
as they expounded the scriptures or exhorted the faithful
on the truths of the faith. James found that this depart-

ment of church-work had become extremely popular. Hence his warning about its serious responsibilities. God will judge us (ii. 12) on the last day with special strictness on account of our influence over others. The reference is not to erroneous doctrine but to the danger of talkativeness, of reckless statements, of frothy rhetoric, of abusive language, of misleading assertions, and the like. It is because the vocation of a Christian teacher or preacher was specially liable to this temptation that James starts from it to portray the perils of the tongue. Walter Bagehot once said of Cobden as an agitator that 'very rarely, if even ever in history,' had a man 'achieved so much by his words and yet spoken so little evil. There is hardly a word to be found, perhaps, which the recording angel would wish to blot out.' James **2** thinks a man might well be termed **perfect,** a finished character (it is the same adjective in Greek), if he could thus avoid the slips (see ii. 10 for these moral lapses) **of speech** to which **all,** teachers and taught alike, are prone, apart from other sources of sin. Indeed he seems for the moment to ignore Sirach's judgment ('Many a man makes a slip, unintentionally; indeed who has not sinned with his tongue?' xix. 16) and to assume that this can be done. Such a **perfect** character (the only safe person to become a teacher in the church), a man who can control his tongue, has self-command enough to control his entire **body.** This is an exaggeration; some of the most reticent men have by no means been able to control their sensual passions. But in his enthusiasm for the man who manages to control his unruly tongue, James declares that to **bridle** (i. 26) the tongue is to master **the 3 whole of the body,** the tongue being as effective as a bridle for horses or a rudder for ships, and proportionately as small. **4**

47

5a These were fairly common metaphors in ancient ethical writings. The uncommon touch comes at the close: **so the tongue,** small as it is, **can boast of great exploits.** Alas, they are often **great** disasters, the **exploits** of a mischievous force in human life ! For imperfect men suffer cruelly from this pernicious and untameable organ of the body, as James now proceeds to describe (5b–8).

5b **What a forest is set ablaze by a little spark of fire ! And**
6 **the tongue is a fire, the tongue proves a very world of mischief among our members, staining the whole of the body and setting fire to the round circle of existence with**
7 **a flame fed by hell. For while every kind of beast and bird, of creeping animals and creatures marine, is tame-**
8 **able and has been tamed by mankind, no man can tame the tongue—plague of disorder that it is, full of deadly venom !**

5b The forest-fire metaphor is familiar enough in ancient literature ; Euripides, in a fragment of his lost play on *Ino*, compares the incautious blabbing of a secret to a spark catching hold of a forest, but James probably means the spread of angry passions stirred by some ill-judged, angry
6 word. **Staining the body** recalls the phrase about the foul nature of **malice** in i. 21, but it breaks the unity of the metaphor. **The round circle of existence** is a rhetorical phrase like the ' orb of creation ' ; it belonged originally to the Orphic mysteries, where it meant technically the endless cycle or circle of death and rebirth. James uses it colloquially, as he had already recalled (ii. 19) another Orphic tag about God ' at whom **the devils shudder.**' Tindal renders it, ' **all** that we have of nature.' The sentence

heaps up burning words to brand the ruinous effects of a loose, malicious tongue. A flame fed by hell comes from Judaism ; hell renders the Greek term Gehenna, where the nether fires were supposed to burn. Reckless talk of this kind is simply hellish, as the spurious, quarrelsome wisdom is devilish (ver. 15). There is no taming this truculent, 8 disorderly (see ver. 16), poisonous thing, he exclaims, in a hyperbole like the opposite exclamation in ver. 2. The deadly venom of misrepresentation, of rancorous or slanderous speech, was a familiar O.T. figure, as in the psalm cited by Paul in Romans iii. 13 ; the popular belief was that the hissing, forked tongue of a serpent darted poison, and this suggested a comparison with the human tongue of Orientals who were singularly gifted in abuse and malignity of utterance. The wisdom-literature abounds with warnings against venomous and vicious speech, but this outburst of James suggests that he had suffered from the strife of tongues in the religious world. Somehow and somewhere he had fallen ' on evil days and evil tongues.' His language is more than picturesque ; it reads like a transcript of bitter experience.

In one wisdom-passage on burning words (Sirach xxviii. 12) the writer remarks, ' If you blow upon a spark it burns up, but if you spit upon it the spark is quenched ; and both come out of your mouth.' This resembles the idea of the closing words in 9–12.

With the tongue we bless the Lord and Father, and with the 9 tongue we curse men made *in God's likeness* ; blessing 10 and cursing stream from the same lips ! My brothers, 11 this ought not to be. Does a fountain pour out fresh water and brackish from the same hole ? Can a fig 12 tree, my brothers, bear olives? Or a vine, figs? No more can salt water yield fresh.

9 To be consistent we should bless not only God but our fellow-men as made in God's likeness. Sirach (xvii. 1–14) declares that God created men ' in his own likeness ' to praise Him, and also gave them ' a command concerning their neighbours ' (i.e. to love them). This ethical obligation, derived from Genesis i. 26, was a marked feature of Jewish moral teaching; some contemporary rabbis connected the command to love one's neighbour especially with the
10 creation of man in the likeness of God, arguing that any sin against man was an attack on the divine likeness. Such
11 is the ethical motive employed here by James. The other figures (in 11–12) are taken from Greek and Roman proverbial lore, to bring out the unnatural habit of using the same tongue for piety and rancorous abuse,
12 though the last words are paralleled by this phrase from a contemporary Jewish apocalypse (Fourth Esdras v. 9), where the writer, in depicting the monstrous phenomena that herald the End, declares, ' Salt waters shall be found in the sweet, friends shall attack one another suddenly.' The general thought tallies with the *Testament of Benjamin* (vi. 5) : ' The good mind has not two tongues, of blessing and cursing, of insulting and honouring, of quietness and confusion, of pretence and veracity.' The metaphors, however, picture life in the religious world of the day, where teachers and preachers uttered lofty sentiments and voiced spiritual truths before their congregations, and also gave way to bitterness in controversy, even cursing their opponents (see v. 12) or dull, slow hearers. Not that James confines

the sins of the tongue to the officials. Talk about religion among ordinary members of the church might be wholesome, but the same people were guilty of spitefulness and scandal in social intercourse, inflaming the passions of others by cruel, careless words or poisoning the mind by insinuations. As Burke wrote to his son, ' A very great part of the mischiefs that vex the world arises from words. People soon forget the meaning, but the impression and the passion remain.'

In the Wisdom literature (e.g. in Sirach xxiv. 30 f.) wisdom is compared often to a stream whose waters benefit the hearers. After the metaphors of 11 and 12, it was natural for James therefore to pass to a searching analysis of the true wisdom which teachers of the church especially should covet and possess. Any wisdom or religious culture which fostered such bitter talk and thoughts was a caricature. He had already mentioned wisdom in i. 5 ; now (13–18) he explains its characteristics and criteria.

Who among you is wise and learned ? Let him show by his 13 good conduct, with the modesty of wisdom, what his deeds are. But if you are cherishing bitter jealousy and 14 rivalry in your hearts, do not pride yourselves on that— and be false to the truth. That is not the wisdom which 15 comes down from above, it is an earthly wisdom, sensuous, devilish ; for wherever jealousy and rivalry exist, there 16 disorder reigns and every evil. The wisdom from above is 17 first of all pure, then peaceable, forbearing, conciliatory, full of mercy and wholesome fruit, unambiguous, straightforward ; and the peacemakers who sow in peace reap 18 righteousness.

'In all (modes of) wisdom there is fulfilment **of the Law,**
13 but to be **learned** in wickedness is not wisdom' (Sirach xix.
20, 21). The Greek term for **learned** (which only occurs
here in the N.T.) denotes a sage or expert. James is still
dealing with teachers or would-be teachers in the church.
Wisdom, in the sense already defined (on i. 5), was the badge
and banner of this class; like religious belief (ii. 14), it must
attest itself practically, in **good conduct** among fellow-Christians, and modestly. Words are not enough without **deeds,**
and the **deeds** of service are not to be done in any spirit of
passion or ostentation. The pursuit of opinions for opinion's
sake, the motive of emulation in the study of knowledge, the
plague of self-conceit which besets teachers and learned persons
both within and without the church, the demoralizing absorp-
tion in rhetoric about morals and religion which the deeper
spirits of the time, from Paul to Epictetus, denounced, and
above all, perhaps, the ambition and intrigues of religious
parties and party-leaders—these are the perils before the
mind of James in this paragraph.

The modesty (see i. 21) **of wisdom** is a paradox, till, as Paul
told the Corinthians (1 Corinthians viii. 1 f.), we understand
14 what true wisdom means. It is out of keeping with the temper
of **bitter jealousy and rivalry** (i.e. party-spirit, selfish ambition,
factiousness). **Do not pride yourselves on that,** on the intensity
and harsh zeal which lead to such unscrupulous partisanship,
and which are sometimes justified as loyalty **to the truth.** This
is really to **be false to the truth** (see on i. 18). The Greek verb
might mean to 'lay false claims to (the truth),' but the other
rendering preserves the profound thought that the **truth of**
Christianity cannot be put forward or defended truly except
in the Christian spirit; religious people may be extremely

provoking, and defeat their own ends by overbearing methods; right views and sound counsels may lose their effect if they are expressed by men who are self-seeking partisans or unscrupulous controversialists. Their so-called **wisdom** is no 15 divine endowment (i. 17) or revelation, but **earthly** (or, as Paul said, ' the wisdom of this world '). **Sensuous** may have the technical sense of Judas 19, or the broader sense of ' unspiritual ' (as Paul uses it in 1 Corinthians ii. 14). **Devilish** is the climax, as in ver. 6 ; malignant temper and strife, the restless spirit which disturbs and degrades human 16 life, is from below, utterly hostile to God. **Disorder** is a favourite term of the Stoics which James, like Paul (e.g. 2 Corinthians xii. 20), applies to the squabbles and disturbances of Christians in their fellowship, particularly in connexion with religious discussions and parties (see below, on ver. 18). True knowledge of religious truth is, to begin with, pure, i.e. ethically. The Greek term has no connexion with doctrinal orthodoxy ; James never enters into any question about the contents of the creed, he brings out the practical criteria of a genuine religious belief.

Wisdom originally and essentially was the knowledge of duties 17 and dangers in the moral life, as revealed in the law of God, and as this study was directed to practical ends, it involved practical qualities in those who professed to teach it. The bearing of **pure** here is best seen in the use made of the verb in iv. 8 or by Peter in 1 Peter i. 22 f. It suggests a life unsullied because it is inspired and influenced by God above, free from impure motives and methods, especially from aggressiveness and quarrelsomeness. **Peaceable** is the opposite of self-assertive ; any statement or application of religious truth leads to differences of opinion and difficulties in handling other people, where a convinced man is apt to be pugnacious or to insist upon his own way inconsiderately, without being **forbearing**, i.e. fair and reasonable in meeting opponents, whether they are reasonable or unreasonable. No brusqueness, no pugnacity! **Conciliatory** (only here in N.T.) is the opposite of stiff and unbending. Manning, wrote Newman, ' wishes me no ill, but he is determined to bend or to break all opposition. He has an iron will and resolves to have his own way.' **Full of mercy**—not of **deadly venom** (ver. 8)—is elucidated by what was said in ii. 8–13. **Wholesome fruit** recalls (see ver. 13) the truth that genuine Christian wisdom is to be a benefit to other people, furthering their health and strength. The Christian teacher or indeed anyone who is interested in the study and progress of religious truth, requires what T. H. Green called ' openings into that active life of charity in which Christian faith is most readily realized ' ; he needs it for his own sake, and others need his insight and aid there. Two negative adjectives end this sevenfold catalogue of qualities. **Unambiguous** never occurs elsewhere in the N.T. ; it means here ' free from ambiguity or uncertainty,' referring to the impression it makes upon others ; you must know what to make of any statement, instead of being left doubtful about its bearing or meaning. Teaching in fact is not to be equivocal or evasive, but **straightforward** (literally, free from hypocrisy or pretence). ' Say what you judge to be best, only say it in a friendly, modest, and **straightforward** manner ' (Marcus Aurelius, viii. 5), so that people know where they are and where you are in the matter (' I do not know,' Newman wrote once to Manning, ' whether I am on my head or my heels when I have active relations with you '). These two last words rule out this habit of using speech to half reveal

and half conceal the mind of the speaker, who has something
(as we say) at the back of his mind all the time ; any subtle
reserve or disingenuous dealing in Christian intercourse is
certain to create friction and misunderstanding. Whereas,
James means, the qualities he has just been praising make
for good feeling and mutual harmony in any community ;
peace of this kind is the one way of promoting right relations 18
with God (see on i. 20). The final clause which brings this
out is remarkable for its double emphasis on **peace ;**
teachers who do their work in the spirit which has just
been commended, to the exclusion of any selfish ends, are
peacemakers, not leaders who stir up strife by their pugnacity and stubbornness and thereby spoil the soil for any
real, religious growth (see i. 21). There is a similar phrase
in Hebrews xii. 11, where **an upright life** is the same as
righteousness here. The only activity which has any outcome in this divine direction is that of men purged from
any taint of self-interest or private ambition, which leads
to **bitter jealousy and rivalry,** since they are thinking more
of their own reputation and party than of the interests of
God. That means the reign of **disorder,** in which good
seed can neither be sown nor ripen. No **wholesome fruit**
or spiritual crop, James is urging, ever comes from quar-
relling and controversy ; to **sow in peace** is to instil and
apply the truth as the **royal law** of love, which can only
be done in the unselfish spirit of that law or wisdom.

‘ But how speak of peace to you,’ James tells his churches,
‘ you wrangling, worldly crew ? To your knees before
God ! ’ The thunder of this call to repentance rolls through
vers. 1–10. The first part is couched in the short, sharp
sentences of contemporary ethical treatises (1–6) ; **the**

second is thrown into the rhythmical style of an O.T. prophet (7–10).

iv.

1 Where do conflicts, where do wrangles come from, in your midst? Is it not from these passions of yours that war

2 among your members? You crave, and miss what you want; you envy and covet, but you cannot acquire : you wrangle and fight—you miss what you want because you

3 do not ask God for it; you do ask and you do not get it, because you ask with the wicked intention of spending it

4 on your pleasures. (Wanton creatures! do you not know that the world's friendship means enmity to God? Whoever, then, chooses to be the world's friend, turns enemy

5 to God. What, do you consider this is an idle word of scripture?—'He yearns jealously for the spirit he set

6 within us.') Yet *he gives grace* more and more : thus it is said,

> *The haughty God opposes,*
> *but to the humble he gives grace.*

1 'The body,' says Socrates in Plato's *Phaedo* (66), 'fills us with desires and cravings . . . it is nothing but the body with its passions that is the cause of conflicts and factions and wrangles'; he explains that the conflicts of war are invariably due to material cravings. James also finds that the feuds by which Christians were being torn are manifestations of something wrong within. But he is not referring to military wars. What are conflicts and wrangles? The latter in Greek could mean disputes or pitched battles over doctrine, and this would carry on the argument of the previous paragraph against the factions and quarrels of Christians, especially

Christian teachers and leaders. But he has more in mind than dissensions. The next four sections (iv. 1–10, 13–16, v. 1–6, 7–11) show that he has begun to handle what a modern would call the social problems of religion. All, poor and rich alike, peasants, traders, and landowners, wanted more than they had. Sometimes they had a right to it. Sometimes they wanted it for wrong ends. Sometimes they wanted it and sought it along wrong ways. The economic aspects do not appeal to James, however ; he does not raise the questions of commerce and property and wages. What occupies his mind as a Christian teacher is the moral aspect of the situation. Hence the **passions** and pleasures to be gratified must be more than the love of pre-eminence or conceit or any of the ugly desires to which the vocation of a teacher or preacher was specially liable. These may be included. But it is the wider craving for more of this world's goods that is responsible for Christians falling out with one another and clashing. Longinus writes sadly about the ruinous effects of 'those passions which in a sense garrison our present life, harrying it and plundering it' (*De Sublim.*, xliv.), especially the love of pleasure and that 'debasing' passion, the love of money. James, from the religious side, uses a similar military metaphor. **These passions of yours,** he says, **war among your members,** again (as in i. 14 f.), tracing the outward manifestations of evil to their inward source. **Your members** are the members of the body, where the human personality is organized for outward action. Paul had spoken of 'the law of sin in my members which wars against the law of my mind and makes me a prisoner' ; Peter spoke of 'the passions of the flesh that wage war on the soul' (1 Peter ii. 12). James does not say what they attack. He remarks that they operate in and through the bodily members. Worldly appetites and interests act through eye, hand, foot, and voice, for example; the emotions come to physical expression; it is in the body that they are rampant.

2 **Crave** is quite general; the rendering 'lust' is too narrow. There are legitimate cravings for outward things, and if people **miss** their objects of desire, it does not follow that this is because they are bad, and therefore withheld by God. James comes back to this in a minute. Meantime, in breathless haste, he turns to selfish cravings. The text is obscure, perhaps corrupt. At an early period one word at anyrate was misread by copyists. The traditional text read **kill** (*phoneuete*), which cannot by any reasonable interpretation yield a relevant meaning; after **kill, covet** is a hopeless anticlimax. Erasmus was the first to guess that the original word must have been **envy** (*phthoneuete*). Envying and coveting the possessions or position of others fail; **you cannot acquire** what you want. Why this was so, James does not explain. Perhaps these people had not power to carry out their insurgent demands for a larger share of outward goods. Still, they seethed with the longings of unsatisfied desire and envious greed. **You wrangle and fight,** doing your best to **acquire** this or that, under the sway of these imperious inward cravings.

3 Here the text is broken, or James breaks off. 'Try prayer to God,' is his next word. 'But we do pray.' 'Yes, but you pray with a selfish, worldly motive, which prevents your prayers being answered.' This is the second reason which James offers for unanswered prayer (the first being in i. 7, 8). **You** do ask God for something (say, some

more money), instead of trying to snatch it violently from the hands of a neighbour, **and yet you do not get it.** Why? **Because you ask with the wicked intention of spending it,** dissipating it, **on your pleasures,** on self-gratification. That proves you have secretly set your heart on the world, not on God ; if you ask Him for something which you mean to take **4** away and lavish on His rival, how can you expect Him to let you have your wish ? God looks to the intention of our prayers. He cannot bear to see us sharing our affection between Himself and the world ; He cares for us far too deeply and passionately to be content with a divided allegiance.

This is the drift of vers. 4 and 5, which are a sharp aside, suggested by the faithlessness implied in the perverted prayer of ver. 3. Some early scribes were puzzled by the abrupt **Wanton creatures** (literally, adulteresses), and put in ' adulterers,' to make it clear that the men of the church were being addressed as well as the women. But **wanton creatures** is, of course, figurative. In the O.T. the sin of forsaking the true God for idolatry was called ' adultery,' the nation being regarded as the wife of God. ' Thy Maker is thy Husband ' ; any apostasy is disloyalty to His love. James applies the same expression pungently to worldly Christians who have broken their baptismal vows to God, transferring their real interest and affection to the world ; he uses the feminine form deliberately, for one turn of special contempt and scorn in the ancient world was to call a community or group by some feminine equivalent. Thus Theopompus the Greek historian denounced the adherents of Philip by saying, ' They were called Friends (*hetairoi*) of Philip, but they were his mistresses (*hetairai*).'

The fifth verse is extremely obscure. James had hailed **5**

59

the pattern believer Abraham as **God's friend,** but instead of urging Christians here to merit that title by devotion to God alone he quotes a scripture passage which seems to describe God's jealous yearning for the human soul. Friendship with Him and with the world is impossible ; He cannot tolerate such a divided affection. You ask, But does He mind it so much ? Are you right in saying that to be on good terms with the world would be seriously resented by God ? ' Well, does He not set His heart on having us all for Himself ? ' That scripture is not idle or unmeaning.

For the third time James cites inspired scripture explicitly (ii. 8, 22). It is some unknown writing of the early church, which has not survived ; possibly it was the Book of Eldad and Modat, which underlies the allusion in ver. 8 (see Introduction). A glance at the text and margin of the English versions will show that the interpretations of this puzzling quotation turn on the point whether spirit is in the nominative or the accusative case. The latter is more likely. To yearn jealously is an echo of the daring O.T. anthropomorphism which emerged from the idea of the People as the Bride of their God, who had an exclusive right to their affections and who grudged the world any share of the love due to Himself. James tacitly rejected the Greek thought of the jealousy of God (see on i. 5), but he could the more readily use language of this kind, as Christians were for him those who love God, and this is the nearest approach he makes to the truth that God loves them ; he preferred to call God the Father, as in i. 17 and iii. 9, with special reference to creation, and so this quotation appeals to him with its allusion to the spirit or breath of life divine (ii. 26) which at creation God set within us. The inward life of man, instead of being abandoned to passions (ver. 1), ought to be surrendered to the original and intense love which throbs in God for the human soul so dear to Him, the soul He endows with such powers and faculties (i. 17). The seriousness of God's devotion is contrasted with the lack of seriousness shown by Christians who felt no scruple about using their religion in order to gratify their desires for the pleasant world around them.

Now James resumes the thought of ver. 3. All this pre- 6 occupation with worldly interests takes men away from the sphere in which God can freely and fully answer their prayers. Whatever is withheld, He never withholds **grace** any more than **wisdom** (i. 5) ; His favour and friendship are bestowed generously ; He never grudges that. To ask **grace** is to get it **more and more,** for His goodwill can be given to one without another being the poorer, and He loves to give (see on i. 5). **Grace** of course does not means for James what it meant for Paul ; he merely quotes a well-known text about **grace** from Proverbs (iii. 34), as Peter does (1 Peter v. 5), to remind his readers of the conditions required for receiving God's help and favour. No wonder they had failed to get what they asked, for they had been too self-reliant, given over to the **proud glory of life** which another writer traced to the spirit of the **world** (1 John ii. 16). Whereas only the **humble** can be helped and blessed. Here **humble** is a broader term than in i. 9 ; it is not social position, but the inward spirit of need and of reliance on God which is meant. **The humble** are those who are penitent and spiritual, who ask God for what they feel the deepest needs of life, who neither envy nor covet what their neighbours own, unlike the haughty or worldly who are so self-reliant that they give up prayer or attempt to use prayer coolly as a means

of furthering some private and personal end. This haughtiness is for James a religious, or rather an irreligious, temper
here ; it is not insolence to one's fellow-men but primarily
the preference of worldly prosperity to anything else. Such
friendship with **the world** means that one is on a footing of
hostility towards God, for it defies His will and despises His
purpose ; disguise it as one may, it is an implicit challenge
to God, James argues, a position so dangerous that it must
be abandoned entirely. Hence the pungent call to repentance
in 7–10.

7 Well then, submit yourselves to God :
　　resist the devil,
　　　and he will fly from you :
8　　draw near to God,
　　　and he will draw near to you.
　　Cleanse your hands, you sinners,
　　　and purify your hearts, you double-minded.
9　　Lament and mourn and weep,
　　　let your laughter be turned to mourning,
　　　and your joy to depression ;
10　humble yourselves before the Lord,
　　　and then he will raise you up.

7　Submissiveness to God instead of any jaunty self-confidence ! Some circles in the early church were perplexed
by wondering if post-baptismal sins on the part of Christians
could be forgiven. Could any such sins be pardoned by God ?
If so, what sins, and how ? James, with practical good sense,
ignores this difficulty, and falls back simply on the duty and
blessing of repentance. Resist the devil in 1 Peter v. 9 means
resistance to the supreme temptation of apostasy, in a time

of persecution ; here it is more general, **the devil** being **the** representative and ruler of the world over against God. As sin gave **the devil a chance** (Ephesians iv. 27), the one way to escape was to break his hold over the soul by repentance, turning to God. James assumes that the human will has this power. As **the whole world lies in the power of the evil One** (1 John v. 19), man must challenge that power ; it is not irresistible. In the *Testament of Naphtali* (viii. 4 : ' If you do what is good, the devil will flee from you and the Lord will love you ') and of *Simeon* (iii. 5 : ' If a man flee to the Lord, the evil spirit runs away from him ') the same metaphor is employed, but James puts it more vigorously and hopefully, summoning his readers to check the evil spirit of self-will which had been allowed to set them against the will of God. In the Book of Eldad and Modat there was a text, ' The Lord is near to those who turn to him ' (quoted in Hermas, *Vis.* iii. 4), which James recalls in ver. 8. To **draw near to** 8 **God** involved a moral purification and consecration of life to His service, which is expressed in the usual metaphors of ritual worship ; the true worshipper who would enter the divine presence must have ' clean hands and a pure heart ' (Psalm xxiv. 4). **Hands** and **hearts** denote (as in Sirach xxxviii. 10 and elsewhere) the whole of life, outward and inward. **Purify your hearts** (the phrase used in 1 Peter i. 22) signifies the consecration of life to God for His ends, instead of the world's, and this throws light upon the meaning of **double-minded** here ; not, ' do this without any hesitation ' (as in i. 8), but ' **purify your hearts** from false compromise between the world and God ' (4, 5). When Jesus said, ' Blessed are the pure in heart,' he meant the single-minded or whole-hearted, whose devotion was free from

63

any alloy of worldly motive or self-interest. So here. The double-minded are sinners, though they may not think so. It is a sin to combine worldliness and religion or to divide one's interest between God and any rival. Instead of being contented and cheerful in your worldly self-satisfac-

9 tion, instead of your gaiety of spirits, mourn sadly over your sins, then ; James speaks in terms of the Hebrew prophets' language about the anguish of repentance, but lament after double-minded looks like another reminiscence of the Book of Eldad and Modat, if that be the scripture cited anonymously in Clem. Rom. xxiii. 3 (' Far be that scripture from us where He says, " Wretched [the adjective corresponding to the verb lament] are the double-minded " '). Depression (only here in the N.T.) is the downcast, subdued expression of those who are ashamed and sorry.

10 James closes with the same assurance as Peter (1 Peter v. 6), but Peter refers to the relief granted by God to loyal Christians who were being oppressed by persecutors, while James means that God will raise up the penitent who have humbled themselves by deploring their offences. The true penitent, like the taxgatherer in the parable of Jesus, does not venture ' to lift up even his eyes to heaven ' ; there is nothing uplifted about him now, till God's pardon raises him to his feet. What James has already said about God raising the humble Christian (in i. 9) is therefore slightly different.

Now for a special case of the pursuit of worldly gain which has just been exposed (1 f.) ! Perhaps this is a note of some address to a mixed audience (ii. 3 f.), but there may have been traders in the church whose methods proved that they left God out of account in their business plans (13–16).

Come now, you who say, 'To-day or to-morrow we are 13
    going to such and such a city ; we shall spend a year
    there trading and making money'—you who know 14
    nothing about to-morrow ! For what is your life ? You
    are but a mist, which appears for a little and then vanishes.
    You ought rather to say, 'If the Lord will, we shall 15
    live to do this or that.' But here you are, boasting in 16
    your proud pretensions ! All such boasting is wicked.

Both this and the next paragraph open with the brusque
Come now. These busy Greek traders have to make plans. 13
James does not censure such foresight ; what he denounces
is their habit of ignoring God. **Say** is of course 'say to
yourselves,' and the religious attitude of James is that of
Proverbs xxvii. 1 : '**Boast** not **about to-morrow,** for **you
never know** what a day will bring.' Life is far too uncertain 14
—for what ? For forgetting your dependence upon the
providence of God, James replies. **A** mist or cloud or vapour
is one of the commonest figures in ancient writers for human
life as transient. It is the impious in *Wisdom* (ii. 4) who
wail that their 'life will be scattered like mist before the
rays of the sun,' but James means the life of man in general.
Another of the quotations in *Clem. Rom.* (xvii.) which
may have come from the Book of Eldad and Modat (see
above, on ver. 8) is a plaint of Moses, 'I am as mist (or
steam) from a pot' ; the word for mist is the same as here,
and human beings, not life, are compared to it, so that there
is a possibility that James had read and recollected this.

If the Lord will had been used by Paul (in 1 Corinthians iv. 19 15
and Acts xviii. 21). It or some equivalent ('if the gods
will') was a familiar phrase of piety in pagan circles ; the

Jewish analogies are all later and derived. James recommends it as an antidote to presumption and an expression of humble submissiveness to God (6, 7). **We shall live to do this or that** is a characteristic touch ; a trader who humbly owns the will of God over him can hope to live and do his work ; as James himself says in another connexion, **he will** 16 **be blessed in his activity,** for faith is always practical. **But here you are** in point of fact **boasting** (see iii. 14) **in** (i.e. as you make) **your proud pretensions.** This last word means in 1 John ii. 16 **the proud glory** of life, but here it is overweening self-confidence, as in Wisdom v. 8, where the impious at the end lament, 'What was the profit of our **proud pretensions ?** ' **All such boasting,** when life is so precarious, is worse than absurd, it is **wicked,** a positive sin, a specimen of the ungodly haughtiness (ver. 6) of which men should repent.

Rich landowners are next attacked (v. 1-6) in a scathing outburst of indignation. The words sound like part of a sermon addressed to a mixed audience by James, an audience which included (see ii. 2) some wealthy proprietors. This outspoken teacher or preacher at anyrate does not toady to them. Indeed he holds out no prospect of repentance, nor does he summon them, as he did the traders, to mend their ways ; this is a threat of doom, in the strain of prophets like Amos and Malachi. It may have been intended to shake some by fear out of their selfishness and injustice, but there is no direct evidence to prove that these plutocrats were members of the church ; indeed the last word of the appalling denunciation indicates that it was their victims who belonged to the church, and that the cruelty was part of what Jews or pagans, who **lorded it over** humble Christian **workers,** made them suffer.

v.

Come now, you rich men, weep and shriek over your impending 1
   miseries !

You have been storing up treasure in the very last days ;   3*b*

your wealth lies rotting,   2

and your clothes are moth-eaten ;

your gold and silver lie rusted over,   3*a*

and their rust will be evidence against you,

it will devour your flesh like fire.

See, *the wages* of which you have defrauded the workmen who 4
   mowed your fields *call out,*

and the cries of the harvesters have *reached the ears of the*
   Lord of Hosts.

You have revelled on earth and plunged into dissipation ;   5

you have fattened yourselves as for the Day of slaughter ;

you have condemned, you have murdered the righteous— 6
   unresisting.

As in iv. 7–10, the style resembles the rhythmical oracles 1
of the Hebrew prophets, though similar threats of doom
against the impious wealthy were a feature of the Wisdom
literature and of apocalypses like Enoch. The nearest
approach to the tone of James is in Luke vi. 24 ('woe to you
rich folk, you get all the comforts you will ever get') and
xvi. 19–31 (the parable of the rich man and Lazarus). The
doom is depicted in highly coloured Jewish phrases, and
the same immediate prospect of the End is held out as a
threat to the rich and as a consolation to the oppressed
poor (in 7–11). Because it was imminent, there was no call
to demand social justice for the victims ; the whole order of
things was to be swept away immediately, and the thought

of any reform and redress on earth never entered the mind
of James. He tells the rich to shriek or howl with anguish
(in the demonstrative Oriental fashion of showing distress)
over their impending miseries on the day of doom.

3*b*　The next clause got displaced at an early period, and
must be recovered from ver. 3 ; you have had nothing better
to do, have you, on the verge of doom, than to store up
treasure ? Any eye can see it already ruined and proving

2　your ruin ! Raiment and coin were two chief forms of
property for a wealthy Oriental : clothes rot and get moth-
eaten (Matthew vi. 19, ' moth and rust corrode '), gold and
silver get rusted over (he means, tarnished). With the
prophetic eye James sees this rust bearing silent witness
against the wealthy for their rapacity in hoarding up their
money instead of giving it away.   In Sirach xxix. 10 we read,
' Lose your money to a brother and friend, and let it not
rust hidden beneath a stone.'   More than that, James adds,
with a Dantesque touch of horror, the rust will devour (or
corrode) your flesh like fire, you are so bound up with your
greedy gains (see on i. 11) ; your wealth perishes and you
perish with it and by it, eaten away in burning pain.

4　The second charge is fraudulent treatment of their farm-
labourers. The Mosaic code ordered the wages to be paid
every evening : ' You must pay him his wages by the day,
nor let the sun go down upon it (for the man is poor and he
wants his wages), lest he cries to the Eternal against you and
you incur guilt ' (Deuteronomy xxiv. 15).   But these farmers,
unlike the employer in the parable of Jesus (Matthew xx. 8),
kept back the pay of the labourers on their farms or estates ;
defrauded covers this injustice, though it need not be confined
to it. The cries of these harvesters, who have filled your

barns for you, **have reached the ears** of the great God, though you would not listen to their protests and appeals. James appositely recalls the language of Isaiah's similar denunciation of selfish landowners ; in the Greek version, which was **the** Bible of James and his readers (Isaiah v. 8–9), **the cries** of their victims **reached the ears of the Lord of hosts** (literally, as in the A.V., Sabaoth), the mighty Judge who avenges such crimes. James, however, makes the doom eschatological and immediate, though he does not hint here, as he does in the case of the two other charges (see vers. 3 and 5), how the imminent punishment was to be inflicted. One of the most relevant passages in the older literature on this charge is Tobit iv. 7–14, where the writer counsels a just and generous use of wealth. ' Give **alms** out of your possessions ungrudgingly . . . for thus **you store up** good **treasure** for yourself against the day of need ' (i.e. the **last** day, when account is taken). This is the point which, in 1–3, James implies these rapacious estate-owners have forgotten, though he does not share the Jewish view of alms as meritorious. Tobit continues, ' in haughty scorn (i.e. of other people) ruin lies and great disorder (the word used by James in iii. 16) . . . let not the wages of any of your workmen remain in your possession, but pay them at once . . . give some of your clothes to those who are ill-clad ' (see James ii. 15, v. 2).

So much for the second charge. The third is wanton luxury, with its social cruelty (5, 6). Your dissipated self-indulgence has been merely preparing you, like the fatted cattle in your stalls, for **the Day of slaughter**. The phrase was coined by Jeremiah (xii. 3), but in the later apocalypses it became eschatological. One of the woes against the

5

impious rich in Enoch (xciv. 8, 9) runs thus : ' Woe to you rich, for you have trusted in your riches, and from your riches you must be parted, because you have not remembered the Most High in the days of your riches. You have committed blasphemy and unrighteousness, and have become ready for the Day of slaughter, the day of darkness, the day of the last great judgment.' And this, says James grimly, is what you have been unconsciously pampering yourselves for ! You must pay with your lives for the wanton indulgence that has cost your victims their lives, the

6 victims of your social and judicial oppression. **Condemned and murdered** echoes what has been already said in ii. 6. Their luxury had been utterly unscrupulous, regardless of human life in its demands. Poor, pious people had been at their mercy, and had received no mercy. **Murdered** had a wider range in Jewish ethics familiar to James. Thus in Sirach xxxiv. (xxxi.) 24 f. ' a man who offers sacrifice which he has extorted from the moneys of the poor is as (bad as) a man who slays a son before his father's eyes. The poor have to live on scanty bread, and anyone who defrauds them of it is a man of blood. He **murders** his neighbour who deprives him of his living, and he who **defrauds** a hireling of his **wages** is a shedder of blood.' But, coming after **condemned,** it probably refers to judicial murders, against which the downtrodden victims could do nothing.

The **righteous** is singular in Greek, the generic singular representing the class of those who are poor because they are pious—a usage stereotyped in the Wisdom literature, which often handled the question. A passage which probably was in the mind of James is the famous determination of the ungodly in Wisdom ii. 10 f. :

' Let us lord it over the poor righteous man. · · ·
Let us lie in wait for the righteous. . . .
He calls the destiny of the righteous happy,
And boasts that God is his Father. . . .
Let us put him to the test with outrage and torture,
That we may find out if he is patient,
And judge his endurance of evil.
Let us condemn him to a shameful death.'

Unresisting (literally, ' and he does not resist ') is a vivid
climax ; the helplessness of the victims aggravates the guilt
of their oppressors. Like the defrauded labourers, these
poor folk had no means of redress, so far as earth was concerned, and they submitted without a murmur to the suffering.
But wait a little, James adds (7-11) ; heaven has not forgotten
you. ' Resist ' is the same word as oppose in iv. 6, and
there is an allusion to that passage taken in a sterner and
special sense ; it is not for the patient, pious Christians to
resist these overbearing tyrants of society, but to leave them
and themselves to the God who is soon to intervene. This
paves the way for the following counsel, which broadens
out into the general thought of all that Christians may have
to endure in ordinary life.

Be patient, then, brothers, till the arrival of the Lord. See 7
    how the farmer waits for the precious crop of the land,
    biding his time patiently till he gets *the autumn and the*
    spring rains ; have patience yourselves, strengthen your 8
    hearts, for the arrival of the Lord is at hand. Do not 9
    murmur against one another, brothers, lest you are 10
    judged ; look, the Judge is standing at the very door !

As an example of fortitude and endurance, brothers, take the prophets who have spoken in the name of the Lord.

11   See, we *call the stedfast happy*; you have heard of the stedfastness of Job, and you have seen the end of the Lord with him, seen that *the Lord is very compassionate and pitiful.*

7   A word of encouragement to Christians (**brothers**) who are still being badly treated in these and other ways. James stirs no class-feeling, e.g. of labourers against their unjust employers; leave the wealthy oppressors to God's imminent vengeance on their cruelty. The religious attitude is what concerns him. The rightful spirit for **the righteous** in the circumstances, with **the arrival of the Lord** (explained on 2 Peter i. 16, iii. 12) so sure and speedy, is patient endurance of grievances and hardships that are soon to be removed, a stedfast courage which is content to wait for God without complaining. **Bide** your **time** like a farmer awaiting **the autumn** (Deuteronomy xi. 14) **rain** in October and November and **the spring rain** so anxiously expected in March and April throughout Syria. The agriculturist was always anxious about these rains; they were of critical importance for his welfare. But the aptness of the figure here depends on the fact that, according to the O.T. interpretation (Deuteronomy xi. 8 f.), this special feature of the Palestinian climate suggested to the pious the providential intervention of God in man's affairs. The farmer had to wait for this rainfall twice in the year; but although he could do nothing to bring it, he did not lose heart, provided that

8 he was obeying the will of his God. So, James implies, with

9 your patient hope: something is coming of it in this order

of God. It is a failure of this patient self-control when the strain is allowed to make people irritable and censorious. In what has just been said about the need of patient endurance, James has embraced the rôle of endurance under the general trials of life which he had already touched in i. 2 f. So in warning Christians not to murmur or complain against one another, he is repeating the admonition of iv. 11-12, 14 f. against quarrelsomeness and carping judgments on one's fellow-members; this sharp, unbrotherly temper will be punished by the Lord. For, like Peter (1 Peter iv. 17 f.), James is alive to the ethical fact that God's judgment will take strict account of Christians' behaviour as well as of their persecutors. What? Falling out with one another, when the Judge is standing at the very door! Fretful, blaming one another, with God on the point of judging men for such breaches of His Law!

Then, from warning, James swings back to encouragement 10 (10, 11), appealing to his readers' recollections of the Bible. Jesus had held up the prophets also as an example to his hard-pressed disciples (Matthew v. 12), but it is strange that James does not appeal to the great example of Jesus himself, as other N.T. writers like Peter (1 Peter ii. 21) did. Why too does he describe the prophets as men who have spoken in the name of the Lord (i.e. by the authority of the Lord)? Not to indicate that even distinguished servants of God have to suffer, but to show that genuine, true prophets had to encounter hardship. Job was traditionally reckoned 11 as a prophet (Ezekiel xiv. 14, 20; Sirach xlix. 9), and his heroic endurance is specially recalled. No other N.T. writer mentions Job, but to James his story shows how the end of the Lord with patient sufferers justifies the ordeal;

those who hold on stedfastly under hardship find, as Job did, that—

> All is best, though we oft doubt
> What the unsearchable dispose
> Of Highest Wisdom brings about,
> And ever best found in the close.

This is the most permanent and profound thought of the whole passage ; patient endurance can sustain itself on the conviction that hardships are not meaningless, but that God has some end or purpose in them which He will accomplish, if sufferers only are brave enough to hold fast to Him (so i. 4). Job was sometimes impatient and fretful, but he never renounced God, and that was his stedfastness. We call the stedfast (those who endure) happy (or blessed). This is an echo of what he had said in i. 12, and stedfastness is the same term as that rendered endurance in i. 3, 4. The blissful conclusion of the story of Job is claimed as an illustration of Psalm ciii. 8, which is freely quoted from the Greek version as, the Lord is very compassionate and pitiful, the word for pitiful only occurring elsewhere in the N.T. in Luke vi. 36, where God is called merciful. The counsel on stedfast endurance thus closes on the note of history and experience as justifying patience.

> Endurance is the crowning quality,
> And patience all the passion of great souls.

James had offered an illustration of this from the farmer's attitude to the slow processes of nature, but he reaches deeper in appealing to what his friends had heard read aloud in the lessons from the O.T. during worship, proving that trial was no new thing in the religious life, and that no one who trusted in God had ever been confounded.

Against oaths (12).

**Above all, my brothers, never swear an oath, either by heaven 12
or by earth or by anything else ; let your ' yes ' be a
plain ' yes,' your ' no ' a plain ' no,' lest you incur
judgment.**

A puzzling fragment, on one sin of the tongue, which 12
James seems to regard as specially serious. **Above all** was
a formula which generally came in as a letter was drawing
to its end (see 1 Peter iv. 8), calling attention to something
particularly important ; but it is an anti-climax to put
forward a prohibition of cursing (see on iii. 10–12) and
swearing as more momentous than anything which has been
said in this epistle. Probably James jotted it down as an
after-thought, to emphasize the warning of ver. 9 ; in excitement or irritation there was a temptation to curse and swear
violently and profanely. Christians, James means, should
have more self-restraint ; they should also be so truthful
and straightforward that their bare word would suffice.
Let your sincerity come out in your speech, when you make a
statement or a promise, and in intercourse with one another
do not give way to frivolous oaths.

Jews had various forms of swearing ; for superstitious
reasons they avoided the name of God, but swore freely **by
heaven** or **by earth** or otherwise, though moralists had already
protested against the abuse of such oaths. Thus Sirach
(xxiii. 9 f.) includes loose swearing among the sins of the
tongue. ' Accustom not your mouth to an oath, nor make
a practice of naming the Holy One. . . . If a man swear
idly, he shall not be justified '—as James put it, he would
incur judgment at the divine tribunal (ver. 9, iv. 11, 12).
The disapproval of swearing was not confined to Judaism.

Thus Epictetus (*Enchiridion*, xxxiii.) writes, ' Refuse absolutely to swear an oath, if possible ; if it be not possible,
refuse as far as you can.' But James's word, couched in
Jewish terminology, is unqualified, probably because common
oaths were to him irreverent, or because they implied and
encouraged untruthfulness, or because he was protesting
against the casuistry which viewed only oaths, and only
some oaths, as binding ; an ungarnished **yes** or **no** was better
than any profuse asseveration backed by an oath. If he was
thinking of the courts before which Christians were sometimes dragged (ii. 6, v. 6), the prohibition might refer also
or entirely to judicial oaths, but this is less likely, either here
or in the curiously similar saying which is attributed to
Jesus in Matthew v. 34–37. It is possible that James had
this saying in mind, though not necessarily in its present
form.

Still dealing with the use of the tongue in the religious
life, he passes on to give some advice about prayer (13–18),
supplementing what he had already said in i. 5–7 and iv. 2–3.

13 Is anyone of you in trouble ? let him pray. Is anyone thriv-
14   ing ? let him sing praise. Is anyone ill ? let him summon
     the presbyters of the church, and let them pray over him,
15   anointing him with oil in the name of the Lord ; the
     prayer of faith will restore the sick man, and the Lord
     will raise him up ; even the sins he has committed will
16   be forgiven him. So confess your sins to one another
     and pray for one another, that you may be healed :
     the prayers of the righteous have a powerful effect.
17   Elijah was a man with a nature just like our own ; but
     he offered prayer that it might not rain, and for three

years and six **months it did not rain ; then he prayed 18 again, and the sky yielded rain, the earth brought forth its fruit.**

To be **in trouble** is the verb corresponding to the noun 13 underlying fortitude in ver. 10 ; prayer is what sustains the spirit when any suffering or hardship has to be bravely borne. Instead of murmuring **against one another** (ver. 9), or complaining peevishly, or breaking out into curses, pray to God. ' Trust in God with all your might,' Haydon wrote to Keats. ' From my soul I declare to you that I never applied for help, or for consolation, or for strength, but I found it. I always rose from my knees with a refreshed fury, an iron-clenched firmness, a crystal piety of feeling that sent me streaming on with a repulsive [repelling, he means] power against the troubles of life.'

James adds, in passing, to complete the picture : And let **anyone** who is **thriving,** in good spirits, **sing praise** to God. Prayer and song are our means of communicating with God. Praise is the sound which ought to rise from a cheerful, prosperous life. Elsewhere in the N.T. the word **to sing praise** refers to public worship, and always, if the usage in classical Greek and in the Greek O.T. be decisive, to songs with a musical accompaniment. But the use of a musical instrument is not bound up with the verb, and in the case of an individual is less likely.

One form of **trouble** is illness, and we now have a word on 14 the functions of prayer at the sick-bed. Social oppression is to be endured, but James believed that some trials could be removed, and among them illness. The sickness of a believer is not a merely physical trouble ; neither is it a purely indi-

77

vidual concern ; these are the two assumptions of his argument. Illness is somehow connected with sin, and the sick man has the right—perhaps we should rather say, he requires —to call in help from the church. The church or churches addressed by James had teachers, but, like the churches addressed by Peter (1 Peter v. 1 f.), they were ruled by **presbyters**, who would **pray over** the sick man as he lay in bed. 'Let the presbyters care for the sick,' Polykarp writes to the church of Philippi (*Ad Philipp.* vi.). Such intercessions were part of their pastoral care and duty. James had spoken about a man praying **in faith** for himself 15 (i. 5) ; he now mentions the presbyters offering a **prayer of faith** for others, which has the effect of restoring **the sick man** to physical health. **The Lord** who hears **the prayer of faith** answers it by raising him from his sick-bed (see Mark ii. 5). And more : **even the sins he has committed,** by which his illness was brought on, **will be forgiven him.** It is natural to assume that the presbyters had the right and power of giving him this assurance, or, as the later church would have said, of pronouncing absolution over him **in the name of the Lord.** This is not mentioned directly, but neither is the man's personal confession of sins, which is plainly implied (ver. 16). Or is the regaining of health the assurance of spiritual pardon ? It is so, among some Chinese Christians to-day, according to Mr. C. N. Moody (*The Mind of the Early Converts*, p. 19). 'It is an everyday occurrence to hear the remark, " My sins are very heavy." This almost invariably means, " My troubles are great " ; for converts believe that special affliction is a proof of special transgression, known or unknown,' and one of 'the main proofs of forgiveness' is deliverance, 'especially a signal deliverance from distress' or ' a remarkable cure in answer to prayer.' For James's age the prevalent belief that sickness was connected with sin is expressed in the *Testament of Simeon* (v. 9) : ' God brought upon me a disease of the liver [the seat of envious passion], and had not the prayers of my father Jacob succoured me, my spirit could hardly have failed to depart.' Here the penitence of the sick man is also assumed, and the cure is due to intercessory prayer. In *Sirach* (xxxviii. 9 f.) the doctor is mentioned. After highly commending the skill of physicians and the science of medicine, the author tells a sick man to do three things. First there is prayer and penitence. ' Pray to God, for he can heal you . . . cleanse your heart from all sin.' Then, offer the sacrifice prescribed in Leviticus ii. 1–3. Finally, call in the doctor, ' for God has created him ' ; the doctor also prays for a blessing on his diagnosis and treatment of the patient.

James describes a curious custom in the churches which he knew, of employing oil, not by the hands of a doctor but as a religious rite of therapeutic power. While prayer is the decisive factor in the cure, the presbyters are not only to pray over the patient but to smear his body with oil, pronouncing the sacred name of the Lord, i.e. ' Jesus,' which was supposed to have potent efficacy in working cures. Oil was a well-known medical remedy in the East, but this is a religious rite of unction, neither mere faith-healing nor purely medical therapeutic. The only other reference to the custom is in one tradition about a mission of the disciples during the lifetime of Jesus (Mark vi. 13), when they ' cast out a number of daemons and cured a number of sick people by anointing them with oil.' If this occasional practice

79

was anything more than a recourse to popular medicine on the part of the missioners, it may throw light on the isolated habit in vogue among these Christians to whom James writes. What interests him, however, is not the oil but **the prayer of faith,** and that as bearing on the forgiveness of sins. So he goes over the important items again, filling in the outline at one point. What follows is not a general statement about mutual confidence and intercessory prayer, but a reiteration : so (as physical health and forgiveness are together won through 16 prayer) **confess your sins to one another** (patients, e.g., to presbyters) **and pray for one another** (as presbyters could not do intelligently and truly, unless they were sure of the patient's penitence), **that you** who are sick **may be healed.** That is, the most vital matter is the personal confession of sins.

Now, in the primitive church this was openly done as a rule, before the congregation. The earliest manual of church practice prescribes : ' you must confess your sins in church, and not betake yourself to prayer with a bad conscience ' (*Didaché* iv.), and again that confession of sins must precede the communion service (xiv.). Clement of Rome (lvii.) tells the insubordinate members at Corinth that they must ' submit to the presbyters and be schooled to repentance.' The context of this admonition of James points to the same practice. To a sick person, unable to attend worship, the visiting presbyters represent the church ; they listen to the patient's confession, and after prayer for his recovery pronounce over him the assurance of God's pardon. James is speaking to presbyters and other members about their respective duties, when he says **Confess . . . pray.** It is in line with the functions assigned here to presbyters that in the English Prayer Book, before the communion service, the minister exhorts anyone disturbed in conscience to ' come to me or to some other discreet and learned minister of God's Word, and open his grief ; that by the ministry of God's holy Word he may receive the benefit of absolution.'

In this second word (ver. 16) on the subject James seems purposely to reverse the order of the first word in 14, 15, where in introducing the topic he had had to speak of the physical side specially. To remove any misconception, he adds his second word. **The prayer of faith** is everything in healing. A marvellous power, this, to ascribe to prayer ? Yes, but **the prayers of the righteous** (a generic singular as usual), i.e. of any true Christian like a presbyter who prays in unquestioning faith, are of extraordinary effect. He cites an O.T. illustration of this. Abraham, Rahab, 17 Job—and now Elijah as an example of efficacious prayer. In the tale of 1 Kings xvii.–xviii. Elijah does not pray either to bring on or to remove the drought, but Jewish tradition in reverence for his prestige as a prophet had ascribed these wonders to his petitions. Thus in the contemporary apocalypse of 4 Esdras (vii. 109), ' we find (i.e. in Scripture) that Elijah prayed for those who received the rain.' One might have expected that James would have found a more telling example in the prayer of the prophet which restored the dead son of the widow to life, but this would have been out of touch with his argument in 14–16 ; he is not thinking there of a patient dead or on the point of death. The O.T. said that Elijah announced or predicted the drought ; then Jewish tradition said that he procured it (this is asserted in Sirach xlviii. 3), and finally, by a not unnatural inference, that he had prayed for it.

Another trace of the Jewish tradition which James follows

in this account of Elijah is the change of the O.T. three
18 years into **three years and six months**. Three and a half,
being the half of the perfect number seven, had become
the period in years for disaster and distress, in apocalyptic
calculations (see Daniel xii. 7, followed in Revelation xi. 2,
where Elijah is one of the two prophets). This interpretation
rose before Christianity ; it is reflected in Luke iv. 25, 26.
On the other hand there is an implicit protest against the
exaggerated Jewish reverence for Elijah as almost super-
human. James calls him **a man with a nature just like our
own**. An example for us, some might say ? But he was a
saint far above our mortal level ; no wonder his prayers were
heard. The reply to this objection is that he was a human
being like ourselves, no more **righteous** than we are or than
we ought to be.

A last word of encouragement in the task of restoring
lapsed Christians (19, 20).

19 **My brothers, if any one of you goes astray from the truth
20 and someone brings him back, understand that he who
brings a sinner back from the error of his way saves his
soul from death and** *hides* **a host of** *sins*.

19 According to Polykarp (see above, on ver. 14), this was
the duty of the presbyters : ' let the presbyters be merciful
to all, **bringing back those who have gone astray**.' James
certainly regards it as one expression of the **mercy** which
God would reward at the end (ii. 13), but the appeal may be
general in its scope ; like Judas (22, 23) he probably thought
it the duty of every Christian to reclaim a brother who had
lapsed **from the truth** (i. 18), i.e. from the faith and obedience
of the gospel. Dealing with a sick, penitent Christian was

82

only one method, for not all sins led to physical suffering. Instead of being sharp and harsh with an erring brother, instead of giving him up as hopeless, a true Christian must endeavour to reclaim him, and a twofold motive for this difficult and gracious effort is suggested. It is 'twice blest,' like Shakespeare's quality of mercy, for a Christian who succeeds **saves his** (the sinner's) **soul from death,** which is the outcome of sin (i. 15) **and** also atones for a number of his own personal misdeeds. James quotes the same O.T. passage as Peter in I Peter iv. 8, and in the same sense. The unselfish Christian love which makes one feel responsible for an erring brother and moves one to **bring him back** to the church, **hides a host of** the good Christian's sins (for **we all make many a slip** in life); such forgiving, redeeming love to a brother will atone for a great deal. It is a good work which the loving God will allow to count in favour of the true Christian—exactly the truth put otherwise in ii. 13, or in another homily (2 Clement xv.), where the writer observes that if a man ' follows my advice, he will save both himself and me his counsellor ; for it is no small reward to **bring** to salvation an **erring,** perishing soul.'

So the homily ends—abruptly, even more abruptly than the First Epistle of John, without any closing word of farewell to the readers, abruptly, but not ineffectively. The Wisdom writings on which it is modelled end as suddenly. Indeed Sirach (li. 30) closes on a note which is not altogether unlike the encouraging note of James : ' do your work [i.e. of seeking the divine wisdom] before the time [i.e. of the final reckoning], and He will give you your reward at its time.' But James promises God's reward to those who do more than seek divine truth for themselves.

THE FIRST EPISTLE OF ST. PETER

INTRODUCTION

This beautiful epistle is addressed to Christians in Asia Minor who needed heartening and encouragement under the strain of a persecution-period. It was a time of tension, due to interference by the State authorities, who had obviously become suspicious of the Christian movement as immoral and treasonable. This set up, in some circles of the church, a feeling of perplexity and hesitation. Christians were suffering from the unwelcome attentions of Government officials, as well as from social annoyances, and they required to be rallied. The purpose of Peter is to recall them to the resources of their faith. Hence the emphasis upon hope, in its special aspect of hope in the near, messianic advent of Jesus Christ. But the responsibilities of hope are also urged ; there is a constant stress upon reverent submission to the will of God as well as upon the duty of living innocent and peaceable lives which will commend the faith to outsiders.

The epistle follows the method of most of the Pauline letters in concluding (iv. 7 f.) with some special admonitions to various classes in the church. Peter may have known some of the Pauline letters, such as Romans. But his type of thought is independent. ' St. Paul's influence scarcely carried him appreciably forward. . . . To compare First Peter with the Pauline epistles is like comparing Schubert

85

with Beethoven.' [1]   Here we miss the Pauline themes of
faith-mysticism, eschatology, and justification. What we
rather find is an original meditation by a primitive Christian
upon the issues of the Christian life as these were visible in
the light of the better messianism fostered by Jewish apocalyptic
piety.

So familiar and congenial is the vocabulary of this
apocalyptic religion to Peter, that he even speaks of Rome
as ' Babylon ' (v. 13).   He sends greetings to these provincial
churches from the church of the capital. They were predominantly
Christians who had been born pagans (i. 1, 14,
ii. 9, etc.), in Pontus, Galatia, Cappadocia, Asia, and Bithynia,
i.e. in Asia Minor north of the Taurus range. It does not
follow that Peter had evangelized these districts. Indeed,
Lightfoot infers, from the way in which Galatia is used in
the provincial sense, that he had not ; ' this is not unnatural
in one who was writing from a distance and perhaps
had never visited the district.' [2]   A glance at the map will
show that the districts are enumerated, for some unknown
reason, from N.E. to S. and W. Possibly the bearer of the
epistle was to follow this route. In any case, facilities of
travel were abundant, and copies of the missive could be
multiplied readily.

The bearer was Silvanus (v. 12), to whom Peter probably
dictated the epistle. How far Silvanus was responsible for
the Greek style of the message, it is impossible to say. He
was not a mere transcriber of what he heard, but neither is
it likely that the bulk of the homily was the deposit of

---

[1] A. H. McNeile, *New Testament Teaching in the Light of St. Paul's*,
p. 138.
[2] *The Epistle to the Galatians*, p. 19.

baptismal discourses by himself, mainly on the 34th Psalm, as has been recently suggested. It is possible that Peter left to him the task of putting his counsels into literary shape. Yet there is nothing in the homily which fairly tells against the Petrine authorship, once the error of regarding it as a product of secondary Paulinism is abandoned. The allusions to persecution harmonize with those reflected in the contemporary Gospel of Mark, behind which lie Peter's spirit and experience ; in these references there is no item which does not suit the seventh decade of the first century. The tone of the religious arguments accords at several points with that of Peter's speeches in the early chapters of Acts, which go back to a good tradition. There are numerous indications of an acquaintance with the primitive tradition of the sayings and sufferings of Jesus, and, once it is recognized that Peter did not set himself to compose a full statement of the Christian faith, there seems no crucial objection, so far as internal evidence goes, to the acceptance of the homily as it stands, viz. as a pastoral letter sent by Peter from Rome during the seventh decade of the first century.

Traces of it appear soon in early Christian literature, probably in Clement of Rome (towards the close of the first century), certainly in Polykarp of Asia Minor, and in Gaul (in the letter from the churches at Lyons and Vienne). It was also known to Papias at the beginning of the second century. It is possible to argue that traces of First Peter are to be found in Ephesians and James ; certainly there are some noticeable affinities with Hebrews, which was the work of a later teacher in the church. But First Peter differs from Hebrews, even while they breathe a common atmosphere. ' Such conceptions as faith (with a different shade of meaning

87

from that in Paul), cleansing through the blood of Christ, inheriting the promised blessing, antitypes of the Christian order as found in the Old Testament, the finality of Christ's sacrifice, must all have been current in the apostolic church. Their appearance in common in two epistles, whose authors are men of such different moulds, reminds us of the rich heritage of religious thought which belonged to the early Christian community, independently of Paul's epoch-making constructions.' [1]

[1] H. A. A. Kennedy, *The Theology of the Epistles*, pp. 173-174.

i.

PETER, an apostle of Jesus Christ, to the exiles of the Dis- 1 persion in Pontus, Galatia, Cappadocia, Asia, and Bithynia, whom God the Father has predestined and chosen, by 2 the consecration of the Spirit, to obey Jesus Christ and be sprinkled with his blood : may grace and peace be multiplied to you.

Apostle means a delegate with powers, one who represents 1 the person who has commissioned him. Whether Peter had founded (ver. 12), or even visited, any of these churches, we do not know ; he simply addresses them as **an apostle of Jesus Christ** (never using the term **Jesus** without adding **Christ**), perhaps to distinguish his position from that of the Jewish ' apostles ' who visited Jewish communities in the Dispersion. Similarly he takes over into the Christian vocabulary the technical Jewish phrase **exiles of the Dispersion** (see ii. 11, v. 9). But on his lips it has a fresh sense and scope. (*a*) The reassembling of the **exiles** is to be in heaven, not on earth in Palestine ; the thought is eschatological, as in Mark xiii. 27 and in the primitive eucharistic prayers of the *Didaché* (ix. 4 : ' As this broken bread was scattered upon the hills and collected to become one, so may thy church be collected from the ends of the earth into thy kingdom ' ; x. 5 : ' Remember thy church, Lord, to deliver her from all evil and perfect her in thy love, and collect her, made pure, from the four winds into thy kingdom which

89

thou hast prepared for her '). Then (*b*) there is no touch of pathos (' poor exiles '), but an exulting stress upon the privilege of membership in this community which is soon to be admitted to its proper glory and privileges in heaven. These Christians of pagan birth are heirs to all that Jews proudly claimed for themselves from God. (*c*) Hence the ethical obligation, which is worked out in ii. 11 f., of pure detachment from the vices of the pagan world ; those who have such a prospect must not disqualify themselves by careless lives.

This Christian position is further described, after the geographical address (on which see the Introduction), as 2 **whom God the Father has predestined and chosen** (literally, **chosen** according to the predestination of **God the Father**). Christians as the true People of God their Father enjoy the prerogative hitherto monopolized by Jews of being **chosen** by God (so ii. 9), whose will of love lies behind everything in life, behind their experience as well as behind the vocation of Jesus Christ (ver. 20). In one sense, the consciousness of being thus **chosen** by the Divine call and choice is what makes them feel **exiles**. **Chosen** refers to the Land where they are really at home but from which they are at present distant ; **exiles** refers to the land where they reside at present but in which they are not at home. The hope of ultimate salvation rests on the consciousness of being **predestined and chosen** by **God the Father,** who has taken up their lives into His eternal will and purpose for all time. Such is the basis and hope of Christianity for Peter as for Paul (Romans viii. 28 f.). The means and process of this Christian life is described as **by the consecration of the Spirit.** Jewish Christians had coined the term *hagiasmos* to express an idea for which the nearest pagan equivalent was *hagismos*, i.e. the hallowing of the People. **Consecration** means the stamping and setting apart for God of those who belong to Him. At baptism they were consecrated (1 Corinthians vi. 11) thus by the Spirit. For what differentiates Christians from the world is not any birth-tie with a nation but their possession and control by **the Spirit,** which marks them off from paganism (iv. 17-18). To belong to God is to obey Jesus Christ (see Matthew xxviii. 19-20), i.e. primarily to believe in Him (so i. 22) and to accept Him as the means of union between the soul and God (i. 21, ii. 25, iii. 18). Hence Peter proceeds to describe the object of Christianity as **to obey Jesus Christ.** 'Obey' is one of the deep words of this epistle; here, as is plain from a passage like ii. 8 or iv. 17, it is practically equivalent to ' believe.' **To obey Jesus Christ** involves moral conduct, but primarily faith. Indeed Peter instantly proceeds to explain the religious and redemptive setting of the term by adding **and to be sprinkled with his blood.** This is not the thought of 1 John i. 7, the continuous forgiveness needed by those who are trying **to obey Jesus Christ.** It is an O.T. allusion, familiar to his readers. In Exodus xxiv. 7 f., the story of the ratification of the covenant at Sinai, Moses ' took the book of the covenant and read it in the audience of the people, and they said, All that the Lord hath spoken will we do, and *be obedient.*' He then ' sprinkled the blood on the people, and said, Behold the blood of the covenant which the Lord hath made with you on the basis of these words,' i.e. their promise of obedience to the laws enacted. Half of the blood of the oxen had been previously sprinkled on the altar, as representing the Lord ; the rest is sprinkled then on the people, who are thereby bound to God. The blood ratifies the compact or bond between God and the people. Peter's point is that the new and true People of God owe obedience to Jesus Christ, not to any Jewish Law, as the authority to be followed; or, more precisely, that their entire relation to God depends upon the sacrificial death of Jesus Christ. But this belief in the significance of the death is merely mentioned, not elaborated.

The final greeting is couched in archaic terms, borrowed from Enoch (v. 7: 'to the elect there shall be light and grace and peace') and Daniel (iv. 1: 'peace be multiplied to you'). **Grace** suggests here as often in Paul the admission of pagan converts to the prerogatives and privileges of God's People; **peace** carries its full Semitic sense of bliss and well-being, due to the goodwill and free favour of God.

The subject of the homily is faith under suffering; it is addressed to Christians who are undergoing a hard time. But Peter begins upon the note of praise (i. 3–12). 'Remember first of all how much you have to thank God for. The right perspective for facing trouble lies in the attitude of grateful thanks to God for His gift of an eternal hope, His sure promises, His purpose for you, and His preservation of you, leading up to the final joy so soon to come; it is a position which the very prophets of old could only anticipate, and which the very angels envy.' This blessing, which in the original is one long sentence (3–12), has three phases, connected with God the Father (3–5), Jesus Christ (6–9), and the Spirit (10–12)—a trinitarian arrangement already suggested in ver. 2.

3 **Blessed be the God and Father of our Lord Jesus Christ!**
  By his great mercy we have been born anew to a life

of hope through the resurrection of Jesus Christ from
the dead, born to an unscathed, inviolate, unfading 4
inheritance ; it is kept in heaven for you, and the power 5
of God protects you by faith till you do inherit the salvation which is all ready to be revealed at the last hour.

Blessed be (the) God was a devout phrase of Jewish religion. 3
Peter, like Paul (2 Corinthians i. 3), expands it as a Christian
by adding **and Father of our Lord Jesus Christ.** What God
has done through Jesus Christ is the assurance of what He
will do for Christians. No need to fear any break or blank
in a life which springs from God's **great mercy,** i.e. His free,
loving choice (ii. 10). By this **we have been born anew.** Our 4
first birth ends in physical death ; this regeneration issues
in life eternal, in **a life of hope,** thanks to **the resurrection
of Jesus Christ.**

For Peter, God is the Father of Christians (i. 2, **17**) as well
as of Jesus, but he does not work out the sonship of Christians
as Paul had done, though he recognizes that sonship carries
with it an **inheritance** or patrimony (Galatians iv. 7). Christians
owe everything to God ; the initiative is with Him. Peter
shares this fundamental conviction, that the undeserved,
spontaneous favour of God is the beginning of everything
in the Christian experience. But he expresses this in new
terms ; for the first time ' regeneration ' enters the Christian
vocabulary. It was not an O.T. metaphor, but it would
be intelligible to Asiatic Christians who knew the mystery-
cults, where the hope of the initiates was often for a re-birth
to immortality through communion with the deity who had
passed through death. One devout initiate thus describes
himself : ' A man, son of A. and born of the mortal womb of

B. and of human sperm, to-day born again by Thee, one of so many myriads rendered immortal at this hour according to the good pleasure of God in His exceeding goodness.' This conviction, that there could be no salvation or immortality apart from regeneration, was widely spread. The cults endeavoured to meet this yearning for a new life through fellowship with some divine Saviour, generally some mythical hero-god or personification of a nature-force. What they offered through sacramental rites and ecstatic experiences on the part of the devotees, generally of a more or less crude nature, Christianity offered in its gospel of the risen Christ. Regeneration issues in a life of hope, i.e. (see on ver. 21) hope of life eternal secured and assured by Jesus Christ the risen Lord, which is further described as an unscathed (a synonym in contemporary Greek for 'immortal' or 'imperishable'), inviolate (unprofaned—see Isaiah xlvii. 6), unfading (see ver. 4) inheritance (such as children receive from their father). In Enoch (xxxix. 9, 10) the prophet exclaims, 'In these days I praised and extolled the name of the Lord of Spirits with blessings and praises, because He hath destined me for blessing and glory according to the good pleasure of the Lord of Spirits. For long time my eyes regarded that place [the predestined dwelling in heaven] and I blessed Him and praised Him, saying, "Blessed is He, and may He be blessed from the beginning and for evermore." ' This is the outline filled up in these verses by the Christian prophet, who now adds that this inheritance is all ready in heaven, kept for you from all eternity (such is the force of the perfect participle). The change from us to you is simply the preacher addressing his people ; in ver. 8 there is an obvious distinction between Peter and those Christians who had

94

never known Jesus on earth, but here he is not dissociating himself from their expectation. Yes, he adds, **and** (lest you **5** think you may never reach it through all this hardship) **the power of God protects you by faith** (as you are loyal, v. 6, 10) **till you do inherit the salvation** (literally, unto the salvation —see Romans i. 16) ; God stands between you and all that menaces your hopes or threatens your eternal welfare, as you rely on Him ; His power works in and for human faith. What is implied in faith is explained later (see vers. 7 and 9, 14, iii. 9, iv. 19, v. 7, 10). Peter meanwhile adds that **the salvation** (see ver. 9, iv. 18) is the final deliverance which issues in life eternal. So the messiah in Enoch (xlviii. 7) ' hath preserved the lot of the righteous, because they have hated and despised this world of unrighteousness,' their lot being called ' the heritage of faith ' (lviii. 5). On the other hand, the protection of the faithful here is entirely and directly the work of God ; Christianity drops the belief of Enoch (c. 5) in guardian angels appointed by God to protect them. The salvation is not merely secure, but soon to come, **ready** (see on iv. 5) **to be revealed at the last hour** after the imminent crisis of the judgment and the second Advent (iv. 5-7, 17-18). **Revealed** always implies something or someone already in existence. **At the last hour** is a Greek phrase which literally (*en kairô eschatô*) might mean, ' when things are at their worst ' ; classical writers used it thus, but the context of this epistle is too eschatological to permit any sense except a reference to the imminent end (iv. 7).

Such bliss endangered by your present hardships ? No, it is reached through them (6-9).

You will rejoice then, though for the passing moment you 6 may need to suffer various trials ; that is only to prove 7

your faith is sterling (far more precious than gold which
is perishable and yet is tested by fire), and it redounds
to your praise and glory and honour at the revelation of
Jesus Christ.

6   The contrast is between then (i.e. at the last hour) and
now, the passing moment of persecution. Peter speaks
elsewhere of a present heroic joy for Christians who bear
rough experiences in the right spirit (iv. 13), but here he is
thinking of the last day. ' I promise you, that will be a
day of joy, a thrilling moment (ver. 8), when you find your
faith ratified and rewarded ! ' In Greek the verb rendered
You will rejoice is a present with a quasi-future meaning,
and most of the early versions understood the word as a
future. The apostle's simple philosophy of suffering is that
(*a*) troubles are merely a temporary episode, (*b*) they do not
last long, for the end (iv. 17, v. 10) is near, (*c*) some may be
spared (may need) the ordeal, and, best of all (*d*), they
are not accidental, but designed to test and attest faith.
You may need to suffer various trials. Some of the acutest
pangs are caused by uncertainty whether God means anything
by allowing trials to befall us ; this mental suffering need
never trouble you, the apostle pleads. In *Samson Agonistes*
(667–670) the Chorus cry :

> ' God of our fathers ! what is man,
> That thou toward him with hand so various—
> Or might I say contrarious ?—
> Temper'st thy providence through his short course ? '

No, Peter would reply, ' You must not say " contrarious.' "
7 The variety of trials which beset Christians is permitted
only to prove something ; persecution shows, as nothing else
can, whether Christians are loyal to their convictions. Trouble

is part of your discipline, to show that **your faith is sterling,** not mere emotion or words. The comparison of discipline to the furnace in which gold metal was tried, to bring out the sound ore, was common in antiquity; Peter's pagan contemporary Seneca wrote in his treatise *De Providentia* (5), *ignis aurum probat, miseria fortes viros.* And it redounds to your own credit, when account is taken of life at the end. Peter speaks later of how the loyalty of Christians redounds to the honour of God (ii. 12, and iv. 11, 16); here, of the **praise** or moral approbation conveyed in the 'Well done, good and faithful servant.' **Glory and honour** are eschatological, as in Romans ii. 7, 10. The signal honour paid by God to the loyal comes at the close of their ordeal, when the world-order with its malign attacks upon the faithful is brought to an end **at the revelation of Jesus Christ.** This revelation of Jesus Christ in glorious authority is never far from the mind of the apostle (see ver. 13, iv. 13, and v. 4); he thinks of it not as the issue and reward of Christ's own sufferings but rather as the supreme encouragement to his loyalists during the sharp interval, when they have to hold on and hold out till they are relieved (v. 10).

Faith and love for Christ will bring you successfully through the brief, hard interval before the end (8, 9); faith has an outcome.

You never knew him, but you love him; for the moment 8 you do not see him, but you believe in him, and you will thrill with an unspeakable and glorious joy to obtain the 9 outcome of your faith in the salvation of your souls.

The original reading, *eidotes*, was at an early period con- 8 fused with *idotes*; hence the rendering, ' whom having not seen.' But Peter means, **you never knew him** in the past, as I did, and yet **you love him** . . . **you** believe in him in the present, though **for the moment** (ver. 6) **you do not see him,** as one day you will, when he is revealed in the immediate future. In Enoch (xlviii. 6 f., lxii. 7) the messiah is only revealed to the elect through O.T. prophecy. The Christian tie with Christ is infinitely richer ; your heart, if not your eyes, can possess him, Peter claims ; the close fellowship of Christians with Christ underlies the thought of passages like ii. 4, 25 and iii. 15. Faith is not a stoical endurance of evil, but a personal affection and devotion to the Lord, and love proves its sterling quality by standing the strain of life in his service. Out of sight but not out of reach : such is Peter's description of Christ. It is one of the most inward and moving sentences in the epistle. Here, as in ii. 6, Christ is the object of faith, and he never disappoints the personal confidence of Christians. Soon **you will thrill** (the verb is future in sense, as in ver. 6) **with an unspeakable** (too deep for words) **and glorious joy.** In the Greek version of Psalm lxxxvi. 3, ' glorious things are spoken of thee, O City of God,' Peter declares that the joy of Christians in heaven will be **glorious,** but that it cannot be put into words. The promise of joy had been made in Enoch (civ. 4) : ' Be hopeful and cast not away your hope, for you shall have great joy as the angels in heaven.' Peter

9 defines the **joy** differently ; you **obtain the outcome** (same word as **receive** in v. 4) **of your faith in the salvation of your souls ;** God will see to it that your **faith** (ver. 7) does not go for nothing.

In the next sentence (10–12), the certainty and magnificence of this **salvation** are extolled, on quite original lines.

Even prophets have searched and inquired about that salva- 10
tion, the prophets who prophesied of the grace that was
meant for you ; the Spirit of messiah within them foretold 11
all the suffering of messiah and his after-glory, and they
pondered when or how this was to come ; to them it was 12
revealed that they got this intelligence not for themselves
but for you, regarding all that has now been disclosed
to you by those who preached the gospel to you through
the holy Spirit sent from heaven. The very angels long
to get a glimpse of this !

How favoured Christians are, when the very prophets of 10
old anticipated but only anticipated this destiny ! **Even
prophets** of old, inspired men who were deeply interested in
your religious privileges, could not do more than predict
the grace or salvation **that was meant for you ;** they could
neither experience it nor understand the hour or method of
its realization. This **grace** includes the thought of God's
goodness in admitting pagan converts to membership in the
People (i. 2, ii. 9 f.), so that **prophets** would mean seers like
Isaiah and Hosea whom Paul had interpreted (see Romans
ix. 25 f., etc.) as foretelling the admission of pagans to the
People by God's merciful favour. But, as the next words
indicate, the apostle's thought is still wider ; he is thinking
of Christians in general, not simply telling these pagan
converts that their religious position is no after-thought
of God, a sudden, new thing, but recalling that the
Christian hope of salvation, which depended upon Christ's
suffering and glory (i.e. upon his resurrection, vers. 3, 21),
as predestined (i. 2, 20) in the mind of God, had been
already the subject of prophecy. **Suffering and after-glory**

99

were essential to the messiah, but under the order of God's grace Christians also pass through suffering to glory (see, e.g., iv. 13) ; they share this experience on the way to their salvation. Even Moses, according to one early Christian writer (Hebrews xi. 26), shared the obloquy of the messiah. Much more those who lived after messiah or Christ had come; with him and for him they suffer.

All this the early Christians found freely predicted in the O.T. ; such a messianic interpretation of the O.T. was common (see Luke xxiv. 26, 27), especially in interpreting passages like Isaiah liii. and Psalms xvi. 10, 11 (see Acts ii. 25 f. for Peter's view of this prophecy) and xxii. Jesus had once told his disciples that many prophets had longed to see what they saw and experienced (Matthew xiii. 16, 17 = Luke x. 23, 24) ; this was to enhance their appreciation of the gospel. In the Fourth Gospel (viii. 56, xii. 41) prophets like Abraham and Isaiah do not long in vain, they actually have visions of the Christ ; Isaiah saw his glory, i.e. the glory of the messiah or pre-existent Christ. So Peter here assumes not only that what occupied the minds of these prophets was the salvation to be realized by Christ, but that 11 they were inspired by the Spirit of messiah within them (the Greek term for messiah being *christos*, the anointed of God, a title which became for Christians the proper name ' Christ '). This was the current opinion in the early church ; ' the prophets, receiving grace from him, prophesied of him ' (Barnabas v. 6). Peter is in line with others when he declares that the Spirit of messiah foretold (*edêlou*, as in Hebrews xii. 27 ; *promarturomenon*, a word coined by the apostle) the suffering of (literally, meant for) messiah and his after-glory, i.e. not merely what Christ as messiah actually and

100

afterwards experienced (1 Corinthians xv. 3, 4, 'according to the scriptures'), but the messianic woes (Mark xiii. 8 f.) which accompanied the end or last hour (ver. 5), and in which these Christians were now involved as the sharp prelude to their final enjoyment of **glory at the revelation of Jesus Christ** (ver. 7).

Such engrossing interest in the storms that were to herald the final bliss was characteristic of the apocalyptic prophets particularly (see Daniel ix. 24 f.), and Peter has them specially in mind as he says that **they pondered reflectively when or how this** consummation was to come (literally, what was to be the time and the character of the time). Would it be soon? What would be the signs of the time? This was not revealed to them—a significant hint, for Peter himself never enters into details about the future in this epistle; he had learned his lesson (Acts i. 7) and is content to be sure that the end is near for Christians, without offering prophetic calcula- **12** tions (iv. 7, v. 6, etc.). All that was **revealed to these prophets** (to Daniel, for example, in Daniel xii. 6, 7) was that their message was for the far future, **not for themselves** (though they would fain have shared in the promised consummation of grace), **but for you** (Peter is speaking from the standpoint of Christians). What the apostle has in view is the apocalyptic confession of Enoch (i. 2), as he predicts the experiences of the righteous on the day of tribulation which inaugurates the final intervention of God; I Enoch 'saw the vision of the Holy One in the heavens . . . which the angels showed me . . . and I understood it not for this generation but for one afar off.' The Greek term for 'understood' is *dienoounto*, and Dr. Rendel Harris shows how this could have been changed into the common reading *diekonoun* by an ordinary palaeographical error on the part of a scribe. Originally Peter wrote that the prophets **got this intelligence** or understood this (i.e. their vision of the coming **grace**), just as in ver. 13 he tells Christians to make their understanding (mind is the noun from this verb) a power in life, they who understood God's **grace** so much better than these prophets of the past.

All this is designed to encourage the readers. The **salvation** in store for them has been the absorbing theme of inspired prophets in the past ; also, they are better off than the prophets, for (*a*) experience is higher than anticipation, and (*b*) even the prophets were limited in their visions ; **to** Christians alone the full truth of God's **grace** in Christ **has now been disclosed.** The preaching of the gospel is **through the holy Spirit** (as in Heb. ii. 4), who **was sent from heaven** (an allusion to Acts ii. 1 f., 32–33) to inspire conviction. The Spirit inspired prophets to predict the gospel, and the same Spirit now in the Christian order (**sent from heaven**) is the dynamic of the gospel mission.

The **very angels** are interested in this **salvation, they long to get a glimpse of it !** The verb is used of the four archangels in Enoch (ix. 1) looking down upon the wickedness of the earth before the Flood, but the sense here is the same as in John xx. 5 (glance). Peter thus closes the paragraph with a rapid, picturesque touch, alluding to the widespread belief in the early church that the saving purpose of God was a fascinating spectacle for the inhabitants of the celestial world. The background of the allusion is the same as in Ephesians iii. 9, 10.

Two paragraphs follow (i. 13–21, i. 22–ii. 10) on the moral responsibilities of this Christian position, but each ends by stressing the spiritual resources that lie behind and below the duties. The first paragraph handles the ethical obligations generally.

Brace up your minds, then, keep cool, and put your hope for 13 **good and all in the grace that is coming to you at the revelation of Jesus Christ. Be obedient children, instead** 14 **of moulding yourselves to the passions that once ruled the days of your ignorance ; as He who called you is** 15 **holy, so you must be holy too in all your conduct—for it** 16 **is written,** *You shall be holy because I am holy.* **And** 17 **as** *you call upon a Father* **who judges everyone impartially by what he has done, be reverent in your conduct while you sojourn here below ; you know it was** *not by* **perish-** 18 **able** *silver* **or gold that** *you were ransomed* **from the futile traditions of your past, but by the precious blood of** 19 **Christ, a lamb unblemished and unstained. He was** 20 **predestined before the foundation of the world, and has appeared at the end of the ages for your sake ; it is by** 21 **him that you believe in God who raised him from the dead and gave him glory ; and thus your faith means hope in God.**

Such a prospect should rally you. **Brace up your minds,** 13 instead of allowing yourselves to become depressed or panic-stricken by the hard times through which you are passing (ver. 6). **Brace,** literally, is ' gird up the loins '—a metaphor common in the ancient world, where loose and flowing garments were tucked up and belted, to facilitate action and movement (Luke xii. 35 ; Ephesians vi. 14). No vague, dreamy thoughts will do, no habit of letting the mind be dominated by appearances, which often contradict the

Christian hope. Realize the great, sure future before you ; your religious position requires mental energy and resolution, in place of any slackness. Otherwise you may become excited and feverish, under the strain. **Keep cool** (iv. 7, v. 8), your faculties all under control, and thus, with calm conviction, **put your hope** (for yours is a life of hope, ver. 3) **for good and all** (as your one resource) **in the grace** (ver. 10) **that is coming to you at the** approaching **revelation of Jesus Christ** (ver. 7). Revelation is always eschatological in this letter (i. 5, v. 1). In some circles (*Didaché* x. 6) the cry was, ' Let grace come, and let this world pass away.' Everything was to be staked upon this future, Peter argued. A man might be a member of several cults and try one mystery-religion after another, to insure his eternal welfare, but Christians must put their **hope for good and all** (absolutely) in the promise of bliss ; Christianity was too great to require to be eked out with other aids.

These words are a bridge between i. 3–12 and the following counsel upon the moral obligations and conditions of the Christian hope. Three serious demands are laid upon the conscience : Christians must resemble God in His nature (14–16), they must fear the last judgment (17), and they 14 must remember the cost of their redemption (18–21). **Be obedient** (i. 2) **children** of the God to whom you owe your life (i. 3), **instead of moulding yourselves** (the word used by Paul in Romans xii. 2) **to the passions** (ii. 11, iv. 2) **that once ruled the days of your ignorance**—a term specially applicable to Christians who had been born and bred in the religious ignorance of the true God which was a characteristic of paganism (so Acts xvii. 30 ; Ephesians iv. 17, 18). The primitive Christians used this language about pagans, as

Muhammad called the ages before Islam, The Times of Ignorance.

(a) **The first motive is put in O.T.** language (e.g. Leviticus 15 xix. 2) ; Christians as **God's people** (ii. 10) **must be holy** like God Himself, as their ancestors (see iii. 5, 6) had been enjoined in the sacred book. Holiness, ' deepest of all words that defy definition ' (Lord Morley), implies here as elsewhere a renunciation of what is worldly and corrupting, in the strength of some higher conception of God. **You shall be holy because I am holy** now means for Christians the call to reproduce what is the real nature of God, His goodness, justice, and moral purity. Moral purity of this kind was sought in some of the contemporary cults like Orphism, with which Peter's readers were familiar ; there were contemporary efforts in pagan religion to secure communion with the gods and immortality by means of a holy life. But Peter simply recalls and broadens the O.T. saying, which for his readers had no associations of merely negative and ritual purity. One specific form of this imitation is mentioned later (ii. 21). Here the injunction is general ; **as He who called you** (ii. 9) 16 **is holy, so you must be holy too.**

(b) Further, stand in awe of the judgment of God ; Christianity is no sentimental religion of the Father, which encourages presumption and moral carelessness. ' Il est bien nostre seul et unique protecteur,' says Montaigne in his essay on prayer (*Essais*, i. 56), ' et peult toutes choses à nous ayder : mais encores qu'il daigne nous honnorer de cette doulce alliance paternelle, il est pourtante autant juste, comme il est bon et comme il est puissante.' **You call upon** 17 (invoke) **a Father** (perhaps a reminiscence of O.T. words like Jeremiah iii. 19 or Psalm lxxxix. 26, but certainly an allusion to the Lord's Prayer) who judges (at the end, iv. 5, 17) **everyone impartially** (only here in N.T.) **by what he has done** (not by his pious language or warm emotions). God your Father will take strict, impartial account of your behaviour in His household, **while you sojourn** (ii. 11) **here below.** So **be reverent** (ii. 17), stand in awe of Him ; God's judgment will soon begin **with us** (iv. 17), and it will be searching, unbiassed, severe.

18   Finally, (c), remember the cost of your redemption **from the futile traditions of your past.** ' Futility ' and ' ignorance ' were two standing epithets for paganism (see Ephesians iv. 17 and above on ver. 14), ' futile ' especially for idolatry (Acts xiv. 15, etc.). Their ancestral customs and national traditions were **futile,** because they led to nothing ; such religious and patriotic rites did not avail to bring them **near to God** (iii. 18), as Christ alone could do and had done. In another sense, of course, they were far from weak ; agelong customs acquire a sanctity and binding force, which in the mission-field have always been found an obstacle. Why should we give up our fathers' religion ? The pull of these old habits is referred to in iv. 3, 4. But they were **futile** because they yielded no sure **hope in God,** and from them these Asiatic Christians had to be emancipated.

19   As usual, Peter does not explain how Christ's sacrifice availed to free men ; with some words of Isaiah lii. 3 in his mind, he appeals to the heart of his friends—**you know it was** *not by* **perishable** *silver* **or gold that** *you were ransomed,* **but by the precious blood of Christ as a sacrifice, a lamb unblemished and unstained.** This may be an allusion to the passover lamb of Exodus xii. 13, sacrificed when the People were emancipated from the slave-pen of Egypt ; **it implies**

at anyrate that the efficacy of Christ's sacrifice lay in his sinlessness, and that it results in a moral emancipation. To be **ransomed** was to be set free, and in the world of that day certain forms of manumission were carried out in temples, the formal ceremony concluding with a sacrifice ; thus the connexion of slaves' emancipation with a sacrificial act would be intelligible to these Asiatics.

The fundamental idea in all such references to emancipation as ransom in the N.T. is not from what but for what one is ransomed, not to whom the price was paid (for **ransomed** is equivalent to **bought**) but to whom one now belongs. The Ransomer owns those whom he has emancipated at the cost of his own life ; remember that, Peter urges—you belong to Another, after what he has done for you (the argument of ii. 24), by a sacrifice which has an eternal value ; it is the sacrifice of One who is not merely sinless but outside the **perishable**, transient order of things. This conception emerges in Hebrews ix. 14, where Christ's sacrifice is made **in the spirit of the eternal.** Peter does not develop the idea, but proceeds to describe Christ in his own way 20 as above the order of time and the universe, **predestined** (he had said this before, in Acts ii. 23) to his vocation as Redeemer **before the foundation of the world.** In i. 2 (as in Ephesians i. 4) Christians are **predestined,** but here the conception of a personal pre-existence is extended to the personality of Christ. The history of the world is determined by a redeeming purpose of God from all eternity, a purpose which was inaugurated when Christ **appeared** (so 1 Timothy iii. 16) **at the end of the ages** (so 1 Corinthians x. 11, Hebrews i. 2, etc.) **for your sake,** and which is soon to be completed (ver. 13). This thought of

Christ's pre-existence expresses the religious sense of his absolute value. It was natural for readers familiar with the book of Enoch and its messianic theology; in Enoch (xlviii.) the messianic Son of man ' was chosen and hidden before God, before the creation of the world, and the wisdom of the Lord of spirits hath revealed him to the holy and righteous; for he hath preserved the lot of the righteous' (so lxii. 7), i.e. he has been revealed through prophecy and has upheld the faithful, till he becomes visible at the final judgment—a rough outline of what Peter has been saying about Christ.

21 The appearance of Christ on earth evokes faith, a faith that expects the final intervention before long; **it is by him that you believe** (' by the faith he inspires,' as Peter had already said, Acts iii. 16) **in God**, the God who raised **him from the dead and gave him glory** (ver. 11); **and thus your faith means hope in God** (ver. 3). Faith is determined by revelation, by the character of the God who appeals for it, here by God **who raised** Jesus from the dead. As the resurrection of Christ is the basis of hope for Christians, their faith becomes confident and hopeful of a similar triumph over death for themselves (the thought of Paul in Romans viii. 11, 13 f.). Thus the paragraph closes as it started, with hope (ver. 13). To Christians of pagan birth their new faith meant hope pre-eminently (see 1 Thessalonians iv. 13, Ephesians ii. 12); in their old religions the outlook upon the state after death had been hopeless; a yearning for the assurance of immortality throbbed in some of the mystery-cults of the age, but, if Peter was conscious of them, he evidently felt that their creeds were not worth mentioning beside the full and clear revelation of hope in Christian faith.

Only, this hope is not a selfish possession ; it involves brotherly love and mutual affection in the members of the community. The general moral obligations of the faith have been already outlined ; now, after the slight digression in 19–21, the apostle goes forward to the special obligations of community-life among Christians (i. 22 f.). The first movement of this long paragraph (i. 22–ii. 10) is in i. 22–ii. 1.

Now that your obedience to the Truth has purified your souls 22
    for a brotherly love that is sincere, love one another
    heartily and steadily. You are born anew of immortal, 23
    not of mortal seed, by *the living, lasting* word of *God* ; for
       All flesh is like *the grass,*   24
          and all its *glory like the flower of grass :*
      the grass withers
        and the flower fades,
      but the word of the Lord lasts for ever—   25
                                ii.

    and that is *the word of the gospel* for you. So off with 1
    all malice, all guile and insincerity and envy and slander
    of every kind !

Peter had once spoken about God cleansing the hearts 22 of pagans by faith (Acts xv. 9). Here he uses another ritual term (like James iv. 8) in a metaphorical sense ; now that (since your baptism—see iii. 21) your obedience (i. 2) to the Truth (instead of futile traditions) has purified your souls (the other side of the holiness mentioned in ver. 15) for a brotherly love (ii. 17)that is sincere, love one another heartily and steadily (not in any formal or perfunctory or casual way not simply when it is easy or when you feel in the mood, but persistently and patiently). **Sincere** is emphatic ; the object of the **Truth** (i.e. the revealed will of the true God, the true Religion—a phrase which came naturally to an apocalypist, as in Daniel viii. 13) is a true affection, devoid of pretence. Paul has twice to give the same warning about Christian **love** (Romans xii. 9 ; 2 Corinthians vi. 6), where he uses the same term as here, literally *devoid of hypocrisy*, *hypocrisy* meaning ' playing a part,' the word rendered **insincerity** in ii. 1.

There is an apt illustration of the thought and term in Marcus Aurelius (xi. 18), who observes, ' A friendly disposition is invincible, if it be genuine and not an affected smile or playing a part (*hypocrisis*).' **Brotherly love** or *philadelphia* was no longer mere affection for one's blood brothers or even for fellow-members of one's nation, as Greeks and Jews interpreted it, but the tie which bound Christians to Christians as members of the brotherhood for which Christ had died, though by birth they might belong to different families and nations, the tie that drew them together and made them join hands in a warm, religious fellowship. Such an affection, Peter implies, does not spring up naturally in human nature ; it is not a sensuous affection, but flows from the heart (**heartily**), from **souls purified** by a spiritual process, otherwise it may become a short-lived impulse or dry up into a formal expression. Even in Christians it requires to be disciplined and trained. This conception recurs elsewhere in the N.T., e.g. in James i. 20 f. (where the royal law of love has to be implanted in the soul), in 1 Timothy i. 5 (' the aim of the Christian discipline is the love that springs from a pure heart, from a good conscience, and from a sincere faith '), and in 1 John iv. 7 and v. 1 (where brotherly love is the outcome of love to

God), above all in John xvii. 17 f. (where the consecration of
life by the Truth leads to brotherly unity).

Love must be taken as seriously as hope, Peter means.
In Christian circles it is constantly spoiled by spitefulness,
self-seeking, censoriousness, fickleness, and formality ; vital
love of this new and exacting kind grows in a regenerated
life, and the practice of it requires a realization of the regenerating power of God.   Brotherly love is a moral task, but
it is also an endowment.   This is the point of the connexion
between ver. 22 and what follows.   Christian **brotherly love,**
which may be defined as devotion to the ends of God in
human personality, comes from the new relation to God in
which He has placed us.   Peter again, as in 19-21, recalls
the roots as he appeals for the fruits of Christian living.
Love one another as **you are born anew** (so i. 3).   **Born** 23
by the Word of the truth, another writer put it (James i. 18) ;
but Peter as usual prefers to use some O.T. lines, quoting
Isaiah xl. 6, 7, to prove that God's word was their vital
force in living the Christian life, the **seed** to which they owed
their being.   **Seed** was appropriate, as it meant not only
human seed but the seed of plant life.   ' The seed is the
word of God,' said Jesus in his parable (Luke viii. 11) of
plant-life ; the further idea of a divine word as reproductive
in human life was already familiar in the Stoic notion of
the *Logos spermatikos* or seminal reason which pervaded
existence, but this Christian application is different.   A
closer parallel is the use of ' sown ' as ' founded ' in a
passage like Enoch lxii. 8 ('the congregation of the elect
and holy shall be sown '), where the founding of the community is due to the revelation of messiah.   Here **the gospel
word of God** is the saving revelation of Christ who **has appeared**

(ver. 20), and the citation is made in order to contrast the
24 living, lasting word of God with mortal seed which can only
25 produce transient life. **You are born of immortal seed,** i.e.
you owe your being as Christians to the revelation of the
living God in Christ incarnate and risen. Such is your
regenerate nature, a nature not only of faith and hope but of
love, it is implied. Let its instincts have full play. **Off**
ii. **with** (see Colossians iii. 8) all habits and tempers that thwart
1 brotherly love in your fellowship ! The regenerate nature
has instincts of love, but it demands a moral effort ; old
inconsistent ways of life have to be thrown aside (Ephesians
iv. 22), all manner of **malice** (ill-feeling, shown in word or
deed), **guile** (pretence or underhand dealing, but specially
deceitful speech—see on ii. 22, iii. 10), **insincerity** (saying
what one does not really mean—a common vice of the
religious world, where pious language may be used by
those who hide their true feelings ; see i. 22), **envy**
('almost the only vice which is practicable at all times and
in every place,' Johnson) **and slander of every kind ;**
Christians might be guilty of slander as well as exposed to it
(ii. 12, iii. 16).

It is not enough to avoid or discard what is inconsistent ;
a taste for the new life must be developed (2–3, 4–5). Peter
then describes again the strong position of Christians in the
purpose of God, the honour of this new life and its responsibilities (6–10).

2 **Like newly-born children, thirst for the pure, spiritual milk**
3   **to make you grow up to salvation. You have had a**
4   **taste of the kindness of the Lord : come to him then—**
    come to that living Stone which men have rejected and

God holds choice and precious, come and, like living 5
stones yourselves, be built into a spiritual house, to
form a consecrated priesthood for the offering of those
spiritual sacrifices that are acceptable to God through
Jesus Christ.

Like newly-born children (babes at the breast)—either an 2
indication that this part of the homily had been originally
addressed to the newly-baptized, or a reminder that, however
experienced, they were not beyond the need of simple spiritual
nourishment for the regenerate life, that they might **grow
up to salvation** (the other side of i. 5). This is a striking and
original expression ; the present attitude of Christians is
more than mere waiting for the imminent **salvation** (i. 9),
it is an active faith and love for the Lord which here and
now brings them into vital contact with him. **Thirst for** (as
the one food you appreciate) **the pure** (unadulterated)
spiritual milk, i.e. for what faith receives from the living
Lord. Peter does not contrast **milk** with solid food, as
Paul had done in 1 Corinthians iii. 2 (see Hebrews
v. 12 f.) ; he describes it as **spiritual,** using, like Paul (in
Romans xii. 1), a Greek term, *logikon*, which in contemporary
religious language had acquired this sense. The mistaken
idea that there was a play on the resemblance between
it and *logos* (Word) led to the rendering ' milk of the
Word,' as though Christ were the content of Scripture or
the Word. By a quaint custom in the later church the newly-
baptized were sometimes given milk and honey as a symbol
of their birth into God's household—a practice for which
there was apparently a precedent in the cults ; the initiated
in some Phrygian rites received milk, to symbolize their new

birth to life eternal. The prevalence of such rites would
lend point to Peter's figure. But what is in his mind is
3 a reminiscence of Psalm xxxiv. 8: **You have had a taste
of the kindness of the Lord.** Here **kindness** is the same
as **goodness** in Titus iii. 4. Any mention of **the Lord** in
the O.T. naturally suggested the divine Christ to an early
Christian, and this sent Peter off again (as at i. 19) to
expatiate upon the vital value of Christ to Christians. The
metaphor is abruptly changed, from child-life to architecture,
but there is no change in the thought : all depends upon
Christians availing themselves of what God has provided in
Christ. In the Greek Bible known to Peter and his friends,
the fifth verse of the 34th Psalm (' they looked to him ') was
mistranslated ' **Come to him.**' Peter quotes this, and turns
to the figure of the Stone and the Building, which he had
heard Jesus use (Mark xii. 10, 11) and which he had himself
4 already applied to the Lord (Acts iv. 11). **Come to him, to
that living Stone,** which had been flung aside as useless by
men like the Jewish authorities ; they had, by a tragic mis-
calculation, **rejected** the messianic **Stone** as of no value for
the fabric of God's House, but in the resurrection God had
shown his true value for the People, proving him **choice and
precious.**

These words echo another passage, from Isaiah, which he
is about to quote. But, before developing this thought, he
5 appeals for a vitally close fellowship with the Lord ; **come
and, like living stones yourselves, be built into a spiritual
house** (iv. 17). **Spiritual** is equivalent to ' not made with
hands,' and there may be an allusion to the Latin *vivus* in
the adjective **living,** for *vivus*, when applied to a stone,
meant a stone that had **not** been worked by hand. Hebrew

thought also associated the building of a house with a family, as in 1 Samuel ii. 35, where to ' build up a sure house for David' was to ensure a succession of children ; indeed the Targum on Psalm cxviii. 22 reads, ' the youth which the builders rejected.' But Peter does not elaborate the figure of the church as a building, as Paul had done ; he continues : **to form a consecrated priesthood** (ver. 9) **for the offering of those spiritual sacrifices** (thank-offerings, of course, not atoning for sins) **that are acceptable** (because **spiritual**) **to God through Jesus Christ.** A priesthood and sacrifices were the normal features of any ancient religious house; the former is spiritualized as usual to mean the Christian body of members, but Peter does not explain what the **sacrifices** are ; this is done in Romans xii. 1, Philippians ii. 17, iv. 18, and Hebrews xiii. 15, 16. What made sacrifices like praise and beneficence and brotherly love **acceptable** was that they were inspired and prompted by **Jesus Christ.** Nothing is said about sacrifice in connexion with the eucharist nor of the martyr's death as a sacrifice (*Martyrdom of Polykarp*, xiv.) ; these lay beyond the horizon of the apostle.

He now comes back to Christ (6–10) as the Stone, before finishing his glowing outline of God's goodness to Christians.

For thus it stands in the scripture :   6
> *Here I lay a Stone in Sion,*
> *a choice, a precious cornerstone* :
> *he who believes in him will never be disappointed.*

Now you believe, you hold him ' precious,' but as for 7
the unbelieving—
> *the very stone the builders rejected*
> *is now the cornerstone,*

8   *a stone over which men stumble* and *a rock of offence* ; **they stumble** over it in their disobedience to God's word. Such

9   is their appointed doom. But **you are** *the elect race, the royal priesthood, the consecrated nation, the People who belong to Him, that you may proclaim the wondrous deeds* of Him who has called **you** from darkness to his wonderful

10   light—**you** who once were *no people* and now are *God's people,* **you** *who* once *were unpitied* and now *are pitied.*

6   The scripture is (*a*) Isaiah xxviii. 16 ; but two other Stone-passages are in his mind, (*b*) the 118th Psalm, in ver. 7, and (*c*) Isaiah viii. 14, in ver. 8. In Luke xx. 17 f. (*b*) and (*c*) are fused, in Romans ix. 33 (*a*) and (*c*). Probably the references are to some book of proof-texts from the O.T., arranged topically for the sake of convenience. The first passage combines the ideas of Christ's value and of human faith in him ; he never breaks down nor gives way ; there is no disappointment in store for the faith of the church that rests upon his divine authority. This is quoted freely from the LXX and without any reference to its original historical

7 meaning ; what matters is the conclusion, **now you believe, you hold him** 'precious' (taking God's view, ver. 4), i.e. you accept Christ as messiah, as the foundation of all your hopes, as the divine revelation upon whom everything depends. But not so all. There are **unbelieving** people in the world. Men come across Christ ; some find and make him the stay and support of life, while others trip over him and collapse. To some he **is**, as the psalm sings, the **cornerstone** of their Sion or sanctuary, the foundation-stone at the angle of the building which determines the whole structure ; to others he is in their way.

And this is the sense of the second Isaiah clause, **a stone** 8
over which men stumble and a rock of offence. If men to-day,
like Ephraim and Judah of old, continue to ignore God's
goodness and strength, He will prove disastrous to them.
The figure is not quite clear ; the Stone may be thought of
as one and the same, the passer-by tripping over the cornerstone of the building which juts out on the road, or two
different stones may be in the apostle's view. But the idea
is plain : the presence of Christ in the world elicits faith and
unbelief. The belief of Christians is thrown into relief against
a background of repudiation on the part of others. These
others include Jews, but they are not confined to Jews.
Peter does not enter into any explanation of the **offence
of the cross,** as Paul does ; we are not told why some do
not believe in Christ, but merely that **they stumble over** the
Stone **in their** fatal (see iv. 17, iii. 1) **disobedience to** God's
word (i.e. to the gospel message and revelation of Christ).
Such (i.e. such a collapse) **is their appointed doom,** as fixed
as the blessed outcome of faith (**never disappointed**) for
Christians. A similar problem is discussed by Paul in Romans
ix.–xi., in connexion with the destiny of unbelieving Israel,
who have rejected Christ. But Peter is not thinking of Israel
specially. He does not mean that a special number of men
were predestined to unbelief and doom, for **the unbelieving**
(ver. 7) merely means ' any who disbelieve.' On the other
hand, he regards unbelief no less than belief as falling under
the will of God.

From this stern reminder that the attitude of men towards
Christ is critical and decisive, and that the world-order **is a**
grave matter for the disobedient (ii. 23), he turns to describe 9
Christians in a mosaic of O.T. phrases drawn from Isaiah,

Exodus, and Hosea, transferring the most honourable predicates of Israel to the Christian church as the true heir of all the divine promises. Some of these predicates had been already combined in Judaism, e.g. in the book of Jubilees (xvi. 18), where it is foretold that Israel should be for the Lord a people who belong to him above all nations, a royal priesthood, and a consecrated nation. **The elect race** is from Isaiah xliii. 20, **the royal** or kingly **priesthood** and **the consecrated** (i. 2) **nation** are from Exodus xix. 6; the former phrase is the only allusion to the King or the Kingdom in the epistle, terms which Peter perhaps avoided on account of their liability to be misconstrued (see on iv. 15). **The People who belong to Him** is a fusion of Exodus xix. 5 and Malachi iii. 17; it refers to the present possession of the church by God as His very own. The object of all this honour and privilege is **that you may proclaim** (from Isaiah xlii. 12) **the wondrous deeds** (from Isaiah xliii. 21) **of Him who has called you** (i. 15) **from darkness to his wonderful light.** The term rendered **wondrous deeds** is almost the same in meaning as **the triumphs of God** in Acts ii. 11; in current Greek it denoted the miraculous or wonderful deeds of a god, for which he was to be praised, his manifestations of power. **Darkness** is often the term for the paganism from which converts have been emancipated (see Colossians i. 13, Ephesians v. 8). Christians are the **People of God,** not that they may exult over the Jews who have been superseded, but that they may exhibit the marvellous goodness of God and by their dutiful life (see, e.g., ii. 12) answer His purposes in the world. This is really the climax of the passage: 10 Such is your destiny. But Peter, like Paul (Romans ix. 25), remembers some apt words from Hosea (ii. 3, 25), which he too transfers boldly to pagan converts. **Pitied** echoes God's great mercy in i. 3.

The transference of the religious consciousness from the city or state to a religious society had been already initiated in cults like those of Isis and Mithras, which were international or rather non-national in scope. For this and other reasons they were suspected by the Romans, either as immoral (which was sometimes true, of Isis at anyrate) or as harbouring anti-social and unpatriotic tendencies. Both criticisms were levelled against Christianity as one of these new Oriental fellowships, and both now engage the attention of the apostle, who issues a series of counsels (ii. 11–iii. 12) on the practical duty of proclaiming **the wondrous deeds** of their God, counsels which close with a renewed emphasis upon (iv. 8 f.) the brotherly love which had been already urged in i. 22–ii. 2. The first is an admonition (11–12) on how the consecrated nation (ver. 9) was to behave in the midst of a pagan society saturated with vice and hostile to the Christian faith.

Beloved, as *sojourners and exiles* **I appeal to you to abstain** 11 **from the passions of the flesh that wage war upon the soul. Conduct yourselves properly before pagans ; so** 12 **that for all their slander of you as bad characters, they may come to glorify God when you are put upon your trial, by what they see of your good deeds.**

The first time Peter speaks in his own person, he affection- 11 ately calls his readers **beloved** (see iv. 12). What was once said of the Jewish nation is now said of the Christian church ; they are appealed to as **sojourners and exiles** on earth (the thought of i. 1 and 17) whose real interests are elsewhere. The classical expression of this other-worldly consciousness occurs in the *Epistle to Diognetus* (v.) : ' they live in their own countries, but as sojourners . . . every foreign country is a fatherland to them, and every fatherland is foreign.' Christians are citizens of Heaven, and here only for a time. All the more reason, therefore, to hold aloof from their surroundings. **Abstain from the passions** (iv. 2–4) **of the flesh that wage war upon** (James iv. 1) **the soul** (the self, the true personality). Both metaphors are combined in Marcus Aurelius, ii. 17 : ' Life is a warfare and a foreign sojourn.' And the call to abjure such passions was common in Greek ethics, e.g. Plato, *Phaedo*, 83 : ' the soul of the true philosopher abstains as far as possible from pleasures and passions.'

One good of this moral discipline is that it forms an effective
12 reply to the pagan **slander** of Christians as **bad characters** (so iv. 15). Among the nuisances and abuses punished during Nero's reign, at Rome, was the religion of ' Christians,' says Suetonius (*Life of Nero*, xvi.), ' a class of men belonging to a new and mischievous superstition ' (where the Latin term *maleficus* rendered ' mischievous ' answers to the Greek term *kakopoios* used here by Peter). It is a vague term to express the ordinary pagan antipathy to Christians as a pest to society. Live down these hateful slanders and insinuations, says Peter (so in iii. 16), by behaving **yourselves properly,** i.e. leading an honest, upright life (Hebrews xiii. 18 —similar phrase), **so that** your accusers **may come to glorify God,** i.e. to own your God, who inspires such innocent, moral lives, **by what they see** (iii. 2) **of your good works.** This refers to the scrutiny at a Roman *cognitio* or preliminary cross-examination of accused persons, which the

magistrate held, when the charges were considered and evidence sought for the case. The apostle confidently hopes that the charges will break down, perhaps even that the accusers will be converted (if this be the meaning of **glorify God**, as in Matthew v. 16). **When you are put upon your trial** is literally ' on the [a] day of visitation,' a phrase used in Isaiah x. 3 of God visiting men in judgment. But Peter uses it for his own purpose, to mean not God's trial of them (i.e. some crisis which will open their eyes to your innocence), but their trial of you as supposed wrongdoers, when they inspect your record or investigate your conduct.

No provocation must lead to rebellion against the authorities (iv. 15) ; a law-abiding, honest life is your duty (13-17). Such is the general principle laid down in these verses.

Submit for the Lord's sake to any human authority ; submit 13 to the emperor as supreme, and to governors as deputed 14 by him for the punishment of wrongdoers and the encouragement of honest people—for it is the will of God that 15 by your honest lives you should silence the ignorant charges of foolish persons. Live like free men, only do 16 not make your freedom a pretext for misconduct ; live like servants of God. Do honour to all, love the brother- 17 hood, *reverence God, honour the emperor.*

In vindicating Christian freedom against the Law, Paul 13 had to issue a similar warning against antinomian excesses (Galatians v. 13) ; the freedom of Christians was not self-indulgence or any escape from moral restraints. But Peter never mentions the Law. His readers had no such problem. The experience of Christian freedom was a temptation to them, but in a different direction. Their danger was to become restive and insubordinate, as though the civil and social order of things had no claim upon them, particularly as it often interfered wantonly with their religion. They belonged to God's People ; they owned allegiance to Him alone ; they were soon to be released from the present, distressful order of things on earth. Why should they pay respect to pagan institutions ? Evidently anarchical and radical tendencies were abroad, fostered by the very consciousness of Christian liberty and hope. In a province like Asia, specially sensitive to loyalty, and with a government intensely suspicious of any secret movements which might cloak political sedition under religious pretexts, such high-flying notions would be compromising and dangerous, Peter felt. Hence, like Paul (Romans xiii. 1), he bids his readers **submit for the Lord's sake** (either because Jesus told you so, when he said, 'Render to Caesar the things that are Caesar's,' or out of loyalty to him, not to bring discredit upon him) **to any human authority** (*ktisis* in the modern sense of ' foundation ' or institution), i.e. not simply because you have to, but for a religious reason ; no spiritual independence absolves you from obedience to the authorities of the State, whose 14 functions are to maintain the moral order of society. **Submit to the emperor** (*basileus*, the Caesar's title among Greeks and Orientals) **as supreme, and to** your provincial (Mark xiii. 9) **governors**, subordinate officials **deputed by him for the punishment of** real **wrongdoers** (same word as ' bad characters ' above) **and the encouragement of honest people**, i.e. of law-abiding, good citizens, who were frequently rewarded with crowns, statues, and inscriptions in their honour, by a grateful community. **Submit**, instead of being resentful and rebellious when you are charged with being **wrongdoers**. Never give

your pagan neighbours a handle for their calumnies. **For 15
it is the will of God** (iii. 17) **that by your honest lives**
(politically and morally blameless) **you should silence the
ignorant charges** (made in disgraceful ignorance) **of foolish
persons.** The pagan ignorance of Christianity was vocal ;
it expressed itself in calumnies and prejudiced criticism, as,
for example, in the insinuation that the Christian kingdom
(Acts xvi. 21 f., xvii. 7) was a revolutionary movement.
There is a touch of righteous indignation in Peter's description
of these senseless critics. Also a very optimistic hope in the
idea that such popular outcries will be silenced by the mere
example of Christian good behaviour. The next two
centuries dissipated this expectation ; the friction between
State and Church proved to be much more serious than
the apostle at this period imagined. But his wise
concern is to check any compromising outburst of
insubordination on the part of the Asiatic Christians. **Live 16
like free men . . . like servants** (literally, slaves) **of God**
(a fine oxymoron, see 1 Corinthians vii. 22), who requires you
to obey the authorities (ver. 13). **Do not make your freedom
a pretext** (literally, a cloak) **for misconduct**—the warning of
a wise leader who knows how fanatical tendencies need to
be disciplined. Religious freedom (i. 18) must never be made
an excuse for moral or social anarchy.

What Christians are really **free** and **bound to do** is now **17**
put in four terse clauses. **Do honour to all,** not only to the
authorities by loyalty and paying taxes, etc., but to all
men ; human nature is dishonoured by being treated as
material for one's own advantage (the temptation of the
strong), or by being flattered (the temptation of the weaker),
or by any cynical temper. Peter takes it for granted that

those to be honoured deserve honour, owing to their position or their character and capacities. He had himself once learned a lesson on this subject (Acts xi. 9). **Love the brotherhood** (v. 9, only here in N.T., a Jewish-Greek term taken over to describe the brotherly union of Christians), as already in i. 22. The words of the next two clauses are partly taken from the Greek version of Proverbs xxiv. 22, 'reverence God and the king,' but Peter inserts **honour before the emperor,** thus closing the paragraph on the note on which he opened it (ver. 13). Awe or reverence is for God alone. The honour is done by obedience. To **reverence God** is the duty of His **servants,** and it is not incompatible with loyalty to the head of the State. Where Christians afterwards felt the strain between the two was over the claim of the State to enforce the worship of the emperor as an official proof of loyalty, which led to the situation reflected in the book of Revelation. But as yet things had not gone so far in Asia.

All Christians were **servants** or slaves **of God.** But some were literally **slaves,** who were specially tempted to be restive. Peter now turns to them (vers. 18–25), calling them to be patient under bad treatment and to give no offence, after the example of Christ.

18 Servants, be submissive to your masters with perfect respect, not simply to those who are kind and reasonable but to
19 the surly as well—for it is a merit when from a sense of
20 God one bears the pain of unjust suffering. Where is the credit in standing punishment for having done wrong? No, if you stand suffering for having done right, that is
21 what God counts a merit. It is your vocation; for when

Christ suffered for you, he left you an example, and you must follow his footsteps.

> *He committed no sin,*   22
> *no guile was ever found upon his lips*;
>
> he was reviled and made no retort,   23
> he suffered and never threatened,

but left everything to Him who judges justly; *he bore* 24 our *sins* in his own body on the gibbet, that we might break with sin and live for righteousness; and *by* his *wounds you have been healed.* You were *astray like sheep,* 25 but you have come back now to the Shepherd and Guardian of your souls.

Peter thinks it possible that pagan husbands may be won **18** over by Christian wives (iii. 1), but he does not contemplate the possibility of Christian servants converting their masters. All he asks is that they be submissive, even under intolerable treatment, with perfect respect (no disrespectful behaviour in any circumstances), even to masters who were not reasonable (i.e. considerate, unwilling to be tyrannical). The term surly means difficult to deal with, harsh. Domestic slaves, such as Peter is specially addressing, were at the mercy of their masters; they had no protection against bad temper or injustice, for they had no rights. As the law did not recognize them as persons, they had no means of redress under the existing conditions of social life. The master could whip his slave, or brand him, if he stole, if he tried to escape; in the last resort, he could crucify him. Such severity sometimes led pagan slaves to rebel, and, short of that, to be impertinent or to retaliate by pilfering (Titus ii. 10). No wonder if Christian slaves were also tempted to resent the degrading duties thrust upon them by some masters, or to be refractory under unfair treatment, as they reflected that they were equal to their masters in the sight of God. Sometimes they were better educated than their masters. For house-stewards (see iv. 10), librarians, and physicians in a large private establishment could be slaves as well as the cooks and porters and personal attendants. When they became Christians, their new sense of personality might intoxicate them, till they forgot to be respectful, when the master proved violent and overbearing.

But if you cannot please these unreasonable masters, you can please your God by bearing **the pain of unjust suffering ;**
19 that is **a merit**, it counts with God, wins His approval. The phrase **from a sense of God** is unexampled in the N.T. ; it means that one is supported by a steady consciousness of God (as **for the Lord's sake**, ver. 13), perhaps by the feeling that God calls the servant to this trial (ver. 21). The term for **standing punishment** includes the narrower sense of being **buffeted** (A.V.), for a sharp blow was the common punishment of a slave who fell under his master's displeasure ; but the range of penalties was wider than whipping or flogging.
20 **Where is the credit** (only here in N.T.) in bending to punishment when you deserve it ? Peter means, the credit with God. **What God counts a merit** (Luke vi. 32) is the patient endurance of suffering that you do not deserve. This
21 indeed is **your vocation** (iii. 9), for Christ calls you to **follow** his footsteps, i.e. (me aemulari, meis instare vestigiis, Pliny's *Epp.*, vi. 11) the **example he left you** of enduring unmerited pain without resenting it or retaliating. **When Christ suffered for you,** his sufferings were redemptive and more (i. 18, 19) ; they set you an example. This is a proof

126

of the honour done by Christianity to the slave-class ; **Christ was actually held up to them as a pattern** ! Never had such conduct been expected from slaves in the ancient world. His innocence is described in words freely quoted from 22 Isaiah liii. 9 (the famous passage which was taken in the early church as a prediction of Christ) ; **guile** was particularly applicable to slaves in the empire, where glib, deceitful speech was one of their notorious characteristics, adroit evasions and excuses being often their sole means of self-protection. But no quotation was needed to describe the bearing of Jesus during his trial ; Peter remembered well what he had seen ; he could not forget (see v. 1) that the execution of 23 Jesus was a piece of human injustice, that it had been preceded by insults, and that the Lord had neither resisted nor resented the outrageous, cruel treatment he had received from the lips and hands of those who had him in their power. **He suffered and never threatened** vengeance upon his tormentors, **but left everything to Him who judges justly** (whatever the Jewish priests and the Roman judge might do in their unjust procedure). So must you, Peter implies, hinting (as in Ephesians vi. 9) that unjust masters will yet be called to account by God.

But the parallelism does not hold his mind. He does not suggest that Christian slaves by their patience under suffering vicariously atone for the sins of those who oppress them. Instinctively he returns to the thought, **Christ suffered for you** (iii. 21), recalling again the Isaiah-prophecy ; **he himself** 24 (the word is emphatic) **bore our sins in his own body on the gibbet** (the slave's punishment—a favourite word of Peter for the cross, to mark the shame of it, e.g. Acts v. 30, x. 39). He bore the consequences of our sins. How, Peter does not explain. **It is** the inimitable element **in** the sufferings **of** Christ, interpreted again from the O.T.: he went up to the cross to suffer there the penalty for our sins, not for his own. This, illustrated in various ways from the O.T. (e.g. i. 2 and 19), was the central truth in Christianity. Indeed for the moment Peter includes all Christians in what he says—he bore our sins that we might break with [die to] sin and live for righteousness (a collective term for the life that answers to the will of God). It is not the method but the object of the atoning death which interests him here as in i. 19. The language echoes that of Romans vi. 2, 11, 18, but there is nothing corresponding to Paul's deep thought of dying and rising again with Christ; this was as far from the mind of Peter as was Paul's conception of the church as the Body of Christ.

The apostle then turns back to the slaves; **and by his wounds** (literally, the weals or scars left by the lash) **you have been healed** (from Isaiah liii. 12), put into a position in which you can **live**, now that sin has been dealt with. The same thought is then put in another form; you have Christ to care for you, in this trying life of obedience, for while **you** 25 **were astray like sheep** (the last three words are a reminiscence of Isaiah liii. 6) once, **you have come back now** (like other pagan converts, 1 Thessalonians i. 9, Acts xi. 21) **to the Shepherd** (v. 4) **and Guardian of your souls.** Guardian or overseer, one who exercises oversight and protection, is literally "bishop"; Christ is the only bishop known to Peter and his churches. Christ had died for them; Christ had left them an example; and, best of all, Christ was living to make himself responsible for them as they tried to follow him in their own way and trusted themselves to his charge and care.

From slaves Peter turns to wives and their duties (1-6) in the home. Women in the churches he addressed had evidently no need of being counselled about behaviour in church, as some of the Corinthian matrons had (1 Corinthians xiv. 33-35).

iii.

In the same way, you wives must be submissive to your 1 husbands, so that even those who will not believe the Word may be won over without a word by the behaviour of their wives, when they see how chaste and reverent 2 you are. You are not to adorn yourselves on the outside 3 with braids of hair and ornaments of gold and changes 4 of dress, but inside, in the heart, with the immortal beauty of a gentle and modest spirit, which in the sight of God is of rare value. It was in this way long ago that 5 the holy women who hoped in God adorned themselves. They were submissive to their husbands. Thus Sara 6 obeyed Abraham by *calling him ' lord.'* And you are daughters of Sara if you do what is right and *yield to no panic.*

The new Christian freedom was apt to make some married women restive as well as slaves, especially when their husbands were pagans. Mixed marriages started an acute problem in the early church. A Christian wife found herself in serious difficulties, domestic and social, when her religion ran across the pagan customs of her position as a married woman. Tertullian, a century and a half later, wrote vividly on these problems, but already they were being felt in Asia Minor, as they had been in Corinth (1 Corinthians vii. 10-16). And even when a husband was Christian, the wife was tempted to be self-assertive as she felt for the first time how her religion invested her with fresh rights as a personality.

1   Peter's first word is that a similar (**in the same way,** as ii. 13, 18) duty of submissiveness lies upon Christian wives, though he does not give the reason of Ephesians v. 22 f. He thinks mainly of Christian women married to pagan husbands (Acts xvi. 1, xvii. 4) **who will not believe the Word** (ii. 8), i.e. the Gospel message. **Be submissive ;** not simply to keep their affections, but that they **may be won over** (the thought of 1 Corinthians vii. 16, and the very word used in 1 Corinthians ix. 19 and Matthew xviii. 15) **without a word.** Your uppermost thought should be their conversion, and this will not be managed by talking at them or even to them ; quiet submissiveness to marital authority will do 2 more than nagging or indeed than any argument, **when they see** (ii. 12) **how chaste and reverent you are.** Chaste because reverent ; *en phobô* here means reverence towards God (i. 17, ii. 17), not (as in ii. 18) respectfulness and deference.

The spectacle of chastity must also include gentle modesty (3–4), evinced in dress. This is the first sumptuary counsel in Christianity. Tertullian afterwards elaborated it into a puritanic protest, in his tract on *The Dress of Women,* against wives taking any care of their persons, which, he argued, simply pandered to lust ; such attention to one's person drew the eyes and sighs of young fellows in the street, whereas husbands wanted chastity alone in their wives ! Tertullian was denouncing fashionable ladies in the Carthaginian church. Peter is also addressing ladies of wealth and position in this fine word upon the real attractiveness of womanhood, with its emphasis upon character, and its protest against showy luxury. He and his readers knew the tradition about the origin of such luxuries, the religious tale voiced in the Jewish piety of the book of Enoch (viii.) and elsewhere, that the fallen angels of Genesis vi. were responsible for introducing them on earth ; these corrupt spirits (of whom he is to speak later, in iii. 19, 20) seduced women by revealing the knack of manufacturing ' bracelets and ornaments,' jewels and cosmetics. Even apart from such sinister associations of luxury in religious tradition, Greek and Roman ethic often frowned upon these meretricious ornaments as pandering to immorality. Probably the provinces followed the capital in fashions. The Roman ladies wore no hats, but there was an elaborate cult of hairdressing with jewelled combs and golden fillets (**braids of hair and ornaments of gold**), and **3** lavish expenditure on dress, among women of means.

Peter's word anticipates some warnings by pagan moralists in the next century. Thus Plutarch (*Conjug. Praecept.* 26, 48) explains that for a woman **to adorn** (*ho kosmos*, the very word used here) herself with **gold** or pearls does not really beautify her ; the real beauty of the sex lies in whatever invests them with seriousness and decorum and modesty. He also makes a point, by the way, which Peter misses, viz. that a husband must not expect his wife to avoid pretentious extravagance if she sees that he is addicted to it himself ; ' you cannot banish extravagance from the women's quarter, when it is unchecked among the men ' (e.g. in decorating the harness of their horses). Lucian stresses beauty of character in women instead of outward adornment (*Imagines*, 11) with similar arguments, and there are other proofs that ethnic critics of social morality were alive to what Peter here urges on religious grounds. The apostle's thought is that such moral beauty never wears out, being immortal (a characteristic touch, absent

from 1 Timothy ii. 9), that simplicity is part and parcel
of chastity, so far as husbands are concerned, and that
4 Christian wives owe it to God (**in the sight of God**) to think
more of their personalities than of external adornments to
their persons. By **a gentle and modest spirit** he means a
spirit that is not self-assertive and aggressive, that will not
flaunt even its religious opinions; to be **modest** in this sense
is to be free not only from indelicacy but from fussiness
and complacency.

Augustine's mother Monica is an apt example of what is
intended here. We are told in her son's *Confessions* (ix.)
how she endeavoured, and not without success, to win over
a pagan husband to God, 'preaching Thee to him by her
character, whereby Thou didst make her beautiful to her
husband, reverently loveable and wonderful.'

5 Peter now (5, 6) urges the example of O.T. women like
Sara, **holy women,** i.e. women who belonged to the Chosen
People of God. All Christian women are now by their faith
daughters of Sara, though they had been born in paganism.
The O.T. tells us nothing of the dress of such women, who
probably wore the usual Oriental jewels and robes. But the
apostle is thinking of the beautiful submissiveness shown by
these women **who hoped in God** (i. 21), as an expression of
their religion, particularly of Sara's. In the tale of Genesis
6 xviii. 12 she was reported to have **obeyed Abraham by calling
him ' lord.'** The instance sounds to us casual, but Jewish
tradition attached high importance to it as a proof of piety;
as such it is cited here, the more aptly as in Greek law the
husband was the **lord** (*kurios*) of the wife. The Roman Pliny
(*Epp.*, viii. 5) has no finer praise for a friend's dead wife than
to declare that ' for thirty-nine years he lived with her,

without any quarrel or disagreement. What respectful deference she showed to her husband, though she herself deserved the greatest deference ! '

And you are true (Isaiah li. 2) **daughters of Sara if you do what is right** (iv. 19, a general term here for a chaste, submissive, married life) **and** (even when your religious principles expose you to risk) **yield to no panic** or alarm. The last phrase is a reminiscence of Proverbs iii. 15, but the idea is entirely different ; keep calm and courageous, even when a pagan husband threatens you with violence if you disobey his orders, e.g. perhaps to throw out a female infant (as by law he had the right to do), or to gratify his passions immodestly, or to give up some religious conviction. A hint of the limits to passive obedience on the part of a Christian wife, but only a hint ! Peter is laying down general principles for wives as for slaves. He does not enter into the question of what a wife's duty should be in cases where a pagan husband went too far. Plutarch, in the tract already cited (xix.), declared that a married woman ought to have no friends except her husband's friends, and that as the chief friends were the gods, ' a wife should reverence and acknowledge the gods owned by her husband. Her street-door should be kept shut against novel forms of worship and foreign superstitions.' This Peter would not have admitted. One lady (the story is told in the Second Apology of Justin Martyr) was obliged eventually to divorce her pagan husband for gross and repeated licentiousness ; whereupon he gave information to the authorities and had her arrested as a Christian. This is the kind of threat which we can read between the lines of Peter's final word to Christian wives who had pagan husbands.

Now for a brief word to husbands (7). It is assumed that

133

their wives were Christians, and it is argued that they have
their dues.

7 In the same way you husbands must be considerate in living
with your wives, since they are the weaker sex ; you
must honour them as heirs equally with yourselves of
the grace of Life, so that your prayers may not be
hindered.

7   **Considerate,** in the light of 1 Thessalonians iv. 3–5 and
1 Corinthians vii. 3–5, includes a reference to sexual rights.
Peter brings three motives to bear upon Christian husbands.
(*a*) Women **are the weaker sex,** deserving courtesy and
chivalrous consideration. The term *skeuos*, here rendered
' sex,' literally means vessel or instrument (a wife in
1 Thessalonians iv. 4). (*b*) The tie is deeper than mere
marital intercourse ; husband and wife in marriage have
equal religious privileges. **You must honour them** (a special
case of ii. 17) **as heirs equally with yourselves of the grace of
Life,** God's **grace** consisting of the Christian life, the only life
worthy of the name. Finally (*c*), **so that your prayers may
not be hindered** (literally ' blocked '—a military metaphor).
Paul mentions how marital intercourse might be interrupted
on occasion for the sake of prayer (1 Corinthians vii. 5).
Peter twice mentions prayer, and in both passages notes the
need of its conditions ; in iv. 7 the need of a collected mind,
here perhaps specially the need of courtesy and kindness
on the part of husbands. God will not hear prayers from a
home where the man bullies and overbears the woman.
The reference is not to prayers in church (1 Timothy ii. 8),
but to home prayers ; it is assumed that both man and
woman pray, and pray together. The previous words tell

against the idea that the prayers are those of a Christian husband for the conversion of his pagan wife, prayers that naturally would be frustrated if they rose from a home where he did not treat her kindly.

' Platon en ses loix,' says Montaigne (*Essais*, i. 56), ' faict trois sortes d'iniurieuse creance des dieux : Qu'il n'y en aye point ; Qu'ils ne se meslent point de nos affaires [the point met by Peter in v. 7] ; Qu'ils ne refusent rien à nos vœux, offrandes et sacrifices.' On the third error he adds, ' il fault avoir l'ame nette, au moins en ce moment auquel nous le prions, et deschargee de passions vicieuses.' Peter would not have limited the demand, however, to ' ce moment auquel nous le prions.' In view of the later tendency in some circles of the church to regard the married life as incompatible with true Christianity, it is important to note that Peter's ethic is free from such ascetic aberration ; he teaches that the ordinary relations of husband and wife may be and ought to be regulated for the highest ends of the Christian religion.

Peter has nothing to say about children and their parents, any more than about the duties of masters to their slaves. He passes forward to offer counsel to the whole body of Christians (iii. 8–iv. 6), beginning with a general word (8–12) which opens out into advice about their bearing under trouble.

Lastly, you must all be united, you must have sympathy, 8
  brotherly love, compassion, and humility, never paying 9
  back evil for evil, never reviling when you are reviled,
  but on the contrary blessing. For this is your vocation,
  to bless and to inherit blessing ;

10 *he who would love Life*
  and enjoy good days,
 let him keep his tongue from evil
  and his lips from speaking guile:

11 *let him shun wrong and do right,*
  let him seek peace and make peace his aim.

12 *For the eyes of the Lord are on the upright,*
  and his ears are open to their cry;
 but the face of the Lord is set against wrongdoers.

8 **Lastly** (the phrase only here in N.T.), **you must all be united.** The Greek word for **united** (only here in the N.T.) is explained by the use in Homer's *Iliad* (xxii. 260 f.): 'wolves and sheep cannot have a *united* mind, but are constantly thinking evil against one another'; to be **united** is to be harmonious—no falling out among yourselves—**you must have sympathy** (only here in N.T.), fellow-feeling, **brotherly love** (i. 22), **compassion** (same word as 'tenderhearted' in Ephesians iv. 32), **and humility** (adjective only here in N.T.; see on v. 5). How needful was this appeal, for communities with such differences of social position among their members! Domestic slaves and noble ladies, for example, summoned to mutual consideration!

Then comes, as in Romans xii. 17, after the call for humility, a prohibition of retaliation which is an echo of Matthew v. 44;
9 **never paying back evil for evil, never reviling when you are reviled, but on the contrary blessing** ('Bless those who curse you,' Luke vi. 28; 'being reviled, we bless,' 1 Corinthians iv. 12). The thought already is including the relation of Christians to the outside world and its hostile atmosphere. **For this is your vocation** (so ii. 21), thus **to bless and so to**

inherit blessing from your God, who only hears the prayers
and undertakes the protection of those who live His life
(see above, on ver. 7).

Then follows (10-12) a free quotation from Psalm xxxiv.
12-16, a psalm which he has already quoted (in ii. 3); he takes
Life, not as earthly life (in the psalmist's sense), but in the
deeper sense of ver. 7, and purposely omits the closing line
(' to cut off the remembrance of them from the earth ').
The last line of his citation echoes the thought of ii. 23,
and it starts the next counsel on the attitude of Christians
towards their enemies in the outside world (vers. 13 f.).

> **Yet who will wrong you if you have a passion for goodness ?** 13
> **Even supposing you have to suffer for the sake of what** 14
> **is right, still you are blessed.** *Have no fear of their*
> *threats, do not let that trouble you,* **but reverence Christ as** 15
> **Lord in your own hearts.**

Wrongdoers ? **Yet who will** (who is likely to) **wrong you** 13
if you have a passion (a strong term, rendered ' a zest ' in
Titus ii. 14) **for goodness ?** An optimistic comfort ! He at
once qualifies this naïve idea by adding, **Even supposing** 14
you do have to suffer for the sake of what is right (as Jesus
foretold, Matthew v. 10), **still you are blessed** by God (ver. 12).
He thus comes nearer to the realities of life. ' You are
certain of God's blessing as you maintain your inward
reverence and homage for **Christ** as your **Lord,** instead of
allowing yourselves to be intimidated into apostasy.' He
clinches the argument by using O.T. words (from the Greek
version of Isaiah viii. 12, 13) which originally meant that
Isaiah's pious followers were to **have no fear** such as the other
panic-stricken Jews felt in the crisis of the Syrian invasion.

Peter had already quoted (ii. 8) from this chapter. **Here he takes the words as 'do not be afraid of your persecutors' threats'; do not let that trouble you.** Your one concern 15 is to be loyal to your Lord, as the pious Jews once had to be loyal to their God.

This is the negative side of their attitude towards pagan oppressors. But occasionally a more positive attitude is demanded (15–16).

**Always be ready with a reply for anyone who calls you to
account for the hope you cherish, but answer gently
16   and with a sense of reverence; see that you have a
clean conscience, so that, for all their slander of you,
these libellers of your good Christian behaviour may be
ashamed.**

15   Fearlessness does not mean contemptuous indifference to pagans, however; when you are questioned informally or interrogated by a magistrate, after arrest, **always be ready with a reply.** Be ready to explain and discuss your religion, not merely to **reverence Christ as Lord in your own hearts,** but to tell others what he means to you. The new outlook upon death and immortality often excited curiosity and keen interest in those who first heard of the Christian religion, but **the hope you cherish** is probably no more than a synonym for Christianity (see ver. 5). Particularly when they were ridiculed about the resurrection or called to account in court (ii. 12), there was a risk of replying arrogantly and scornfully. Hence Peter bids them not only take every chance of clearing away misconceptions of the faith, but also to do this **gently** (no indignation, no supercilious temper) **and with a sense of reverence** (towards God—as i. 17, iii. 2); to bear testimony

138

before men tactfully and wisely requires a sense of serious
responsibility to God.

To these two conditions of an effective reply, freedom from
any lecturing tone and a deep consciousness of God's presence,
the apostle now adds a third, viz. that Christians must be 16
conscious of their own innocence (the thought of ii. 12, and
the phrase of iii. 21) ; any misconduct or inconsistent
behaviour (i. 15, 16) would spoil their reply. The charges
which they had to meet were obviously against alleged
immoral conduct on the part of Christians. **Christian is**
literally ' in Christ,' a phrase coined by Paul and used by
him in a special and mystical sense. Peter hopes for some
good result of such testimony ; it may make an impression
upon the pagan authorities ; if they are not actually converted (ii. 12), they **may** at least **be ashamed** of their base
and baseless misrepresentations.

Now, resuming the thought of ver. 14, he shows how the
sufferings of Christians resemble those of Christ himself, as
in ii. 21 f., where also the thought of Christ's example passes
at once over into the larger thought of the redemptive
efficacy of his sufferings.

For it is better to suffer for doing right (if that should be the 17
   will of God) than for doing wrong. Christ himself died 18
   for sins, once for all, a just man for unjust men, that he
   might bring us near to God ; in the flesh he was put to
   death but he came to life in the Spirit.

God's will is personified here, like His **patience** in ver. 20. 17
Suppose you are punished or ill-treated unfairly ? At anyrate
it is not arbitrary or accidental, but **the will of God** for you
as once it was for **Christ himself.** He had to suffer death 18

itself to overcome the obstacle of the sins that separated us from the presence of God (the other side of ii. 25). Peter had already spoken of Christ as ' The Just One ' (Acts iii. 14), a messianic title first current in Enoch (see xxxviii. 2), and this lies behind the phrase a just man for unjust men. But how could he secure this free access to God, if he died ? The answer is (as in 2 Corinthians xiii. 4) that he came to life in the Spirit as a ' Christ of power.'

From the turn of thought here, as at ii. 21 f., we might again expect that Peter would proceed to show how Christians can vicariously suffer for others, as Christ did, by patient endurance of an unjust death. But he never does. He goes on to indicate that their suffering has a beneficial result upon themselves (iv. 1 f.). Before passing to this, however, the mention of the Spirit and the resurrection leads him into an aside upon baptism as the manifestation of Christ's risen power in the Spirit (19–22). Only as baptized persons can Christians be nerved to lead a clean life in the flesh, with the suffering which it may entail. What takes place in the flesh, in the present bodily sphere, is explained by what takes place in the sphere of the Spirit.

19
20 It was in the Spirit that Enoch also went and preached to the imprisoned spirits who had disobeyed at the time when God's patience held out during the construction of the ark in the days of Noah—the ark by which only a few souls, eight in all, were brought safely through the
21 water. Baptism, the counterpart of that, saves you to-day (not the mere washing of dirt from the flesh but the prayer for a clean conscience before God) by the resurrection of Jesus Christ who is *at God's*

right hand—for he went to heaven after angels, author- 22
ities, and powers celestial had been made subject to him.

You remember, says Peter, how it was **in the Spirit** (i.e. 19
after his translation to heaven) that **Enoch went** down on
his famous mission **to the imprisoned spirits.** One tradition
placed this commission during Enoch's lifetime ; ' Enoch,
though a man, acted as God's envoy to the angels, and
was translated,' says Irenaeus (iv. 16, 2). Peter seems to
follow the other tradition (so Enoch xii. 1), which gave
Enoch the honour of being commissioned by God to go down
from heaven to announce a sentence of final doom to the
rebellious angels who had (Genesis vi. 1–7) demoralized
mankind so deeply that the Flood had to be sent. They were
spirits who had defiled themselves with the flesh (Enoch xv. 4),
and were punished by being **imprisoned** at the Flood (Enoch
liv. 7 f.) **in chains eternal** (Judas 6). In vain they pled to
God for mercy. At His bidding **Enoch went and preached**
doom to them (Enoch xii. 2–xiii. 3), telling them from God
that they were to have ' no peace nor forgiveness of sin '—
a grim preaching ! (Peter never uses this word in the epistle
for preaching the gospel.) Enoch's activity **in the Spirit**
was very different from Christ's : the one **went down,** on a
mission of doom ; the other **went up** (ver. 22), triumphing over
all that kept men from receiving the mercy of God.

But what interests Peter is baptism, not Enoch. The
contrast of **flesh** and **Spirit,** on which he is dwelling (iii. 18,
iv. 1–6), suggests to him the supreme case of sin in the flesh
being punished, and also the contrast between the two
missions of Enoch and Christ **in the Spirit.** But his aim is
to remind his readers that this activity of Christ **in the Spirit**

has inaugurated the sacrament of baptism, which saves the spirit from the defilement of the flesh. We moderns have to spend words on explaining the mission of Enoch, because the allusion is to a world of belief which is remote and misty for us ; but the first readers of the epistle required no explanation. They were familiar with the story of Enoch. The legend was so intelligible that their minds easily passed on to the subject of baptism, the reference to the Flood being the bridge between it and the mission of Enoch. The Flood ! What a terrible warning (see Matthew xxiv. 37 f.) of the end of the world ! Only eight souls saved then ! **Only a few**—and will salvation be easy now (iv. 18) ? There was an interpretation of Genesis vi. 3 (' yet shall man's days be a hundred and twenty years ') which took it as the declaration of a respite before the Flood, and to this 20 Peter refers when he speaks of **the time when God's patience held out during Noah's construction of the ark** (Hebrews xi. 7). Then no more than eight souls **were brought safely through the water.** The Greek preposition *dia* has the same convenient vagueness as our ' through ' ; the water was at once the means of destruction and the agent of salvation. (Hence one rabbinic legend made Noah and the others find their way to the ark by wading up to the knees through the water which had already begun to rise.) Now 21 there is water in our sacrament too, **the counterpart to** this rescue of Noah and his family through water. Paul found a counterpart in the waters of the Red Sea (1 Corinthians x. 1–2) ; Peter chooses what some of these Asiatic Christians would appreciate as a local allusion, for early traditions connected both Enoch and the ark with Phrygia ; indeed the city of Apamea on the river Marsyas was identified as the spot at which the ark rested, partly owing to its byname of Kibotos (Ark). But Peter appeals to far more than local interest. **Baptism saves you to-day by the resurrection of Jesus Christ ;** the faith (i. 21) of Christians made them participate at baptism in the new life opened by Christ's supremacy in the spiritual world. Again, the language would appeal to those who knew the contemporary representations of resurrection in cults like those of Cybele and Attis, or the aim of the Eleusinian mysteries to effect regeneration and salvation from evil through baptism (see above, on i. 3). But the thought of Peter is quite intelligible in the light of common Christian experience: had Christ not risen, there would have been no baptism at all ; baptism in the name of Jesus Christ meant from the first (Acts ii. 31–41) a recognition of his living power to pardon sin and to confer new life.

In an important parenthesis Peter explains the human side of the sacrament. The Greek term (*baptisma*) still carried its original sense of **washing** (see Ephesians v. 26), but the effect of the sacrament was not skin-deep, as we say, **not the mere washing** or removal **of dirt from the flesh.** Instead of saying that it meant the cleansing of the spirit or heart (Hebrews x. 22), Peter defines the inward, essential factor in baptism as **the prayer** (only here in N.T.) **for a clean conscience** (ver. 16) **before** (in presence of, a reverential use of *eis* in connexion with petitions to authority) **God.** The reference is to the strict ethical obligations laid upon catechumens at baptism, perhaps to their solemn renunciation of the world. When Pliny cross-examined some Christians in Bithynia, about A.D. 112, he found that they ' bound themselves by an oath (*sacramento*) not to commit theft or robbery or adultery, not to break their word, and not to deny having received a deposit when demanded '—a practical expression of the clean conscience for which Christians at baptism prayed, and to which Peter summoned them for the sake of impressing the outside public as well as for their own sake.

As for the closing words of the paragraph, they allude to the accepted belief of the church that the resurrection was 22 followed by the ascension (**went to heaven**), the session **at God's right hand** (as Peter had said long ago, Acts ii. 32–35) and (as he had already mentioned, i. 12) the despatch of the holy Spirit. It is a picturesque way of delineating the supreme honour and authority of Christ. In the book of Enoch, Enoch is on a footing with the angels and celestial powers, but no more. Christ is superior to **angels, authorities, and powers celestial** (the same enumeration of celestial forces occurs in the contemporary Jewish apocalypse of *The Ascension of Isaiah*, i. 3) ; this supremacy in heaven belongs to the **glory** (i. 11, 21) he has won through death. Paul makes more of this triumph in the spirit-world, but Peter's practical interest only touches the belief in order to remind Christians how secure they might feel with so exalted and powerful a **Guardian** (ii. 25) over them and theirs. In the flesh Christ had to die, his body laden with sins that were ours, not his. But now in the Spirit he has a saving ministry for us, who are still in the flesh.

Note on iii. 19, 20.—The text of ver. 19 as rendered above is ΕΝΩΚΑΙ ΕΝΩΧ. The common text is ΕΝΩΚΑΙ, i.e. by or in which (**the Spirit**), but an early copyist dropped ΕΝΩΧ, owing to their similarity to the preceding ΕΝΩΚ, a blunder not uncommon in MSS. This conjecture was originally suggested by some English scholars in the eighteenth century, made independently by the Dutch scholar Cramer in 1891, and put in improved form by Dr. Rendel Harris recently. The ordinary reading makes the preaching to the imprisoned spirits the work of Christ. Some scholars, it is true, recognize the mission of Enoch in iii. 19 even under the traditional text, but suppose that Christ acted through Enoch. The majority, however, take the words to mean a personal mission of Christ. This is sometimes referred to (*a*) the pre-existent Christ who is supposed to have preached in vain to the disobedient contemporaries of Noah (now in durance vile as imprisoned spirits for their rejection of his warning). More often, though no more convincingly, it is assigned to (*b*) Christ between the crucifixion and the resurrection, when, his body lying in the grave, he went in the Spirit to preach in Hades, the world of the dead. But to whom? To these impenitent contemporaries of Noah, offering them salvation ; they were examples, good examples, just because they were so bad, of the gospel being presented after death to sinful men (an idea which is frequently read into iv. 6). This would be an unparalleled application of the common early Christian belief that Christ did descend to the lower world ; the more usual view was that he preached there to the O.T. saints or that he released all in Hades, pagans as well as good Jews. The idea of disembodied spirits being released from Hades and the devil may underlie the allusion to the celestial powers having been made subject to Christ (ver. 22) ; such a result of the conquest of Hades by the descent of a divine victor was familiar in ethnic circles already, and soon entered into primitive Christianity as well as into apocalyptic Judaism. The later ' Petrine ' literature throws no light upon the passage. In Second Peter the entire conception is ignored ; Noah is the herald of righteousness

(ii. 5) to his incredulous generation. In the Gospel of Peter (x. 39–42), when Christ, supported by two angels and followed by the cross, emerges from the grave, a Voice from heaven asks, 'Hast thou preached to them that sleep?' The cross replies, 'Yes.' Those who sleep are the dead, but the reference is deliberately vague.

Peter now resumes the thought of iii. 17, 18, applying the antithesis of flesh and the Spirit to the Christian life. In iii. 19–22 the Spirit of Christ has been uppermost; now it is the flesh of the Christian.

iv.

1 **Well, as Christ has suffered for us in the flesh, let this very conviction that he who has suffered in the flesh gets quit**

2 **of sin, nerve you to spend the rest of your time in the flesh for the will of God and no longer for human passions.**

1 We are living in a new era and order of experience, since Christ has suffered for us in the flesh. Therefore, he had already said, 'We must break with sin and live for righteousness' (ii. 24); the same thought is now put differently, in the form of a general axiom, **he who has suffered in the flesh gets quit of sin.** Some in the later church held that martyrdom was an atonement for sin, a second baptism which washed the soul clean. But this is not the meaning here; the words about **the rest of your time in the flesh** suggest that capital punishment was not expected as the normal outcome of faithfulness. The idea rather is that suffering in the flesh, i.e. in our sensuous nature, has a purifying and liberating effect. When Christians undergo suffering for conscience' sake, there is a real virtue in it, a blessing (iii. 14) from God; it enables them to participate more fully in the Spirit (iv. 14).

This is the deep thought expressed by Paul in his aspiration to *know Christ in the power of his resurrection and the fellowship of his sufferings, with my nature transformed to die as he died* (Philippians iii. 10), i.e. to sin. Peter puts it thus: people who for the sake of maintaining a **clean conscience before God** endure pain or face trials in order to advance his cause, are thereby detached from the grip of sin. Self-denial and hardship of this kind contribute a moral and spiritual factor of development to our nature (see ii. 20). It proves that they are done with sin, sitting loose to the passions and instincts of the flesh.

Experience is the best exegesis of such tense words, particularly the experience of those who have lived through similar phases of endurance in the Christian cause. Thus when Hus went to the Council of Constance in 1414, he wrote a letter to his friends in Bohemia about his persecutors in the Roman Church which contains a passage bearing on our text. 'I shall not be led astray by them to the side of evil, though I suffer at His will temptations, revilings, imprisonments, and deaths—as indeed He too suffered, and hath subjected His loved servants to the same trials, leaving us an example that we may suffer for His sake and our salvation. If He suffered, being what He was, why should not we? In truth, our suffering by His grace is our drawing from sins and our deliverance from eternal torments' (*The Letters of John Hus*, ed. Workman and Pope, p. 148). The same profound thought reappears in lines which he wrote during his imprisonment (*ibid.*, p. 198):

> The hours pass lightly ; for this road
> The Master went, who bore our load.
> This is my passion, naught indeed
> Or slight, if I from sin be freed.

May Christ the Lord stand by His own,
Lest Antichrist do gulp us down !

2   This is the **conviction** needed to **nerve you** for such moral
loyalty ; it is an heroic and trying enterprise. Literally
the phrase is, ' arm yourselves with ' this **conviction**. It
is a common phrase, which has even passed into English.
Thus the Roman general Cominius, in Shakespeare's play,
exhorts the high-spirited Coriolanus to summon up his
powers of self-control in order to meet the critical tribunes :

> Arm yourself
> To answer mildly ; for they are prepared
> With accusations.

What matters is not so much the actual trials incurred in
a consistent obedience to **the will of God** (ii. 15, iii. 17) as
what we think about them when we encounter them **in the
flesh**, where **human passions** still make their appeal. These
human passions were primarily impurity and self-seeking.
What impressed the world in the early Christians was their
charity and their chastity. The former has been already
mentioned. The latter, for which they were liable to be
affronted and abused as well as admired, is now discussed.

With a touch of grave irony, Peter tells them that they
have lived long enough in pagan vices, and consoles them
by predicting the imminent judgment of God which will
vindicate their staunchness (3–6).

3 It is quite enough to have done as pagans choose to do, during
    the time gone by ! **You** used to lead lives of sensuality,
    lust, carousing, revelry, dissipation and illicit idolatry,
4   and it astonishes them that you will not plunge with them

still into the same flood of profligacy. They abuse you, 5
but they will have to answer for that to Him who is
prepared to judge the living and the dead (for this was 6
why the gospel was preached to the dead as well, that
while they are judged in the flesh as men, they may live
as God lives in the spirit).

A sixfold description of the **human passions** of pagan 3
society. **Sensuality** is indecent, lascivious conduct, wanton
and unashamed. **Lust** is sexual passion in immoral forms
(same word as that rendered ' passions ' in ver. 2). **Carousing**
(only here in N.T.) is immoderate indulgence in wine. **Revelry**
means protracted drinking-bouts, often in connexion with
celebrations of pagan religion, and **dissipation** refers to social
drinking-parties (only here in N.T.). All **idolatry** was **illicit,**
from the Christian point of view (i.e. contrary to the law and
worship of God), but some forms of pagan worship in the
Oriental cults were mixed up with practices which, from
the point of Roman law, were abominable and illegal. ' What
you were makes them astonished at what you are ' : this is
the thought of ver. 4, where **profligacy** means a reckless 4
waste of time and strength and means. The reverberating
effect of the participle *blasphemountes* at the end of the
sentence is best preserved by taking it as the beginning of
the next ; from amazement at your new strictness they pass
to abuse, taunting you as kill-joys and morose creatures.
But they will have to answer for that abuse (which did not 5
stop with words) **to Him who is prepared** ere long, at the second
Advent, **to judge the living and the dead,** i.e. God the Father
(i. 17, ii. 23), though, in speaking to Cornelius (Acts x. 42),
Peter had followed the theology of Enoch (lxix. 27) that

149

all judgment was entrusted to Christ. He is **prepared to judge the dead** as well as the living, in the immediate future, for the dead have had their chance of hearing the gospel already. The living include the present abusive enemies of Christians, for it is assumed that they will be alive at the judgment, so near it is. The Christians will also be alive and be judged strictly by their God (i. 17, iv. 17, 18), passing into life eternal in the spirit.

Peter mentions **the dead** for a special reason and with an explanation by way of parenthesis. Christians who have died before the second Advent are not excluded from this blissful vindication ; though they have had to suffer the penalty of death in their mortal sinful natures (**judged in the 6 flesh as men**), their acceptance of the gospel when they were alive insures their immortal life **as God lives** (see i. 15) **in the spirit**. Peter thus meets in his own way the anxiety felt by some Macedonian Christians (1 Thessalonians iv. 13). In Asia, too, the vivid hope of the second Advent made believers feel disappointed and discouraged when some of their fellows died before this crowning triumph ; they asked in perplexity, ' What was the use of preaching the gospel to them at all, if they miss the outcome of it ? ' Peter's reply is that the reason why **the gospel was preached** once (i. 12) to those who are now **dead as well** as to those still living was to secure that in adhering to it they, like Christ (iii. 18), should reach the divine life **in the spirit**, though first they had to be **judged in the flesh**.

Another view is possible. While it is naturally out of the question to take **the dead** here as ' dead in trespasses and sins ' (the dead in ver. 5 are dead people, and **the dead** here are the same · they are not spiritually dead, but dead in the

150

sense that they have experienced death on earth), yet **the dead** here might refer to those who had not heard the gospel during their lifetime, and therefore had an opportunity granted them somehow. In the early church there was a belief that Christ preached in Hades, the underworld of the dead, between the crucifixion and the resurrection, either to all the dead or to the O.T. saints, and Peter may be alluding to this idea (see above). There would be an implicit contrast between Enoch's mission (iii. 19) and Christ's ; Enoch had only a message of doom, whilst Christ had one of hope ; Enoch addressed fallen angels, whilst Christ dealt with disembodied human spirits, in the spirit-world.

In any case the words are an allusion in passing to some belief which was familiar to the writer and his readers, too familiar to require explanation. But it is hard for us to reconstruct the context of the belief from the scanty materials at our disposal. Peter was not writing a theology ; he was simply addressing himself to a special situation, to harassed Christians who were in need of encouragement, and he reminds them that the relief is sure and near, vindication for themselves, retribution for their foes—and also that their dead fellows were quite safe with God. Modern Christians ask larger questions. What becomes of the pre-Christian dead ? How are men treated, who at the end have never heard the gospel ? But these questions were not present to the apostle's mind here.

The next paragraph (7–11) is an epilogue, recalling the tone of iii. 8–12.

Now, the end of all is near. Steady then, keep cool and 7
    pray ! Above all, be keen to love one another, for *love* 8

9
10

hides a host of *sins*. Be hospitable to each other, and do not grudge it. You must serve one another, each with the talent he has received, as efficient stewards of

11

God's varied grace. If anyone preaches, he must preach as one who utters the words of God ; if anyone renders some service, it must be as one who is supplied by God with power, so that in everything God may be glorified through Jesus Christ. The glory and the dominion are his for ever and ever ; Amen.

7 No panic or excitement, however, though the end of all is near (ver. 5) ! Steady (the word translated ' sane ' in 2 Corinthians v. 13) then, instead of losing your heads, as some early Christians were apt to do (see 2 Thessalonians ii. 2, iii. 11, 12), dropping their work and duties in hectic anticipation. Keep cool (i. 13) and pray (literally, ' keep cool for prayer ') ; your prayers must not be wild screams or reasonless cries. The judgment was to be a trying time (iv. 17, 18) as well as a relief, and serious prayer was the best preparation for it.

8 Another vital preparation was the habit of mutual love (i. 22, ii. 1, iii. 8), answering to the demands of God. Keen is the adjective whose adverb is rendered ' steadily ' in i. 22. The community must hold together, instead of allowing their love to ' grow cold ' (Matthew xxiv. 12) in the latter days of strain ; it is a warning against loving others by fits and starts, a plea for steady affection, persisting through the irritations and antagonisms of common life in a society recruited from various classes of people. For much will be forgiven to a loving heart ; God counts that too (ii. 20) a merit. Love hides a host of sins, says Peter, quoting a

Greek version of Proverbs x. 12, to remind his friends that
brotherly love will atone for a good deal in the sight of God.
The original meaning of the proverb was that the loving
temper does not rake up faults but seeks to pass them over
with forbearance (the idea of 1 Corinthians xiii. 7).   But here
the sins are a man's own, not his neighbours'.   As he forgives,
he is forgiven (Matthew vi. 14, 15) ; hides or ' covers ' implies
forgiveness (Psalm xxxii. 1).   The imminent judgment was
to be a serious scrutiny of Christians (ver. 17), who would be
tested by their measure of brotherly love.

As in Hebrews xiii. 2, one special form of love is urged. 9
Be hospitable to one another. This duty of entertaining
travelling Christians was still the duty of the members,
though later it fell specially to the clergy (1 Timothy iii. 2).
It was needful, for inns in the East were often not only
expensive but morally deteriorating ; an itinerant Christian,
whether he was a preacher or not (see 3 John 5–8), was safer
in the house of some local member of the church. **And do
not grudge it,** despite the trouble and expense ; naturally
the burden would fall on one or two as a rule in each community, and fall repeatedly. In the pre-Christian *Psalter
of Solomon* (v. 15), drawing a contrast between God's kindness
and man's, the author writes : ' If a man repeats his kindness
and does not grudge it [the very phrase used here], you
would be surprised.'

The point of 10–11 is that the exercise of the various
talents or endowments of Christians must be carried on in
a deep sense of responsibility to God, as designed for the
service of the community, not for self-display nor in any
self-reliance. We do not make them ; **each has received 10
his talent** (Romans xii. 6, 1 Corinthians xii. 4) to serve others,

and we are called to be efficient stewards in the household of God, administering His varied grace. The house-steward distributed the rations and pay regularly to his fellow-slaves. Jesus had used the figure (Luke xii. 42), and so had Paul (1 Corinthians iv. 1), for the responsible duty of exercising one's gifts in the service of the church.

Hospitality (Romans xii. 13) was one of these talents, but Peter passes on to mention preaching specifically, as Paul does in Romans xii. 7, 8 ; this, and not the administration of the sacraments, was the prominent function (so Hebrews xiii. 7). **Preaches** is a word that covers teaching and prophetic utterances, any official or unofficial exhortation to which a member was moved by his **talent.** The temptation of the talent of hospitality was to be grudging, i.e. to regard one's possessions as more for oneself than for others. The temptation of preaching was to forget that one was no more than a **steward,** giving out what God had in store for the good of others. Hospitality was stewardship of money and a home ; preaching was stewardship in which a man depended on God

11 for what he said. **He must preach as one who utters the words of God,** not his own opinions, not rhetoric of his own which he parades ; he must depend upon the inspiration of Another for what he says.

So with any other form of practical **service** (Romans xii. 7, 1 Corinthians xvi. 15) ; the person must render it with due recognition that he is **supplied by God with power** (the term rendered ' supplied ' is that rendered ' furnish ' in 2 Corinthians ix. 10), therefore humbly, without self-display. Ignatius (*Ad Polyk.* vi.) bids the members of the church at Smyrna live together ' as God's stewards and assessors and servants.' The range of stewardship here is equally wide ;

it is not confined to apostles or presbyters or any special ministers. Such a spirit of service in the community will bring out the full power of God, as it was intended to do— **so that in everything God may be glorified through Jesus Christ** (the thought of Matthew v. 16 and John xv. 8). The brotherly love which is the life of the church is devoid of any self-glorification. The more efficient a community is, the more it suggests how great and good is the God to whom it owes everything. **The glory and the dominion** (over the celestial world, the earth, and the church, iii. 22, iv. 5, 11, see v. 6 and 11) **are his** (God, or, as in Revelation i. 6, Jesus Christ) **for ever and ever ; Amen** (i.e. so be it, so it is—a liturgical affirmation).

Here the homily might have ended. Here indeed it may have ended. But letters then, as now, were not always written at a sitting, and we may assume some interruption at this point ; the epistle had to be laid aside for a time, and then resumed. In what follows Peter reiterates afresh the main thoughts of the earlier sections : iv. 12–19 corresponds to iii. 8–iv. 11 and v. 1–11 to iv. 7–11. On both topics he found he had more to say.

'And now for a last word upon your sufferings.' The apostle has two things to say, the first in 12–16, the second in 17–19.

Beloved, do not be surprised at the ordeal that has come 12 **to test you, as though some foreign experience befell you. You are sharing what Christ suffered ; so rejoice** 13 **in it, that you may also rejoice and exult when his glory is revealed. If** *you are denounced* **for the sake of** *Christ,* 14 **you are blessed ; for then** *the Spirit* **of glory and power,**

155

15   the Spirit of *God* himself, *is resting on you.* None of you must suffer as a murderer or a thief or a bad character

16   or a revolutionary; but if a man suffers for being a Christian, he must not be ashamed, he must rather glorify God for that.

12   Beloved, as in ii. 11, is a touch of affectionate sympathy, as he handles the sensitive question of their trials. It is as though he overheard some saying, 'Why have we been plunged into this trouble? What relevance has all this to our character and record?' His first point is (*a*) that it is a test (as in i. 7). The term rendered **ordeal** occurs in the LXX of Proverbs xxvii. 21 ('the fining pot for silver and the *furnace* for gold'). Only valuable metal is smelted in a furnace, and smelted to bring out its brilliance and lasting value. Then (*b*) the **ordeal** is not a **foreign experience**, not something irrelevant and abnormal, but in the direct line of Christ. Peter does not bring forward the example of the prophets, like Jesus (Matthew v. 11–12) and James (v. 10); he again (ii. 21) recalls how Jesus was badly treated by the world of his day, and summons his friends to **rejoice in sharing what**

13 **Christ suffered.** To be maligned and molested for his sake brings his followers into touch with him. Theirs is the inward joy of which he spoke (Matthew v. 10), and there is a thrilling joy (so i. 6, 8) to follow at the end of the rough experience. What promotes this heroic enthusiasm cannot be thought **foreign** to the Christian discipline. Peter, like Paul, only speaks about the 'sufferings' of Christ in connexion with Christians sharing them (see 2 Corinthians i. 5 and Philippians iii. 10). And in elaborating his argument (**ver. 14**) he is speaking of what he himself knew by sharp

experience (see Acts v. 41), as well as of what he had once
heard Jesus say (Matthew v. 11).

Rejoice. Why? Because (see iii. 14) you are already
being blessed, as Jesus promised ; there is a divine compensa- 14
tion to be enjoyed under the outward contempt and scoffing,
as **you are denounced** for being Christians. Sometimes this
denunciation led to arrest and punishment at the hands of
an excited mob or of the authorities (see ver. 16), but Peter
is here thinking primarily of the sneers and taunts and
slanders from pagans which were apt to make Christians feel
depressed and uneasy. He would have them deserve the
praise awarded to Milton's Abdiel (*Paradise Lost*, vi. 32 f.),
who, ' for the testimony of truth,' had borne—

> Universal reproach, far worse to bear
> Than violence ; for this was all thy care—
> To stand approved in sight of God, though worlds
> Judged thee perverse.

Injuries and outrages reveal the spirit of your pagan
neighbours, who try to crush your strength, but there is
for your loyalty another revelation of God's **glory and power**
(the presence of God in glorious power) which inwardly
rewards and rallies you. The phrase **you are denounced . . .
Christ** may be an echo of Psalm lxxxix. 51, 52 (the LXX) ;
certainly there is an echo of Isaiah xi. 2 in **the Spirit of God
is resting on you,** i.e. inspiring and endowing you permanently.
Only, this inner glow is reserved for those who are suffering
innocently **for the sake of Christ ;** it is not for any Christian
who is punished as a criminal, e.g. as a really (contrast ii. 12)
bad character (see on ii. 12). This Greek term has been 15
taken in the narrower sense of the Latin *maleficus*, i.e. poisoner
or magician. but we should expect then a word like *goês*

157

(2 Timothy iii. 13) or *magos* (Acts viii. 9 f.). **Revolutionary** again suggests the danger of Christians laying themselves open to the Roman suspicion of the church as a seditious, secret organization, aiming at the overthrow of the State. A Christian, especially under the influence of apocalyptic hopes, might incur the suspicion of treason by encouraging disobedience among slaves, for example, or by sympathizing with revolutionary movements, in exasperation against the persecuting authorities. The risk of an extreme left wing among Christians was not unfounded at this period. The anti-Roman tone of an apocalypse like the book of Revelation shows how the apocalyptic hope might be used to foster social discontent and political disorder. The Greek term, however, has been also taken to mean " busybody," i.e. a tactless interference with social customs, as when a Christian gave needless offence by tampering with social relationships or by ill-timed protests which roused dissension and discord. It might further refer to imprudent, though generous, representations to the authorities on behalf of some ill-used fellow-citizen, which laid the objectors open to the law against treason. Peter seems to have coined the word, and **revolutionary** answers to the sense of the context better than any allusion to indiscreet interference or meddling tactics.

16   **But if a man suffers for being a Christian, he must not be ashamed,** and so apostatize (see Mark viii. 38, 2 Timothy i. 8, 12), **he must rather glorify God for that,** i.e. in words, by thanking God for this opportunity of proving his loyalty and honouring the Christian cause, and also in deeds, proving by his stedfastness and patience what a good God he has **and thus reflecting credit on his God**—perhaps even by a

martyr death (as in John xxi. 19). The name of **Christian** (see on Acts xi. 26) had already become a nickname on the lips of the Roman mob, as Tacitus implies. But it is noticeable that Peter never alludes to the three charges of atheism, cannibalism, and immorality, which were afterwards brought against Christianity by the suspicious Romans. Here, as elsewhere in the homily, the situation reflected seems to be merely one of popular suspicion directed against what was considered to be an illicit, foreign cult or secret religious society, largely recruited from the slave class and ominously antagonistic to social harmony.

Peter's second word of consolation is eschatological. ' Deliverance is at hand: you have not long now to wait.'

It is time for the Judgment *to begin with the household of God ;* **17**
> **and if it begins with us,**
>> **what will be the fate of those who refuse obedience to God's gospel ?**
>> **If** *the just man is scarcely saved,* **18**
>> *what will become of the impious and sinful ?*

So let those who are suffering by the will of God trust **19** **their souls to him, their faithful Creator, as they continue to do right.**

It was an O.T. axiom that God's judgment should **begin** **17** **with the household of God** (see Isaiah x. 12, Jeremiah xxv. 29, and Ezekiel ix. 6, which is in the apostle's mind here). That is, it **begins with us,** God's People (ii. 9, 24) who live His life. Peter, like Jesus in the parable (Luke xix. 15), is sterner and stricter than the book of Enoch, which (see civ. 5, etc.) occasionally exempts the righteous from judgment. **He views the** sufferings of Christians as the prelude to **the final**

159

judgment, or rather as the initial scene in the last act of judgment, and trying (the apocalyptic thought of Mark xiii. 20) because they involve the possibility of failing under the 18 severe test. **The just man is scarcely saved,** so hard is the trial, so weak is human nature. The consolation is (*a*) that it will be over soon, and (*b*) that failure will be unspeakably awful. Trust yourselves to God, **continue to do right** (see on ver. 8), and all will be well; however severe this ordeal may be, it is nothing compared to the fate of outsiders. In Proverbs xi. 31 the Hebrew couplet ran:

> The just will be punished on earth—
> How much more the impious and sinful!

That **is,** retribution will overtake sin in the present world. The LXX omitted **on earth,** which suited Peter's purpose better. He is content to leave his question unanswered, What will be the fate of the impenitent? Which is more impressive than the explicit threats of Enoch (xxxviii. 1 f.: ' sinners shall be driven from the earth,' xlv. 6, etc.).

19 **So,** in view of what has been urged in 12–16 as well as in 17–18, let those who **are suffering by the will of God** (iii. 17) **trust their souls to him** for safe keeping—the thought of Psalm xxxi. 5, which Jesus quoted on the cross (Luke xxiii. 46). Do as Jesus did (ii. 23), leave yourselves in the hands of a **faithful Creator,** faithful in upholding the moral order, punishing the evil and preserving the faithful. The appeal to God as **Creator** is as early as Acts iv. 24, but this is the only place in the N.T. where the title is used. The implication here, as in Hebrews ii. 10, is that the redemptive purpose is part of creation. The **Creator** has the forces of the universe at His disposal to punish the disobedient (Enoch xciv. 10:

' He who hath created you will overthrow you '—the woe upon rich oppressors) and to safeguard the loyal lives which He has Himself created, **as they continue to do right.** Their trust in Him implies moral activity (the thought of 15–16). There must be no presuming upon faith in God; only a clean, obedient life can be securely committed to God's care.

A word to the presbyters (v. 1–4) broadens into a general plea for humility (5–7), which brings the apostle round again for the last time to the critical situation of his readers (6–11).

v.

Now I make this appeal to your presbyters (for I am a presbyter myself, I was a witness of what Christ suffered and I am to share the glory that will be revealed), be shepherds to your flock of God; take charge of them willingly instead of being pressed to it, not to make a base profit from it but freely, not by way of lording it over your charges but proving a pattern to the flock. Then you will receive the unfading crown of glory, when the chief Shepherd makes his appearance.

1
2
3
4

Presbyter, the official title for the ministers of the primitive communities, meant literally ' senior.' Not all the seniors in a community would be presbyters, but the presbyters would be as a rule chosen on account of their experience and age. Peter plays on the double sense of the term; **I am a presbyter myself,** i.e. old enough to have seen Christ suffer. **Presbyter myself** (literally, fellow-presbyter) is a touch of modesty from an apostle (i. 1)—there is nothing overbearing about Peter (ver. 3). **Witness** means not only an eye-witness, but one who witnesses to **what Christ suffered,** i.e. to their significance and reality. But he cannot speak of these

1

sufferings without adding their climax of **the glory that will be revealed** (see iv. 13), in which he is to **share** with Christ (the thought of John xiii. 36). Behind the suffering of the present world for Christians as well as for Christ, Peter always sees the gleam of the final glory. Even in an aside like this, the thought rises instinctively to hearten his readers.

2 **Now . . . be shepherds.** The adverb and the aoristic imperative of the verb (here, as in i. 13, 17, 22, referring to a specific period, the interval before the end—ver. 4) imply that one means of upholding the faith of Christians under a strain (iv. 19) is the proper discharge of ministerial duty. The faithful must not be left to themselves ; ministers ought to fulfil their pastoral responsibilities, supplying Christian discipline and direction, and giving a lead to the people. The pastoral metaphor has lost its appeal and significance for modern readers. Nowadays a mature layman will resent a clergyman calling ' me one of his sheep. I am not a sheep relatively to him. I am at least his equal in knowledge, and greatly his superior in experience. Nobody but a parson would venture to compare me to an animal (such a stupid animal too !) and himself to that animal's master' (P. G. Hamerton, *Human Intercourse*, p. 191). But in the ancient world the metaphor denoted a vigorous and responsible authority. It was applied to kings and rulers, who had to provide for their people, protecting and ruling them with close personal supervision. The Oriental shepherd had to protect his flock as well as guide them to good pasture. He was never away from them. He had to stand between them and danger, to think for them, and to be responsible for them with his own life, if occasion required. No relation so expressed the twofold functions of control

and devotion. Hence the term came into use for ministers of the church. **Be shepherds to your flock of God.** The flock belongs to God; Christ is the chief Shepherd (ver. 4); Christian ministers are subordinate shepherds. The word **your** (literally, among you) means that part of the great church wh ch falls to your charge; the flock is wider than those within the Asiatic communities; it is invariably the **flock of God,** the divine flock ('My sheep,' John xxi. 15, 16); and Peter has three directions for the presbyters.

(a) They must show no reluctance in undertaking or in carrying out their duties. **Take charge of them** (*episcopountes*, i.e. discharge your episcopal functions) **willingly, instead of being pressed to it.** Sometimes the presbyters were selected by the apostles who founded the community (Acts xiv. 23). But, however chosen, they had a divine commission; Paul reminds the presbyters of the Ephesian church of their duties 'to all the flock of which the holy Spirit has appointed you guardians (*episcopous*, bishops): shepherd the church of the Lord' (Acts xx. 28). They must not grudge time and pains in the service, nor resent the onerous responsibilities of the position. In periods of persecution there was a real danger in accepting office, for officials enjoyed an unpleasant prominence, which led to them often being singled out by the State authorities. Hence some were indisposed to take office at all.

Others, again, were quite willing to serve, and threw themselves into the work, but evidently for the sake of what it brought them. Such presbyters (b) are warned **not to make a base profit from it** but to serve the church **freely,** i.e. without making the stipend the main end. Peter protests against mercenary aims, against the temper which makes men do no more than they are paid for. The presbyters had some control of church finance; they had to do with the funds, and this started temptations to make a lucrative thing of their position. Polykarp, in his epistle to the church of Philippi (ch. xi. 1), mentions the sad case of a local presbyter called Valens, who had evidently succumbed to this temptation.

But the desire for position is stronger in some than the love of money, and the apostle proceeds to warn (c) other 3 presbyters against **lording it over** their **charges**, the overbearing temper against which Jesus had already put his disciples on their guard (Mark x. 42 f., Luke xii. 45). A pre-Christian Jewish warning is quoted in the Chagiga (5b, i. 32) against any president of a rabbinic school 'who deals arrogantly with the congregation.' How this autocratic or self-important temper worked in the primitive Christian communities we are not told, but this is not the only hint of it (see 1 Timothy iii. 3). Such a domineering spirit defeats the ends of Christian discipline, produces bad feeling, and lowers the atmosphere of brotherly love.

Charges translates the plural of the term *klêros*, which here has its untechnical sense of 'an allotted portion'; the **charges** are the different churches entrusted to the care of the presbyters. The Vulgate rendered the Greek literally, 'dominantes in cleris,' but the distinction between clergy and laity is much later than this, and the words cannot mean 'domineering over the lower clergy.' Instead of driving and bullying the faithful, the presbyters are to prove **a pattern to the flock**; their best influence will be through personal 4 example. Then, at the second Advent, **you will receive** (the same verb as 'obtain' in i. 9) the unfading (i. 4) **crown (consisting) of glory**, when the chief Shepherd makes his

appearance (same verb used of the first Advent in i. 20). **In** the Hellenistic world distinguished statesmen or public benefactors received crowns of gold from the community **as** a recognition of their services.

A brief sentence to the younger men (5) passes on to a general counsel upon deference and humility (6–7).

> **You younger men must also submit to the presbyters. Indeed** 5
> **you must all put on the apron of humility to serve one**
> **another, for**
>> *the haughty God opposes,*
>> *but to the humble he gives grace.*
>
> **Humble yourselves under the strong hand of God, then,** 6
> **so that when it is time, he may raise you ; let all your** 7
> **anxieties fall upon him, for his interest is in you.**

The younger men are junior subordinates in the ministry 5 (see Acts v. 6, 10). They **also** (same word as ' in the same way,' iii. 1) have their temptation, to be restive under authority, and are bidden **submit to the presbyters.** Later in the century serious trouble arose in the church at Corinth over insubordination on the part of the younger men ; the epistle of Clemens Romanus is elicited by this. Peter probably had this risk of forwardness and insubordination in mind when he warned the senior presbyters against rough ways (ver. 3). A tyrannical spirit among authorities does not make submissiveness easy among subordinates. **Indeed you must all** (seniors and juniors alike, officials and members) **put on the apron of humility,** as Jesus did at the last Supper (John xiii. 4 f.). Peter had not forgotten his lesson. The **apron** was worn by slaves, to protect their tunic when at **work.** Ministers are to help or **serve one another ;** they require mutual aid and support, and this is impossible when they put on airs. Age and youth in the ministry are equally liable to a proud independence. But the common spirit of humility demanded by Peter from the rank and file as well implies a readiness to learn from others, a willingness to work with them ; each must humbly recognize what the other may have to contribute, instead of holding aloof in a proud superiority. The comparative length of the admonitions may imply that the senior presbyters required more warning than the juniors ; but it may simply mean that the senior position was more responsible and therefore involved greater perils.

The quotation from Proverbs iii. 34, with which the counsel is clinched, widens and deepens the duty of humility. Friends used to say of Bishop Westcott that ' he was humble to God but not exactly humble to man.' Peter insists upon 6 humility in both directions, and now on submission to the **strong hand of God**—an O.T. phrase (Exodus iii. 19, Ezekiel xx. 33 f.) for protection and deliverance as well as for the downfall of proud persecutors. The pressure of His hand in suffering must be submitted to humbly ; **so that, when it is time** (when His time comes, as come it will), **he may raise you,** uplifting the lowly who have lain still under His discipline. For—

> Tho' His arm be strong to smite,
> 'Tis also strong to save.

7 **Humble yourselves** by letting **all your anxieties fall upon him** (a reminiscence of Psalm lv. 22). No impatience or fretfulness, as if you had to carry the burden yourselves. **His interest is in you.** ' There are gods, and they are interested (*melei*, the same word as here) in human affairs ' (Marcus Aurelius, ii. 11). Be sure of His ultimate relief, but mean-

while do not think that He is careless or indifferent. **His**
and **you** are emphatic.

But this does not mean that you can relax your efforts ;
be alert and stedfast till you are finally relieved (8–11).

Keep cool, keep awake. Your enemy the devil prowls like a 8
roaring lion, looking out for someone to devour. Resist 9
him ; keep your foothold in the faith, and learn to pay
the same tax of suffering as the rest of your brotherhood
throughout the world. Once you have suffered for a 10
little, the God of all grace who has called you to his
eternal glory in Christ Jesus, will repair and recruit and
strengthen you. The dominion is his for ever and ever : 11
Amen.

Trust is not idle security (so in iv. 19) ; the confidence in
God which throws off anxieties only leaves one more able
to be morally alert against temptations to apostasy. **Keep** 8
cool (as in i. 13, iv. 7)—no need for panic, when God's care
is over you—**keep awake** (Peter remembered the incident of
Matthew xxvi. 41). For the first time in the epistle the
origin of persecution is assigned to the ill-will of the devil ;
Satan is the inspirer of the attacks upon Christians. **Your**
enemy the devil prowls like a roaring lion round the flock
(1–3), roaring in hunger and eager ferocity, **looking out for**
someone to devour, i.e. to force into apostasy. The devil's
aim is to induce weak Christians to deny God and thus to
incur eternal death (see the phrase of Hus cited above on
iv. 1). Peter does not explain how this activity of the devil
was permitted by the will of God (which is the problem of
the book of Job) ; he is simply putting his friends on their
guard. The best comment on the verse is Latimer's in his

Sermon of the Plough, where he quotes and applies the text to prove that the devil is 'the most diligent prelate and preacher in England'; in Sirach xxi. 2,

> The teeth of sin are the teeth of a lion,
> Slaying the souls of men.

9 **Resist him** by refusing to give up your faith, **keep your foothold in the faith**, firm and unyielding, with a courage on which no hardship makes any impression, **and learn to pay the same tax of suffering as the rest of your brotherhood** (ii. 17) **throughout the world.** Suffering is the penalty of your position, and there is nothing exceptional about it; it is the common lot of Christians. Peter then repeats his assurance of final relief. The prayer of the angels for the pious who are persecuted, in Enoch (xlvii. 2), is that 'judgment may be done them, and that they may not have to suffer for ever.' Peter ignores all such ideas of angelic intercession, and announces that after suffering **for a little**

10 (i. 6) they will be refreshed and settled in God's heaven, **by the God of all grace.** The mark of His **grace** is that **He has called you** (so i. 2, 10, 15, etc.) **to his eternal glory** which is bound up **in Christ Jesus.** God's choice, predestinating them to share in His purpose, will carry them through all opposition on earth, provided they remain loyal. The suffering passes, but the **glory is eternal.** There and then God **will repair** (refit the church broken by persecutions) **and recruit** (their powers—the same word as 'be a strength to' in Luke xxii. 32) **and strengthen** (verb only here in N.T.) **you;** some manuscripts add *themeliôsei* (settle), needlessly. The whole promise refers to the shattering and disabling effects of persecution, which are to be undone in

heaven. The liturgical formula of ver. 11 is practically the 11 same as in iv. 11, but the stress on the divine **dominion** is significant ; during times of persecution it was usual to contrast the transitory authority of the Empire with the lasting Reign of God. Thus Polykarp is said to have been martyred, in A.D. 155 or 156, at Smyrna, ' when Statius Quadratus was proconsul but when Jesus Christ was reigning for ever ' (*Martyrdom of Polykarp*, xvi.).

A brief postscript follows (12-14).

By the hand of Silvanus, a faithful brother (in my opinion), 12 **I have written you these few lines of encouragement, to testify that this is what the true grace of God means. Stand in that grace.**

Your sister-church in Babylon, elect like yourselves, salutes 13 **you. So does my son Mark. Salute one another with a** 14 **kiss of love.**

Peace be to you all who are in Christ Jesus.

Silvanus was a Jewish Christian who spoke Greek, and 12 therefore had been employed by Peter in the composition of the homily (see Introduction), as his amanuensis or secretary. Peter vouches for him as **a faithful brother (in my opinion),** i.e. as a reliable messenger, just as Cicero had vouched for Cossinius in one of his letters (*Ad Attic.*, i. 19 : ' Cossinius hic, cui dedi litteras, valde mihi bonus homo et non levis et amans tui visus est '), perhaps because he was unknown to some or all of the recipients, perhaps because he was commissioned to expand orally the **few lines** enclosed. The verb in **encouragement** is *appeal* in ii. 11, v. 1, but here includes its wider sense of exhorting and inspiriting. (The A.V. ' as I suppose ' suggests an uncertainty about Silvanus

which is not in the original.) The object of the apostle in
writing has been to **testify** (only here in N.T.) to **what the
true** (real, see Colossians i. 5) **grace of God is**—a sure revelation of the future hope, resting on the purpose of God for His
People, and not incompatible with hardship for the time
being. **Stand** (ver. 9) **in that grace** (so Romans v. 2). The
aorist imperative *stête* is better attested than *estêkate* (' wherein
ye stand ') and more vivid ;   take your stand upon the
Christian position as I have outlined it briefly.

13   The first of the two greetings is from the local church
where Peter is writing, **your sister-church in Babylon, elect
(i. 2) like yourselves.** This is as figurative **as son** in the next
sentence ; it is a phrase of the apocalyptic outlook which
has so often marked the homily. As Babylon had been the
supreme oppressor of the People in the O.T., the name had
already begun to be applied in Judaism and Christianity to
Rome, as a telling and cryptic epithet, e.g. in the contemporary
Apocalypse of Baruch (xi. 1) and the Sibylline Oracles (v. 143)
as well as in the early sources of the book of Revelation
(xiv. and xvi. f.), where the term is used as traditional and
familiar. No one in the early church ever dreamt of any other
meaning ; the first tradition (which may be as early as Papias,
the Asiatic bishop, early in the second century) explains that
Babylon here is a mystical figurative name for Rome (Eusebius,
Hist. Eccles., ii. 25). It was not till much later, when the
apocalyptic setting had been forgotten, that **Babylon** was
identified with the Egyptian Babylon (a fortress at old Cairo)
or Babylon in Mesopotamia. No tradition ever connected
Peter or Mark with either locality.

14   The **kiss of love,** or, as Paul termed it, the **holy kiss,** was a
naïve custom among the primitive communities, who met

for worship as real families of God. It was a simple, warm expression of the genuine fellowship which knit the members. ' What prayer is complete,' says Tertullian, ' apart from the holy kiss ? ' But, as Jesus had been betrayed by a kiss, it became customary to omit the kiss on Good Friday. As the meetings became larger and more formal, the habit of kissing was abused ; Clement of Alexandria reports indignantly that some churches were noisy with the loud smack of kisses, and in the *Apostolic Constitutions* (ii. 57, viii. 11) it was expressly ordered that promiscuous kissing was to be stopped, men to kiss only men. The epistle was read aloud at public worship.

Peace as a farewell greeting occurs in 3 John 14 ; here, as in Hebrews xiii. 20, etc., it denotes the full bliss of God's saving presence (see above on i. 2). **In Christ** (iii. 16) is practically equivalent to ' Christians.' Of the just it is said in Enoch cv. 2, ' I and my Son the messiah will be united with them for ever in the paths of uprightness in their lives, and ye shall have peace.'

THE SECOND EPISTLE OF ST. PETER

INTRODUCTION

THE atmosphere of this tract is described in the introduction to the epistle of Judas. Indeed the writer has drawn upon that earlier pamphlet, since it seemed to him to characterize the false teachers against whom he is warning the churches. Antinomian errors are still rampant. But the specific feature of the later development of the movement is a repudiation of belief in the second Advent, and the author seeks to rehabilitate this doctrine as the source of good, Christian faith and morals. He writes a pastoral letter for Christendom in general. It is a strongly worded manifesto against unworthy antinomian teachers, who were propagating a view of Christianity which, under a cloak of liberalism, seemed to him to produce moral indifferentism in the lives of its adherents.

The course of the argument is easily followed ; there are no real difficulties in the transition from one paragraph to another. Everything becomes plain, once it is borne in mind that the writer has the tract of Judas before him, and that he is writing under the name of Peter, throwing himself back (e.g. at iii. 1) into the position of the apostle as a prophet and defender of the authentic faith. The latter feature is characteristic and unique. Here we find a second-century author who writes under the name of Peter, modestly employing the apostle's name in order to discredit views which,

173

he felt certain, were unapostolic. The Greek style is totally unlike that of First Peter; so is the tone of the manifesto. And the differences of language cannot be explained by the supposition that Peter used two different amanuenses or dictated the two letters roughly to different secretaries. Second Peter stands by itself, in its florid, Hellenistic vein. The discrepancies of language and thought are too well-marked to allow of both homilies coming from the same author. The author of Second Peter has First Peter before him, as well as the tract of Judas; but he writes with much less ease and lucidity. His object is to controvert the dangerous teachers of his age, and he does so by appealing to the prestige of St. Peter as the representative of the primitive, orthodox faith. The literary device was recognized in these days. It was a development of the method which allowed an historian to compose speeches for characters in his narrative, and an author evidently felt no scruples about adopting this literary device in order to win a hearing for counsels which he felt to be both timely and inspired.

' The real author of any such work had to keep himself altogether out of sight, and its entry upon circulation had to be surrounded with a certain mystery, in order that the strangeness of its appearance at a more or less considerable interval after the putative author's death might be concealed.' [1]   Hence, the origin of the manifesto is obscure. One or two scattered echoes of its phraseology are heard in the literature of the second century, as for example in a letter written by the churches of Lyons and Vienne in Gaul, during the reign of Marcus Aurelius, and in a treatise written about the same time by Theophilus, the bishop of Antioch;

[1] Dr. V. H. Stanton. *Journal of Theological Studies*, ii. 19.

but the first time it is definitely mentioned is by Origen, who admits that ' there are doubts about it,' i.e. about its title to be in the canon. In the next century Eusebius of Caesarea declares that of all the writings under the name of Peter he recognizes ' only one epistle as genuine,' i.e. First Peter. ' As for the current Second epistle, it has not come down to us as canonical, though it has been studied along with the rest of the scriptures, since it has seemed useful to many people ' (he means, to Origen and others). One reason why so many denied the genuineness of the Second epistle was, as Jerome allowed, its disagreement in style with the First. No N.T. writing won so limited and hesitating a recognition. So far as its connexions with the other Christian literature of the early church go, they prove no more than that it must be later than the tract of Judas, which it incorporates freely, and earlier than the reign of Marcus Aurelius. Possibly, like the tract of Judas, it emanated from some circle in the Egyptian church ; but all theories that attempt to link it to a definite community are sheer guess-work.

THE SECOND EPISTLE OF ST. PETER

As in the case of the epistle of Judas, the greeting or address (1–2) is directed to Christians without any specific note of i. their residence.

1 Symeon Peter, a servant and apostle of Jesus Christ, to those who have been allotted a faith of equal privilege with ours, by the equity of our God and saviour Jesus Christ :
2 grace and peace be multiplied to you by the knowledge of our Lord.

1 **Symeon,** the Semitic form of ' Simon,' is used by James in Acts xv. 14, where he tells the council of Jerusalem that ' Symeon has explained how it was God's original concern to secure a People from among the Gentiles to bear his Name.' This may be the meaning of **those who have been allotted a faith of equal privilege with ours ;** but probably the distinction here is not between the Jewish and pagan origins of Christians, but between the apostles (in whose name Peter writes) and the ordinary Christians who owed their faith to apostolic preaching (iii. 2). **Allotted** implies the free favour and goodness of God, and **the equity of our God** points to the divine freedom from favouritism ; supreme as the work of the apostles was, their religious position was no higher than that of other Christians. The later generations enjoy a faith and fellowship as real, thanks to the impartiality of God ; as the ages pass, and as the

176

apostolic faith is transmitted, it does not become less direct
and immediate.

The description of **Jesus Christ** as **our God and saviour**
is unique ; the adoring cry of Thomas, ' My Lord and my
God ' (John xx. 28), is the nearest parallel to it in the N.T.
Elsewhere in the epistle **our Lord and saviour** is the
favourite phrase. But the habit of calling Christ, God
was becoming more common ; thus Ignatius can write that
' Mary was pregnant with our God, Jesus the Christ '
(Ephesians xviii. 2).

The prayer of First Peter (i. 2) is rounded off by the 2
significant addition of **by the knowledge of our Lord** (which
later editors expanded into ' the knowledge of our God and
of Jesus our Lord '). ' Knowledge ' (*gnosis*) was a catchword
of the age in religious circles ; it had associations of inward-
ness in Hellenistic mysticism, which recommended it to the
writer and others in his age, but it also expressed speculative
and esoteric theories which are here tacitly set aside in
favour of a personal acquaintance with Christ as divine.
The term employed (*epignôsis*) is a more or less intensive
form, but the central idea is that the progress and development
of the Church's life depend on the inward knowledge of
Christ, not on fantastic and mystical insight into aeons and
theosophic mysteries. Here the theme of the homily is laid
down, and in the next paragraph the writer proceeds to
expand it. As the meaning of Christ is realized by Christians,
they enter more and more into what God's **grace** means, i.e.
His free favour and forgiving power ; also, they experience
more and more of His **peace,** i.e. the bliss and security
realized by Christ in the lives of believers. **The knowledge
of our Lord Jesus Christ** is everything. How it works and

how it calls upon Christians to work with it, the writer now explains, in 3–7 and 8–11.

3 Inasmuch as his power divine has bestowed on us every requisite for life and piety by the knowledge of him who called
4 us to his own glory and excellence—bestowing on us thereby promises precious and supreme, that by means of them you may escape the corruption produced within the world by lust, and participate in the divine nature—
5 for this very reason, do you contrive to make it your whole concern to furnish your faith with resolution,
6 resolution with intelligence, intelligence with self-control,
7 self-control with stedfastness, stedfastness with piety, piety with brotherliness, brotherliness with Christian love.

3 Us answers to ours in ver. 1 ; the apostles originally receive the revelation, which they transmit to others. The faith was opened up to them that it might be passed on ; divine promises were bestowed on us so that by means of them, handed on by the authoritative apostolic tradition (iii. 2), you may enjoy your share in their saving power. But, as the writer has spoken of our God and our Lord, it is plain that he is already grouping apostles and other Christians together, and that he uses you as a preacher addressing his audience ; the stress on the validity and authority of the apostolic transmission of the gospel is not so marked as in Hebrews ii. 3, 4. These words played a large part in bringing John Wesley through his spiritual crisis in 1730. About five o'clock on the morning of May 24th, he opened his Bible at the words, ' There are given to us exceeding great and precious promises, even that ye should be partakers of the divine nature '; that day relief came to him, and (on

June 4th) he notes in his diary : 'All these days I scarce remember to have opened the New Testament, but upon some great and precious promise. And I saw, more than ever, that the gospel is in truth but one great promise, from the beginning of it to the end.'

The ideas and even the language about **divine power** 4 manifesting itself to human beings in order that they might **participate in the divine nature** through some **knowledge** of the deity, gained by sacramental or semi-physical means, often of an ecstatic character, were current in the Hellenistic philosophy and religious cults of the age. In terms of this contemporary faith the writer expresses his Christian beliefs, availing himself of forms and conceptions familiar to his readers. The personal fellowship with Christ, first verified by the apostles, is adequate for real life and piety, i.e. for the true life which, in a world of moral corruption, consists in piety or practical religion (see iii. 11 f.). This rules out theosophies which depreciated the historical revelation of Christ or reduced him to a position of relative importance in the saving order of redemption. The divine self-manifestation in Christ is complete ; as conveyed in the apostolic tradition it does not require to be eked out by any scheme of aeons and angels, nor is it to be revised (iii. 4), as though some elements in it had been superseded. It is further defined as the intimate **knowledge of him who called us to his own glory and excellence,** i.e. to share his pre-eminent divine life, fully and finally manifested in the next world (ver. 11). Usually God 'calls' Christians, but the writer of a contemporary homily called 2 Clement (ix. 5) could write that 'Christ, the Lord who saved us, though originally Spirit, became flesh and called us,' and this is the meaning here, especially as Christ had personally called the apostles during his lifetime on earth.

The object and end of Christian **knowledge** is moral and spiritual communion with Christ. But this destiny requires active participation on the part of believers. The historical revelation endowed men with exceptional **promises** of an undying divine life beyond this transient, material order of things; what Christ was and did opened a new outlook for men, encouraging them to hope and all its responsibilities, for **thereby** refers loosely to **every requisite for life and piety.** The revelation of the divine nature in Jesus Christ was full of promise. It is assumed that these **promises** will be fulfilled by the Lord, but what needs to be argued is the moral demand that they make upon Christians (as in iii. 14). Plutarch, in his *Life of Aristides* (vi.), laments that men feel the passion for immortality (a quality of God which they cannot share) far more than the passion for God's moral **excellence,** which is within their reach; but our author links both together. Immortality is a sure promise of God, and hopes of immortality are a moral power and responsibility; to **participate in the divine nature,** i.e. to reach the final **glory and excellence,** involves an **escape** from the moral decay or **corruption produced within the world by lust.** This is directed against the libertinism of the errorists (see ii. 19, 20). The spirit of lust is the spirit which prompts men to demand, ' Give me the portion of goods that falls to me,' the grasping desire for earthly things which results in moral deterioration. Ever since Plato, the idea of resembling God by shunning material preoccupations had been a current thought in religious philosophy; here it is applied to the renunciation of the world by those who aim at the **Christian hope.**

The positive response to the divine **promises** is now sketched 5 (5-7) in a series of seven Christian graces or acquirements with which **faith** is to be supplied. **Faith** here, as in ver. 1, is the personal belief which is fundamental. But it must be provided with **resolution,** moral and mental energy. Someone has described conventional Christian experience as ' an initial spasm followed by a chronic inertia '; what our writer demands is a challenging, vital quality in faith. The Greek term (*aretê*) here carries its specific sense of prowess and power. **Faith** lives in a world of difficulties which have to be met frankly and courageously instead of being dodged. But zeal must be according to knowledge, and this energy requires to be supplied with **intelligence,** i.e. with insight and understanding, otherwise it may be misdirected. The Greek term (*gnôsis*) is deliberately applied to this quality of practical wisdom, instead of to the more speculative flights of contemporary theosophy. A resolute faith may be aggressive and enterprising, but it cannot afford to do without sagacity or shrewd **intelligence.** Nor can **intelligence** work 6 effectively apart from **self-control**—a warning much needed in view of the passionate, lax conduct of the errorists (ii. 10 f., iii. 3). The appetites to be mastered were not simply those of the flesh, but any passions of self-assertion and individual impulse; continence is included, but **self-control** is the opposite of any lack of self-restraint.

Life has to encounter trials, however, as well as incitements to self-indulgence, and so **stedfastness** is further required in maintaining the Christian hope when it is contradicted (iii. 3 f.), and in adhering to Christian truth when it is denied (i. 16). This tenacity must be religious; supply it with **piety.** It is not a close-lipped stoical endurance or a dogged determination to hold on, but inspired by a sense of the divine purpose which is running through the trials of life. **Stedfastness** is to be reverent, not defiant. It acquiesces in God's will, and it also turns kindly to other members of the brother-

7 hood. Supply your **piety with brotherliness,** i.e. with brotherly kindness (see on 1 Peter i. 22) ; there was then, as there has always been, the danger of a **piety** or godliness which was inhuman, wrapped up in its own hopes and fears, and indifferent to the needs of the community. Even this is not enough. The affectionate temper must not be confined to members of the Christian community ; supply **brotherliness with Christian love** for all men.

Only by this discipline and development of the religious life is it possible to attain heaven (8–11).

8 **For as these qualities exist and increase with you, they render you active and fruitful in the knowledge of our Lord**

9 **Jesus Christ ; whereas he who has not these by him is blind, shortsighted, oblivious that he has been cleansed**

10 **from his erstwhile sins. So be the more eager, brothers, to ratify your calling and election, for as you practise**

11 **these qualities you will never make a slip ; you will thus be richly furnished with the right of entry into the eternal realm of our Lord and saviour Jesus Christ.**

8 The practical development of the Christian life along these lines deepens and widens our personal experience and sense of Christ ; it enables members of the community in their common life to penetrate into the meaning of the Lord's life and purpose. We learn him as we live with him and for

9 him. Anyone who neglects these graces shows that he has forgotten all about the change wrought in his life at baptism,

when he was cleansed (so ii. 22) from his erstwhile sins ; the
great experience has meant nothing to him, for he has failed
to follow it up by developing the new nature and understanding what the divine promises involved. So, in view of 10
all this, be the more eager yourselves. It is an urgent imperative, as in iii. 14. Ratify or attest by a full, consistent life
your calling and election (a hendiadys). To make a slip,
such as a careless, indifferent Christian might make, is to
collapse on the road to the eternal realm ; it is a fall into
deadly sin (see Judas 24).

The term furnished echoes ver. 5 ; furnish your Christian 11
faith with all that it requires, and you will be furnished in
turn with the entry into the future realm of the Lord. The
Greek term for right of entry carries with it a sense of triumph.
The phrase, the eternal realm, is quite original, but the
thought is the same as in I Peter v. 11 ; it is the character-
istically Christian expression for what Hellenistic piety called
participating in the divine nature (ver. 4), though realm is
nowhere else employed in the epistle.

My one aim and constant endeavour is to keep you mindful
of this vital creed (12–15), which is guaranteed by apostolic
testimony (16–19a).

Hence I mean to keep on reminding you of this, although 12
    you are aware of it and are fixed in the Truth as it
    is ; so long as I am in this tent, I deem it proper to 13
    stir you up by way of reminder, since I know my tent 14
    must be folded up very soon—as indeed our Lord Jesus
    Christ has shown me. Yes, and I will see to it that 15
    even when I am gone, you will keep this constantly in
    mind.

12   In view of the critical importance of the issues, **I mean to keep on reminding you** of them. The Greek is awkward but the sense is plain. So is the courtesy (as in Romans xv. 14 and Judas 5). **The Truth** (see on 1 Peter i. 22) **as it is** means the Christian creed of life in the complete form in which it has reached them (a similar phrase in Colossians i. 5, 6) ; there is no allusion to any larger experience or insight

13 which may be expected. The metaphorical use of **tent** for the body was common, and had been introduced into the

14 Christian vocabulary by Paul (2 Corinthians v. 4). **Very soon** is a poetical term, meaning 'imminent.' When and how Christ revealed this to Peter we do not know ; the story in John xxi. 18, 19 refers to something quite different, to a long life crowned by martyrdom. The line of thought is, that while he proposes to recall them to their Christian duty during the short time left to him, he will make provision for some lasting record of it, to serve after he has gone.

15 But what was this permanent record by means of which the readers might **keep constantly in mind** the apostolic testimony ? (*a*) The present epistle as a written statement of the faith, to which reference could be made ? (*b*) The gospel of Mark, in which Peter's reminiscences were embodied ? Or, if the words are taken to mean a direct composition, (*c*) some Petrine writing like *The Gospel of Peter* or *The Preaching of Peter* ? The future tense of **I will see to it** tells against (*a*), unless he is referring to measures taken for the wide circulation of the epistle. It is in favour of (*b*) that the earliest tradition (preserved in Irenaeus) about the date of the gospel of Mark ascribes it to Mark 'after the decease' of Peter (the same Greek term as is used here for **when I am gone**). when 'Mark the disciple and interpreter of Peter

transmitted to us what Peter had preached.' The data are
too few and faint, however, to enable us to do more than
guess, at this point. What the writer does make clear,
in the following passage (16–19*a*), is that such apostolic
testimony is worth recalling, since the Christian hope was
guaranteed not merely by O.T. prophecy, but by apostolic
eye-witnesses of Jesus Christ.

**For it was no fabricated fables that we followed when we 16
reported to you the power and advent of our Lord Jesus
Christ ; we were admitted to the spectacle of his
sovereignty, when he was invested with honour and 17
glory by God the Father, and when the following voice
was borne to him from the sublime Glory, ' This is my
son, the Beloved, in whom I delight.' That voice borne 18
from heaven we heard, we who were beside him on the
sacred hill, and thus we have gained fresh confirmation 19
of the prophetic word.**

The **we** now is the apostles once more, as in ver. 1. ' Our 16
testimony is not a handful of illusions ; we repudiate the
charges and the methods of the errorists.' The reference
in **fabricated fables** is either to teachers who thus discredited
the historical testimony of the gospels, or to the fantastic
speculations of some gnostic schools ; the Greek word for
fables is rendered **myths** in passages like 2 Timothy iv. 4
and 1 Timothy i. 4. Ultra-spiritualists derided particularly
the divine promise of the second Advent (iii. 4), and this
promise is reaffirmed ; it was no hallucination, our account
of the power and advent of our Lord Jesus Christ, i.e. the
risen power which will be manifested fully at his second
Advent (so Mark viii. 38, ix. 1).

The term for advent (*parousia*) suggested a royal visit or arrival, and this regal significance is brought out in what follows ; we were admitted to the spectacle (literally, initiated into the supreme mystery) of his sovereignty or divine majesty at the transfiguration, when we first realized his divine honour and authority. The apostolic report of his power and advent was a testimony to what was yet to be manifested fully ; but there had been a significant anticipation during his lifetime, of which Peter and his fellows had been eye-witnesses. For some reason the transfiguration is appealed to as a fore-shadowing of the second Advent rather than the resurrection ;

17 there Jesus received honour and glory from God the Father (i.e. his Father), shown in the dazzling light which we saw shining from his person. There too from—the original *apo* of the Latin Vulgate and the Syriac versions was soon altered into the *hupo* of the traditional text (i.e. ' by ')—the sublime Glory (a reverential periphrasis for heaven or the divine Presence), the voice came to him, which is quoted freely. The writer assumes that his readers knew the synoptic tale, but his citation agrees with none of the three versions ; he inserts the Greek term for ' I ' in the clause in whom I delight, for the sake of emphasis. We heard that voice, he

18 declares, we who were beside him on the sacred hill, sacred because it was the scene of this divine manifestation. All this stress on the transfiguration as heralding the second Advent sounds at first sight strange, for in the gospels no such interpretation of the scene is suggested. But in all three traditions (Matthew xvi., Mark viii.–ix., and Luke ix.) it is introduced immediately after a reference to the second coming of the Lord ' in glory ' or ' with power,' and in the Ethiopic text of *The Apocalypse of Peter* (see M. R. James,

The Apocryphal N.T., pp. 518 f.) the transfiguration is blended with the ascension, whilst Peter speaks of 'the hill on which he showed us the second coming in the kingdom that passeth not away.'

It is not difficult to understand why the writer omitted the words 'hear ye him' from the divine voice, for this concentration of attention upon Jesus in contrast to the O.T. law and prophets, who are thereby superseded, would not have suited his purpose. So far from viewing the transfiguration as superseding the O.T. prophecies, he explains that thus (by our experience of the transfiguration) we have 19 gained fresh confirmation of the prophetic word, i.e. of the O.T. prophecies about Christ, especially in connexion with his glory and second Advent ; this fulfilment has strengthened our faith in these prophecies. It is an argument on the lines of that urged in the apostle's speech in Acts iii. 18 f., where he finds O.T. predictions of the second Advent as well as of the sufferings of Christ, who is 'kept in heaven till the period of the great Restoration,' of which 'ages ago God spoke by the lips of His holy prophets.' By the time that this epistle was written, the engrossing interest of Christian apologetic lay in the proof from prophecy. Not long afterwards Origen declared that 'clear proofs of the inspiration of the O.T. could not well be given until Christ came to earth. Till then the Law and the prophets were liable to suspicion as not being truly divine, but the coming of Christ set them forth clearly as records made by the gracious aid of heaven' (*De Principiis*, iv. 6). It was all the more important for the writer to emphasize this value of the O.T., as some errorists depreciated it.

But the connexion between this sentence and the following

lies here ; ' if we apostles have been led to appreciate the
O.T. prophecies, how important they must be for you ! '
Hence he pleads for close attention to them (19*a*–21).

19 Pray attend to that word ; it shines like a lamp within a
    darksome spot, till the Day dawns and the daystar rises
20   within your hearts—understanding this, at the outset,
    that no prophetic scripture allows a man to interpret it
21   by himself ; for prophecy never came by human impulse,
    it was when carried away by the holy Spirit that the
    holy men of God spoke.

19   ' The O.T. prophecies, especially. as they are confirmed
by such facts as the transfiguration just mentioned, will
illuminate your minds sufficiently about the second Advent
till it actually happens.   So ponder them ' amid—

> The smoke and stir of this dim spot
> Which men call Earth.

The present world is a darksome spot, where you need this
lamp of prophecy to guide your steps ; all will be clear when
the Day of the Lord's Advent dawns.   The writer twists the
metaphor to suit his purpose.   The daystar rises before the
dawn, but here it is the outward signs of the Day which
clear up the inward uncertainties of Christians ; the open
manifestation of the Advent is the means of enlightening
them.

20   Attend to the prophetic anticipations of Christ, but understand the principle of their interpretation.   False teachers
(ii. 1, iii. 2 f.) were disseminating novel views of the O.T.,
claiming revelations which superseded the prophets of old
or which undervalued their witness to Christ as the Church

understood it ; hence this protest against such unauthorized interpretations as out of keeping with the nature of the prophecies themselves. **No prophetic scripture allows a man to interpret it by himself,** out of his own head ; it is not susceptible of 'any private interpretation,' the Greek term for 'private' or 'out of his own head' being the familiar opposite to 'authoritative' or 'inspired.' Individual ingenuity cannot solve the problems of prophecy, because individual ingenuity was not at the origin of prophecy ; **prophecy never 21 came by human impulse,** by any conscious cleverness on the part of an individual, but **it was when carried away by the holy Spirit** (under an overpowering divine impulse) **that the holy men of God spoke,** i.e. the prophets, **holy** as possessed by God.

Here, as in iii. 16, the writer warns his readers against the danger of unauthorized interpretations of the O.T. Apart from the Spirit which produced the prophecies, how can they be understood ? It is implied that the Spirit belongs to the Church where the apostolic testimony is preserved, but the writer does not enter into further details. He is simply putting members on their guard against plausible contemporary misapplications of the O.T. ; no interpretation is valid if it ignores the Spirit, for that is to miss the genius of prophecy. We to-day ask, how are such prophecies to be interpreted according to the Spirit ? but there is no answer to this question any more than to the other, How did the Spirit act upon the consciousness of the original prophets ?—except that the use of **carried away** as an equivalent for 'inspired' suggests that the writer considered the prophets had been mouthpieces of God in the sense popularized by the Hellenistic theology of a man like Philo. 'Those who prophesy,' says

189

Justin Martyr (*Apol.*, i. 33), speaking of the O.T. prophets, 'are divinely inspired (literally, **carried away by God**) by nothing but the divine Word.' This current view went back to Philo, who (e.g. in *Quis Rerum Div. Haer.*, 51, 52) explains that the state of inspiration is an ecstasy, in which the human faculty of reason is replaced by the divine Spirit ; the true prophet is rapt into a frenzy in which the Spirit uses his unconsciousness to predict and reveal the future. Such ecstasy is only possible to pure, godly souls ; ' for the prophet utters nothing that belongs to himself ; Another is prompting him to utter what lies beyond his own range. And as it is wrong for any worthless man to be an interpreter of God, so no rascal can be divinely inspired, in the strict sense of the term ; the wise alone is the echoing instrument of God, sounding as he is invisibly struck by Him.' This corresponds to the theory behind our writer's words on **holy men of God** alone being swept into prophecy by the divine Spirit.

Prophecy ? Yes, but while there were **holy men of God,** there were pseudo-prophets too, as there are to-day. This leads the writer to the special theme of his letter ; the next section (ii. 1–22) is a sustained indignant exposure of their practices and principles, moulded on the epistle of Judas.

ii.

1 Still, false prophets did appear among the People, as among you also there will be false teachers, men who will insinuate destructive heresies, even disowning the Lord who ran-somed them ; they bring rapid destruction on themselves,
2 and many will follow their immorality (*thanks to them*
3 the true Way *will be maligned*) ; in their lust they will

exploit you with cunning arguments—men whose doom comes apace from of old, and destruction is awake upon their trail.

False teachers, the term for these pseudo-leaders of religion, 1
does not occur elsewhere in the N.T. ; in Justin Martyr's
Dialogue (lxxxii.), ' as there were false prophets in the days
of your holy prophets, so among us to-day there are many
false teachers,' and *The Apocalypse of Peter* begins with this
statement of the Lord, ' many of them will be false prophets
and teach various destructive dogmas and ways.' The
heresies which they adroitly and subtly spread affected both
faith and morals, though the only explicit charge on the
former score is that they actually disowned **the Lord** (literally
liege, as in Judas 4) who ransomed them—probably alluding
to some heretical view of the person of Christ. But the
repudiation of the Saviour might refer to inconsistent life ; it
is to this at anyrate that the writer turns, to **their immorality**
(the charge of Judas 4), which brings discredit on true
Christianity (here called **the Way,** as the practical aspect is
to the front).

In the homily called 2 Clement (xiii.) we read : ' When
pagans hear from our lips the oracles of God, they marvel at
their beauty and greatness ; but afterwards, when they
discover that our deeds are unworthy of our words, they
turn to malign the faith, declaring that it is a fable and a
delusion '—a comment on Isaiah lii. 5 which is quoted
here as by Paul (in Romans ii. 23, 24). **Many will follow** 2
their lead, so plausible and persuasive are their arguments ;
in their lust (particularly for money—the writer uses deliberately a term which suggested lower sensual cravings such as

3 those to which their principles pandered) **they will exploit you** (see on Judas 11, 16) cunningly, turning their religious views to personal profit. This is to put the readers on their guard. But before describing the deplorable and deadly effects of their teaching on their victims (in 18–22), the writer depicts the **rapid destruction** which they bring **upon themselves.** It is swift and certain. God's judgment may seem to be delayed, as these teachers actually declared (iii. 3 f.), but the Advent is imminent ; they may pooh-pooh the idea of a final retribution, but they are doomed men, on the verge of punishment. The writer does not find any prophetic prediction of their fate, as Judas did (4, 14–15), but it was a commonplace of Christian apocalyptic that the appearance of such errorists was a sign of the last days (Matthew xxiv. 24 and 1 Timothy iv. 1). The doom that **from of old** overtook such impious offenders is hot **upon their trail.**

Then follows in one long, involved sentence (4–10*a*) a denunciation of the errorists, combined with reassurance for the faithful. Three historical examples of God punishing sin are given, but the second and the third suggest the companion thought of God preserving the loyal minority ; so, instead of concluding that God will punish these errorists, he alters the thought in ver. 9, putting foremost God's mercy to the good.

4 **For if God did not spare angels who had sinned, but committing** **them to pits of the nether gloom in Tartarus, reserved** 5 **them under punishment for doom :** if he did not spare **the ancient world but kept Noah, the herald of righteous-** **ness, safe with seven others, when he let loose the deluge on** 6 **the world of impious men :** if he reduced the cities of Sodom

and Gomorra to ashes when he sentenced them to devasta-
tion, and thus gave the impious an example of what was
in store for them, but rescued righteous Lot who was 7
sore burdened by the immoral behaviour of the lawless
(for when that righteous man resided among them, by 8
what he saw and heard his righteous soul was vexed
day after day with their unlawful doings)—then be sure 9
the Lord knows how to rescue pious folk from trial, and
how to keep the unrighteous under punishment till the
day of doom, particularly those who fall in with the 10
polluting appetite of the flesh and despise the Powers
celestial.

The underlying thought is that God will act as He has
always done, to punish sinners and to preserve the faithful.
This is His character in the moral order, and it may be
relied upon ; history offers examples of His procedure which
are a salutary warning and a consolation. Instead of beginning with the first instance cited by Judas (5, 6), he starts
more chronologically with the second, the doom upon the
rebellious angels, adding some touches of his own (ver. 4).
The Greek term for pits, *seirois*, is so unusual that it was soon 4
altered to *seirais* (' chains '), which had the recommendation
of agreeing with the language of Judas. Tartarus had been
already introduced into Jewish apocalyptic by the book of
Enoch (xx. 2) ; it had a certain appositeness, since in Greek
mythology it was the place of punishment for rebellious
celestial powers like the Titans.

In the second example, of the deluge, Noah is called the 5
herald of righteousness, herald meaning ' preacher ' as in
I Timothy ii. 7. ' Noah preached repentance, and those

who obeyed were saved' (Clem. Rom. vii.). This tradition went back to Jewish sources, where Noah had already acquired the halo of a preacher to his evil generation. 'Many angels of God,' says Josephus (*Antiquities*, i. 3, 1), 'lay with women and begat sons who were violent and who despised all good, on account of their reliance on their own strength ; for tradition goes that they dared to act like the giants of whom the Greeks tell. But Noah, displeased and distressed at their behaviour, tried to induce them to alter their dispositions and conduct for the better.'

6   In the allusion to the destruction of Sodom and Gomorra (the third example, as in Judas), the Greek word for **reduce to ashes** is an out-of-the-way term, which commonly meant 'covering with ashes' (as in an eruption of Vesuvius). A punishment by fire follows a punishment by water. In the third book of Maccabees, which for a time had a vogue in the Eastern Church, this passage occurs (ii. 4, 5) : 'Thou didst destroy those who aforetime worked iniquity, among whom were Giants relying on their strength and boldness, letting loose on them a boundless flood of water. Thou didst burn up with fire and brimstone the men of Sodom, workers of arrogance, who had become notorious for their crimes, making them an example to all who should come afterwards.' Our passage seems like a reminiscence of this as well as of Judas 7, but the writer proceeds to dwell on the

7 rescue of **righteous Lot**. *The Wisdom of Solomon* (x. 6, 7) had already spoken of the rescue of this 'righteous man, while the impious were perishing, who fled from the fire falling on Pentapolis, of whose wickedness a waste land still smoking is still appointed as a testimony' (see on Judas 7). **Sore burdened** may be another reminiscence of 3 Maccabees (iii. 2),

where the prayer is, ' Give ear to us who are **sore burdened**
by an unholy and profane man.' **Lawless** (only here and in 8
iii. 17 in the N.T.) means those who defy the divine law. In
Clem. Rom. xi. 1, ' For his hospitality and piety Lot was
saved from Sodom when the entire countryside was condemned by fire and brimstone, and the Lord made it clear
that he does not forsake those who hope in him, but delivers
to punishment and torture those who turn to others.' This
is the thought of 9 and 10, where trial is exposure to sur- 9
roundings that bear hard on faith and goodness. **Pious folk**
sometimes, like Noah, can do their best to testify publicly ;
sometimes they can do no more than be shocked and distressed as they maintain their character. (' Our great security
against sin,' said Newman, ' lies in being shocked at it.')
But they are never left to themselves. **The Lord knows**
how to rescue them, and that soon, by a similar catastrophe
(iii. 9 f.), it is assumed.

The writer now returns to the errorists, their antinomian 10
practices (as in ver. 2), and their irreverent attitude towards
angels (as in Judas 8). This blasphemous depreciation of
angels leads him into a bitter attack on their general bearing
and behaviour (10*b*–16). The severity of tone is not unexampled. Thus Bunyan (see on Judas 19) speaks of the
' cursed principles ' of the Ranters, the seventeenth-century
English analogue to these antinomians ; and Richard Baxter,
who also loathed and lashed them as he encountered them in
the Commonwealth army, declared, ' I am an unreconcileable
enemy to their doctrines. I had as lieve tell them so as hide
it. The more I pray God to illuminate me in these things,
the more I am animated against them. The more I read
their own books, the more do I see the vanity of their

conceits. But above all, when I do but open the Bible I can seldom meet with a leaf that is not against them.' This is one of the most pugnacious leaves.

10 Daring, presumptuous creatures ! they are not afraid to scoff
11 at the angelic Glories ; whereas even angels, superior in might and power, lay no scoffing charge against these
12 before the Lord. But those people !—like irrational animals, creatures of mere instinct, born for capture and corruption, they scoff at what they are ignorant of ; and
13 like animals they will suffer corruption and ruin, done out of the profits of their evil-doing. Pleasure for them is revelling in open daylight—spots and blots, with their dissipated revelling, as they carouse in your midst !—
14 their eyes are full of harlotry, insatiable for sin ; their own hearts trained to lust, they beguile unsteady
15 souls. Accursed generation ! they have gone wrong by leaving the straight road, by following the road of Balaam son of Bosor, who liked the profits of evil-
16 doing—but he got reproved for his malpractice : a dumb ass spoke with human voice and checked the prophet's infatuation.

10 The first charge is repeated from Judas (8, 9), but in rebuking their audacity the writer generalizes the allusion to Michael and omits the details about Satan, so that **against**
11 these (i.e. the devil and his angels) is left vague, whereas in Judas it is pointed. **Before the Lord** is a pictorial detail,
12 added to make up for the omission of the retort, ' The Lord rebuke you.' In ver. **12** the thought of Judas (**10**) is less happily expressed. The fatal result of scoffing at angels was often noted in connexion with the story of Sodom, as,

e.g., in *The Testament of Asher* (vii.) : ' Be not like Sodom, my children, which sinned against the angels of God and perished for ever.'   **Done out of the profits of their evil-doing 13** is a play on words already present in the Greek—*adikoumenoi* . . . *adikias* ; but as this use of *adikoumenoi* was unfamiliar, it was changed into *komioumenoi*, or ' receive,' in the traditional text.

The writer had already mentioned (in ver. 3) the self-seeking temper of the errorists, and he returns to it in ver. 15, but meantime he dwells on their immoral practices. **In open daylight** seems to be a reminiscence of *The Assumption of Moses* (vii. 4 f.), where the proud religionists are ' cunning in all their affairs, loving banquets at every hour of the day . . . filled with lawlessness and iniquity from sunrise to sunset.' They were luxurious and self-indulgent, disgracefully **dissipated.** The Greek term *apatais* literally meant ' deceivings ' (A.V.), but in Hellenistic Greek had acquired the sense of ' pleasure ' or ' delight ' (as in Mark iv. 19) ; at an early period it was changed to *agapais* (love-feasts), perhaps owing to the parallel in Judas 12.   The context 14 shows that lust here (see above, on ver. 3) denotes sensual indulgence ; the doctrine that spiritual natures could with impunity indulge in sexual excesses and that these might even be practised as expressions of mystical love, was only too likely to appeal to certain natures, **unsteady souls,** as the writer calls them (in contrast to i. 12). But he turns back to the errorists themselves (15, 16), who like **Balaam 15** claimed prophetic visions and set their hearts on gain (see Judas 11). He leaves out Cain and Korah, but expands the reference to Balaam by mentioning the incident of the ass (Numbers xxii. 21 f.). **Bosor** was the name of a town in 16

Gilead, which had no connexion with Balaam; it is a mistake for Beor, and the correction was made in some early texts.

A closing paragraph (17–22) on their iniquities describes the disastrous effect of their teaching upon their adherents.

17 These people are waterless fountains and mists driven by a squall, for whom the nether gloom of darkness is reserved.
18 By talking arrogant futilities they beguile with the sensual lure of fleshly passion those who are just escaping from
19 the company of misconduct—promising them freedom, when they are themselves enslaved to corruption (for a
20 man is the slave of whatever overpowers him). After escaping the pollutions of the world by the knowledge of our Lord and saviour Jesus Christ, if they get entangled and overpowered again, the last state is worse for them
21 than the first. Better had they never known the Way of righteousness, than to know it and then turn back from
22 the holy command which was committed to them. They verify the truth of the proverb :

' *The dog turns back to what he has vomited,*
the sow when washed will wallow in the mire.'

17 The writer changes the rainless clouds of Judas (12) into waterless (same Greek word as rainless) fountains (yielding nothing to help men, for all their appearance) and mists (darkening the light, for all their pretences to enlightenment), but this leaves the allusion to nether gloom out of place.
18 The seductive appeal of their moral or rather immoral principles, backed by rhetoric (which is contemptuously called arrogant futilities), has been already denounced (14), but the writer is indignant and underlines his warning. Beguile

198

implies the clever use of a bait or lure. ' I, using adroit
words,' says Milton's *Comus*—

> ' Baited with reasons not unplausible,
> Wind me into the easy-hearted man,
> And hug him into snares.'

What chance have recent converts from paganism against
the specious argument of these religionists that Christian
freedom means freedom from the moral law ? The words
throb with the righteous passion of a man who had seen
such men and women suffering a moral collapse under libertine
' spiritual' teaching. **Promising them freedom** from the 19
law of God, **when they are themselves** the slaves of passion !
The inconsistency of it !

> Licence they mean when they cry Liberty ;
> For who loves that must first be wise and good.

Paul had had to warn his converts long ago (Galatians v. 13)
on this very point, but our writer is dealing with leaders
who instilled religious teaching that led to moral anarchy,
and in 20-22 he depicts the ruinous consequences of it for
the victims. If newly converted people (he uses the language
of i. 3-4) relapse, i.e. give way to the very immorality from
which Christianity saves them, then **the last state for them
is worse than the first.** This is a reminiscence (see on iii. 10) 20
of the saying of Jesus preserved in Matthew xii. 45. The
responsibility is placed upon the converts themselves. They
may be unsteady souls, inexperienced and raw, but they are
not mere dupes ; those who mislead them are blamed and
doomed, but the converts themselves are treated as morally
accountable for their actions. **The Way of righteousness** is 21
practically synonymous with **the true Way (ver. 2)** or the

straight road (ver. 15), and another expression for Christianity as a practical authoritative code of life is **the holy command** (see iii. 2) **committed to** Christians (see Judas 3), i.e. the faith viewed as the revelation of God's will as the standard and inspiration of life for His People. For individuals just emancipated from paganism and still swayed by the associations of the lax morality of the age, to make the inner light the supreme criterion of right and wrong, or to regard mere morality as beneath the level of an emancipated Christian, was to court wild dangers. It was the sense of this that helped to recommend the O.T. with its decalogue and ethical teaching to the church, when gnostic religious philosophers would have rejected it. Our writer does not enter into this, however; he simply reiterates that Christianity is a revelation which involved moral enterprise and moral obedience.

22　As for apostates, who forsake true Christianity for such circles of sanctified licentiousness, they merely illustrate the old adage about the dog and the sow! It is a double proverb. The first part occurs in Proverbs xxvi. 11, the second is from an ancient Oriental story preserved in *The Book of Ahikar*, a pre-Christian collection of parables and sayings, where we read, ' My son, thou hast behaved like the swine which went to the bath with people of quality, and when he came out, saw a stinking drain and went and rolled himself in it.' The combination of the dog and the pig as proverbial illustrations of unclean instincts was not uncommon; Horace (*Epp*. i. 2. 26) says that if Ulysses had drunk the cup of Circe he would have sunk to the low level of ' a dirty dog or a pig that loves the mud.' There is an implicit allusion here to the cleansing water of baptism (as in i. 9). The stern,

severe warning of the whole passage (20–22) is clinched by
this rough proverb ; the writer evidently felt that plain
speaking was wisest in the circumstances, and his speech is
even more plain than the equally serious warning in Hebrews
vi. 4–6 that any deliberate renunciation of Christ is past
forgiveness ; in ver. 22 there is a note of contempt for low
natures upon whom baptism has produced no effect what-
soever. The leaders had been dubbed mere animals (ver. 12),
actuated by physical instincts, for all their spiritual pretensions. Their adherents are now compared to what an Oriental
regarded as the dirtiest of brutes, not simply worse than
any ' pagan suckled in a creed outworn ' (21), but on a
level no higher than the existence of dogs and pigs.

Now the writer resumes the first person singular, as he
returns to the theme of i. 5–21, after the outburst of ii. 1–22.

iii.

**This is the second letter I have already written to you, beloved, 1
stirring up your pure mind by way of reminder, to have 2
you recollect the words spoken by the holy prophets
beforehand and the command given by your apostles
from the Lord and saviour.**

The first letter, to which this is a sequel, is First Peter, 1
which had by this time become well known to the Church
at large, and it is to this catholic Church that the present
epistle is addressed by the writer in the name of Peter. ' It
is not sufficiently considered,' says Dr. Johnson as a moralist,
' that men more frequently require to be reminded than
informed.' Our author had considered this. His allusion
to the **pure mind** of Christians is another touch of courtesy,
such as in i. 12. Philosophers like Plato had spoken of ' pure

intellect or mind,' meaning thought detached as far as possible from the bodily senses, and the writer uses this phrase for the Christian mind which had been uncontaminated by any taint of heresy (i. 4, ii. 20). It is a loose, untechnical application of the phrase.

2   The language of Judas 17 is then expanded by the addition of an allusion to the holy prophets of the O.T., with their predictions of the Advent—the idea already urged in i. 19 f. He has already referred to Christianity as an authoritative revelation or command (see above on ii. 21), embodying the divine will for life. This language of command became popular in Johannine circles, particularly in connexion with the new command of love. But the writer here does not refer to any specific command of Jesus; he is thinking of the Christian creed as the decisive rule for regulating faith and morals, for determining not only what was to be believed (3–10) but what Christians were to do in the light of their beliefs about the Advent. He prefers command to 'law,' possibly to avoid confusion with the Mosaic code of Judaism.

The words your apostles are not unambiguous. Had the epistle been directed to a special church or group of churches, the apostles might be those missionaries who had founded them. But in a general pastoral like the present, the phrase means the twelve apostles (i.e. men like myself, i. 16) regarded as the transmitters of the gospel to the church at large. They were in closer touch with the church than the prophets of the O.T.; hence he calls them your apostles, as Judas had called them 'the apostles.' One writer calls them 'the holy apostles' (Ephesians iii. 5); our writer, however, confines the term holy to the O.T. prophets (i. 21). He reminds Christians that they must attend to the apostolic gospel no less than to the prophetic messages (i. 19) which anticipated it, and especially to that prediction in the apostolic tradition which announced the rise of scoffing objections to the doctrine of the immediate Advent.

In what follows, the writer starts from Judas 17–18, but he develops his argument (3–7) along independent lines. No prospect of any change in the universe, such as the Advent implies? Yes, there has been a violent change already, and there will be another and a final.

To begin with, you know that mockers will come with their 3 mockeries in the last days, men who go by their own passions, asking, 'Where is His promised advent? 4 Since the day our fathers fell asleep, things remain exactly as they were from the beginning of creation.' They wilfully ignore the fact that heavens existed long 5 ago, and an earth which the word of God formed of water and by water. By water the then-existing world was 6 deluged and destroyed, but the present heavens and earth 7 are treasured up by the same word for fire, reserved for the day when the impious are doomed and destroyed.

In some quarters the death of Christians before the return 3 of Jesus from heaven roused anxious fears, for their friends wondered whether they had not thus missed salvation. This perplexity, felt by genuine believers, we have already met in 1 Peter iv. 6. In other quarters the same fact roused sceptical questionings about the Advent itself, especially as the first generation passed away and there was no sign of the end at all. **Our fathers** have died, men said; the Advent 4 of the Lord promised in their day has not come; the Advent was to be the end of the present world, and the world is as it has always been. This objection had apparently passed into writing. Clement of Rome (xxiii.) quotes a 'scripture' in which sceptics are rebuked for doubting the Advent by saying, 'We have heard these things even in the days of our fathers, and here have we grown old and none of these things has happened to us.' The same word is cited in the homily called 2 Clement (xi.) from 'a prophetic word,' evidently some primitive Christian apocalypse which has not come down to us. Our author has it in his mind here. The objection he has to meet is not merely that the Advent has not occurred during the previous generation when it was promised and expected, but that it is contradicted by the stability of the universe. His answer is (5–7) that the deluge proves the universe is not stable, and that it is to be ended by fire. A convulsion of water ended the first world with 5 its heavens and earth which had been **formed** or composed **of water and by water.** This is an allusion to the cosmogony of Genesis i., where God's **word** fashioned the earth or dry land out of the primaeval watery chaos by separating the waters of the sea ; it is a loose, amplifying phrase such as the writer loved, to bring out the fact that water was the medium of the original earth's creation. The sentence is awkwardly expressed. **Heavens existed long ago** stands by itself, but the skies were also composed by **the word of God,** and both skies and earth (the Hebrew equivalent for the universe) represent **the then-existing world** which was **deluged and destroyed** at the flood ; water constituted the first world and water destroyed it. Another loose term is *di* 6 *hôn* (the plural), rendered by **water ;** the singular would have been correct, but the plural probably was used to suggest **the** two waters referred to above. In the vision of the deluge seen by Enoch (Enoch lxxxiii.), ' the heaven collapsed and fell on the earth . . . and the earth was swallowed up in a great abyss,' whereas in Second Peter the doom concentrates upon the earth, at the inundation. The argument is that while water once destroyed the world—so that things have not **remained exactly as they were from the** **beginning of creation**—fire is to be the doom of **the present** **heavens and earth**, which **are treasured up** (a grim destiny !) **by the same word** (as created the first universe) **for fire,** i.e. for God's doom on **the impious** (see ii. 5).

This is the solitary reference in the N.T. to the current idea of the universe ending in a conflagration. Josephus (*Antiquities*, i. 2) mentions a prediction of Adam that the world would be twice destroyed by water and by fire, and the far-spread idea of a final bonfire of the universe had entered Jewish apocalyptic ; it is voiced specially in the Sibylline oracles, where it differs from the Stoic cosmogony, in which there was a periodic renovation of the universe by means of fire. ' The Sibyl and Hystaspes,' says Justin Martyr (*Apol.*, i. 20), " said that corruptible things would be dissolved by fire ; the philosophers who are called Stoics declare that God himself is to be dissolved into fire, and that after this change the world will be renewed. . . . In asserting that there will be a conflagration we use the language of the Stoics, but,' he adds, our doctrine is not theirs in essence. The belief was popular in Roman as well as in Greek mythology, and it entered Christian apocalyptic at an early period. The writer alludes to it here as a familiar conception of the end, in order to meet the first objection taken to the doctrine of the Advent. He shows some independence in his levelopment of the general theme. Thus he follows the iook of

Enoch in adding **the heavens** to the earth as having been destroyed at the deluge ; the tale of Genesis spoke only of the earth in this connexion. But he adds **the heavens** to the earth in the expectation of the future (ver. 13), whereas the book of Enoch confined its outlook to a new heaven ; thus in xci. 16 :

> The first heaven shall depart and pass away,
> and a new heaven shall appear.

Our author, like the prophet John (Revelation xxi. 1), expects a new earth as well as a new heaven, though, unlike John, he anticipates the removal of the first stained universe by fire. This idea caught the imagination of the later church, as is plain from the opening lines of the great mediaeval hymn :

> Dies irae, dies illa
> Solvet saeclum in favilla.

George Herbert echoed it in the last stanza of his poem on Decay :

> I see the world grows old, when as the heat
> Of Thy great Love, once spread, as in an urn
> Doth closet up itself and still retreat,
> Cold sin still forcing it—till it return,
> And calling Justice all things burn.

His second argument is against misconceptions of the divine delay (8–9). It is addressed to believers who were apt to be impatient.

8 Beloved, you must not ignore this one fact, that *with the Lord* a single day is like a thousand years, and *a thousand*
9   *years are like a single day.* The Lord is not slow with what he promises, according to certain people's idea of

**slowness ; no, he is longsuffering for your sake, he does
not wish any to perish but all to betake them to
repentance.**

The scoffers **wilfully** ignored one fact ; believers were apt 8
to **ignore** another, namely, the truth underlying the words
of Psalm xc. 4, ' with the Lord a thousand years are like a
single day.' Jewish writers had used this text, as Christian
writers afterwards did, to explain the use of the term ' day '
in the Creation-tales of Genesis, but this is a new application
of it. The writer ignores any doctrine of a millennium.
That line of prophecy was popular in his day, but evidently it
did not appeal to him. He simply quotes the text to show
that delay as measured by actual time does not apply to the
eternal God ;

> Long the decrees of Heaven
> Delay, for longest time to him is short.

What is time to God ? If He seems to delay, it is not, as
certain **people** imagine, because He is careless or powerless, 9
but because He is merciful and patient, **longsuffering** (see
I Peter iii. 20) **for your** sake. The early reading *dia* brings
this out better than *eis* (' to us-ward '), and *your* is more
apposite than *our*. **He does not wish any to perish, but all
to betake them** (only here in N.T.) **to repentance.** Do you
not know, says Paul, speaking of this patient longsuffering,
though not in connexion with the Advent, ' that his kindness
is meant to make you repent ? ' In I Timothy ii. 4, ' God
our Saviour desires all men to be saved.' This is the interpretation of the delay offered by the writer ; God is really
putting off the end as long as He can, to give you a fuller
chance. If He seems slow with what he promises, it is in

order to make the promise available to as large a number as possible.

The day of the Lord is sure to come (5–7), and its delay is a proof of the divine generosity (8–9). These two truths are now reiterated, the former in 10–14, the latter in 15 f.

10 The day of the Lord will come like a thief, when the heavens will vanish with crackling roar, the stars will be set ablaze and melt, the earth and all its works will disappear.

11 Now as all things are thus to be dissolved, what holy and pious men ought you to be in your behaviour, you who

12 expect and hasten the advent of the Day of God, which dissolves the heavens in fire and makes the stars blaze

13 and melt ! It is new heavens and a new earth that we expect, as He has promised, and in them dwells righteous-

14 ness. Then, beloved, as you are expecting this, be eager to be found by him unspotted and unblemished in serene assurance.

10 **Like a thief** is another (see on ii. 20) reminiscence of a saying of Jesus about the unexpectedness of the Advent ; ' like a thief (in the night) ' was one of the most uncommon figures for the sudden return of the Lord in primitive Christianity. But the writer lays more stress on the cosmic conflagration at the end. ' Heaven and earth will vanish,' Jesus had predicted ; our author adds, **with crackling roar**, using an onomatopoetic word in a rare sense. **Set ablaze** is another unusual term, generally employed for feverish heat. The Greek term *stoicheia*, rendered ' elements ' in A.V., means the literal stars here, not the Elemental Spirits or

angels closely connected with the planets and constellations (see on Judas 6) as in Galatians iv. 3.

The last word of the sentence is obscure. The primitive reading is not **shall be burned up,** as we might expect, but *heurethêsetai*, 'be found' (as in ver. 14). The old Egyptian Sahidic version reads 'not be found,' i.e. **disappear,** which yields quite a good sense, and is a common phrase in similar connexions (e.g. in Revelation xvi. 20). Other conjectures have been offered, of verbs meaning destruction or burning, but the hypothesis that the negative was omitted by accident by the author or some early copyist meets the case adequately. What **the earth and all its works** denotes, is shown by the description in *The Sibylline Oracles* (ii. 251 f., translated by Professor Terry) :

> For stars from heaven shall fall into all seas.
> And all the souls of men shall gnash their teeth,
> Burned both by sulphur stream and force of fire
> In ravenous soil, and ashes hide all things.
> And then of all the world the elements
> Shall be bereft, air, earth, sea, light, sky, days,
> Nights ; and no longer in the air shall fly
> Birds without number, nor shall living things
> That swim the sea swim any more at all,
> Nor freighted vessel o'er the billows pass,
> Nor kine straight-guiding plow the field.

The terror and pathos of this are not what the writer **11** stresses ; it is (11–14) the moral and spiritual effects which such an expectation ought to have upon life to-day, on those who **expect and hasten the advent** of this **Day of God. 12** Good men hasten the Advent by their repentance (see Acts iii. 19 f.), for it is the sins of men that retard the coming of the Day (see above, ver. 9). Even by their prayers, like

' Thy kingdom come,' they bring faith to bear upon the fulfilment of the divine purpose; for the order of the world is not mechanical but moral, and Jesus had taught that his followers might, as it were, thus shorten the interval of 13 waiting. The expectation of a **new** order of things, embodying **righteousness,** calls for a clean, honest life to answer to it. One writer put the thought thus : ' Everyone who rests this hope on him purifies himself as he is pure ' (1 John iii. 3).

14 Our author writes, **be eager** (so i. 10) **to be found by him** at his coming (see Philippians iii. 9) **unspotted and unblemished** (not like these errorists, ii. 13), **in serene assurance, as you are expecting this.** A pure and consistent life is the one ground for **serene assurance,** the **peace** of i. 2, and the deep thought is that the Christian hope ought to produce a moral and spiritual quickening of conscience. It is a privilege, but it is also an obligation. For the writer it was impossible to give up the hope of the Advent without ethical deterioration. He had already marked the disastrous consequences of this in the errorists, and now he drives home the positive counsel to his readers.

The permanent lesson of the passage (as of i. 3–4) is that Christian hope must react upon the lives of those who entertain it. As Ruskin puts it in his famous application of the passage in *The Stones of Venice* (vol. iii, chap. iv) : ' It is indeed right that we should look for, and hasten, so far as in us lies, the coming of the Day of God ; but not that we should check any human efforts by anticipations of its approach. We shall hasten it best by endeavouring to work out the tasks that are appointed for us here.'

The writer now returns to the thought of ver. 9, but this leads him to assure his readers that the teaching of the apostle Paul is in agreement with his, whatever these errorists might say to the contrary (15-16).

And consider that the longsuffering of our Lord means salva- 15
  tion ; as indeed our beloved brother Paul has written
  to you out of the wisdom vouchsafed to him, speaking of 16
  this as he has done in all his letters—letters containing
  some knotty points, which ignorant and unsteady souls
  twist (as they do the rest of the scriptures) to their
  own destruction.

The thought of God's longsuffering is more prominent in 15
Romans (see ii. 4, iii. 25, ix. 22, and xi. 22) than in any other
of Paul's extant epistles, but the writer is not alluding to
this or to any one epistle which the readers were supposed
to have received for themselves. The you means the catholic
church. All the Pauline epistles were held to be meant for
the church at large. In the Muratorian canon it is expressly
argued that while Paul wrote to separate churches by name
yet ' one church is recognized as spread over all the world,'
i.e. the Pauline epistles are catholic. So here. No one
epistle, neither some lost epistle nor one of the canonical, is
meant. By a natural hyperbole the writer declares that
Paul treated the doctrine of God's saving patience in all his 16
letters, but he hurries on to explain that the errorists had no
right to claim as they did the authority of Paul for their
antinomian views. If Paul said, ' You are free from the
Law,' he did not mean ' free from moral claims.' The knotty
points (only here in N.T.) refer to Paul's views on Christian
freedom and the like, which even in his lifetime had been
misrepresented (see Romans vi. 1) and exaggerated. By

the time this epistle was written, they were being warped into a defence of moral laxity as the right of truly ' spiritual ' persons, by ignorant and unsteady (see ii. 14) souls. What N.T. writings are included along with the O.T. in the rest of the scriptures we do not know, but it is clear that the Greek term *loipas* means not ' the scriptures as well,' but the rest of the scriptures, and that *graphas* means scriptures in the technical sense, not ' writings or books' in general. Fatal (see ii. 1) distortions of Paul's meaning were abroad when this epistle was written, and this implies that his epistles were being appealed to as authoritative.

A last word of exhortation (17, 18) : be on your guard against error and grow in grace.

17 Now, beloved, you are forewarned ; mind you are not carried away by the error of the lawless and so lose your proper
18 footing ; but grow in the grace and knowledge of our Lord and saviour Jesus Christ. To him be the glory now and to the day of eternity : Amen.

17 Error is the word rendered misconduct in ii. 18, but it means here the pernicious principles and practices of the lawless (see on ii. 7) errorists, not pagan morals. To lose your proper footing (only here in N.T.) answers to the warning
18 of Judas (24) about slipping. The writer then repeats (i. 2–8) his counsel about Christian growth ; all depends on personal communion with Christ, a personal communion which deepens steadily. The knowledge of our Lord and saviour Jesus Christ is not a mere means of rescue (ii. 20), but the one means of maturity and health, which enables the Christian to throw off pernicious errors. And it is a knowledge which

depends upon the Lord's **grace,** not on speculative acuteness and individual enlightenment (see on i. 2). In the doxology, addressed to Christ (a rare practice in the N.T.), the phrase **to the day of eternity** is unexampled, though it does occur in Sirach xviii. 10. There, ' as a drop from the sea or a grain of sand, so are man's few years to the day of eternity ' ; but here it seems chosen **as a** special variant for the **day of the Lord** or **of God,** no period or episode but **an** eternal Day.

THE EPISTLE OF JUDAS

INTRODUCTION

IN the rhymed preface to his *Pilgrim's Progress*, Bunyan explains that he was drawn into writing the allegory when he was occupied with another book.

> I had undertook
> To make another, which when almost done,
> Before I was aware, I this begun.

So Judas meant to write upon the general theme of the Christian salvation, but, says he, I am forced to write you this special appeal, in view of a sudden emergency. Only, Bunyan's alteration of purpose was literary. In Bedford gaol he had been thinking and indeed writing already about—

> The Way
> And Race of Saints, in this our Gospel-day.

Fortunately for the world, the allegorical handling of the subject suddenly appealed to him with such force that he struck off into allegory, instead of composing a theological treatise as he had originally intended. Judas had to drop a wider project for a special piece of counsel and warning; he had to change his message rather than his method. So far as we know, he never wrote the book or epistle which he had in mind, when he turned to dictate this urgent call. Pindar opens his first Isthmian Ode by apologizing for

writing it when he had already begun to compose a paean
for Delos, which he is obliged to put aside meantime. But
the poet lived to complete the paean in question; it has
been preserved. Whereas, if Judas ever finished his original
plan of composition, it has not survived, unless, as some
have thought, he had a hand in the composition of the church-
manual called the *Didaché*. Probably it is another of the
books which early Christians meant to write and never
wrote. Ignatius, for example, in his letter to the Ephesian
church, said that if it was the will of Christ, ' I will proceed,
in the second treatise which I propose to write to you, to
explain the divine plan relating to the new man, Jesus
Christ, which I have begun to discuss.' But he did not live
to write this treatise. So, for some reason, Judas has only
left us this brief manifesto.

What moved him to write it was an outburst of antinomianism. Antinomianism is an ugly word for an uglier
thing. In religion it is the belief that a truly spiritual man
is exempt from the moral law, in virtue of his relationship
towards God. For certain religions it has never been
binding on a so-called ' saint ' to be what his fellow-
beings would call a moral person. But Christianity from
the first insisted on faith and fellowship being bound up
with a good life, and therefore the appearance of antinomian tendencies within its communities caused instant
and indignant protests.

That such tendencies should manifest themselves, however,
was only natural. Antinomianism, like Pharisaism, is a
perversion of religion at its very best. It is the exaggerated
extreme of a merely legal view of religion. Once people awake
to the truth that God's favour is not to be earned by an

accumulation of merits, nor by merely doing this or that in obedience to a prescribed code, they turn to the evangelical or mystical line ; ' faith is everything, we are not under law but grace.' Pushed to an extreme, this may become, and in the history of the church it often has become, for mystics and evangelicals alike, a repudiation of any moral restrictions or regulations as inconsistent with inner freedom. Mediaeval outbursts of the Free Spirit, the sectaries whom Luther had to check, and the English Ranters, are notorious cases in point. Paul had already met this spirit, which he denounced as a caricature of his teaching about salvation by faith. But towards the close of the first century it began to assume formidable proportions, as it became connected with a ramified movement of thought in Egypt, Asia, and Syria, which exploited the revival of Platonism in the interests of an ultra-spiritual conception of the world ; a theoretical basis for antinomianism was afforded by those who sought to explain the origin of evil as part and parcel of the material world. The Christian church, says Judas, adores the one and only God, our Saviour, the same God in creation and in redemption. But the creation of the world was ascribed in some circles to an inferior deity, the O.T. Creator, and redemption was the emancipation of the soul from the trammels of the senses by means of some higher God, the Father, who in Jesus intervened to rescue the pure spirit. Perfection was of the spirit alone. Hence an enlightened spirit might either take an ascetic view of evil, or regard anything done in the flesh as irrelevant to the well-being of the spirit—the more so when the O.T. decalogue was regarded, as it was by many, as the code of the inferior creator-god, whose sway was cancelled for the redeemed.

It is against a background of this kind that pastoral letters
like those of Judas and Second Peter are intelligible. The
details are obscure, for the precise data of the controversy
cannot be recovered, but the general trend is fairly plain.
Judas, for example, is an earnest, honest leader of the church,
not a keen analyst or cool religious critic of heresies. He
denounces the errorists, instead of describing them. Indeed
this would have been superfluous, as his readers are assumed
to know them at first hand. It is therefore difficult to
identify them amid the movements that swarmed between
the last quarter of the first century and the middle of the
second within the Christian churches of the East. The
pastoral is no transcript of the errorists' opinions and
practices, and the hints dropped by Judas do not fit any one
party known to us. But some suggest that he must have
been attacking an incipient phase of the gnostical tendency
which characterized, for example, what Irenaeus called ' the
party of Simon and Carpocrates,' who were antinomian on
principle and held erroneous views of the person of Christ,
besides disparaging angels. Thus the Simonians believed
that redemption emancipated the elect from the sway of the
rebellious angels and celestial powers who ruled or mismanaged
(according to them) the universe. As Judas put it, they scorn
the Powers celestial and scoff at the angelic Glories. They
also held that the distinctions between good and evil were
the arbitrary work of these angels, and that the free man,
saved by grace, could do as he pleased ; morality, as usually
understood, was a matter of opinion, due to the angels of the
present world. Besides, said some, one ought to try all
experiences, good or bad. Thus, said the indignant Judas,
they pollute their flesh, and pervert the grace of our God into

immorality. And when he charges them with disowning **Jesus Christ,** it may be a reference to their view, resembling that of Cerinthus the traditional opponent of St. John, that the Supreme Power descended in Judaea in the form of man (yet not a man), who only seemed to suffer (since the flesh and suffering were incompatible with the deity). Some did not believe Jesus to be the Son of God, and they claimed, says Irenaeus angrily, to be not only like Jesus, ' but sometimes even better.' Obedience to the moral law might be good enough for ordinary church believers, who did not possess the Spirit, but the emancipated spiritualists held that perfection belonged to the spirit, not to the flesh. Hence, they not merely took a docetic view of the person of Christ, but regarded the passions and impulses of the body as indifferent; in some cases adherents of such parties openly held that men ought to obey these instincts and were entitled to do so freely—like irrational creatures, Judas puts in !

They made extensive use of dreams and visions, these visionaries ! They scoffed at the O.T. prophecies as inspired by the inferior angels, arrogantly preferring their own revelations. And they practised their religious rites and cures for money—for what it brings them, as Judas sneered, to benefit themselves. Like the prophet John, who found similar lax movements in the Asiatic churches of Ephesus and Smyrna and Thyatira towards the close of the first century, Judas took the effective line of stamping the errorists with O.T. names of notorious offenders—Cain, Balaam, and Korah ; but he is controverting a more subtle and speculative movement, though it evidently was tinged with the same tendency to moral laxity. Clement of Alexandria, in his *Stromateis* (iii. 2), declares that what Judas wrote (8-17) seemed to him an actual prediction of what went on at religious gatherings of the Carpocratians and other sects in Egypt. He even accuses some of **vice and sensual perversity,** i.e. of sodomy. This was nearly a century later than Judas, and probably the movement had degenerated in the interval. But if the errorists belonged partly to a rudimentary phase of the movement which was organized definitely by Carpocrates the Alexandrian early in the second century, it would throw light on some of their traits, for the Carpocratians believed that Jesus was born of human parents (a disowning of **our sole liege and Lord Jesus Christ**) ; they also disparaged the world and the angels who were supposed to have created it, and from this principle further deduced the practical conclusion that all things ought to be common (including wives), and that such mundane scruples as moral restrictions on vice and theft were not binding on the free soul, which was only concerned with faith (no **most holy faith,** this !) and free love. Love ! says Judas angrily—these fine advocates of spiritual love are simply **stains on your love-feasts !**

It is through glimpses like these of various rampant tendencies, all speculative and antinomian, that we can form some idea of the teachers against whom this emphatic pastoral is directed. It is alive to the unholy alliance between speculative theosophy and practical immorality, just as the first epistle of John is, though the latter faces the Cerinthians with their doctrine of a truly human Jesus who was endowed with the divine spirit of Christ only between the baptism and the passion. The prophet John in the book of Revelation denounces Nicolaitans, who were connected somehow with the followers of Carpocrates or at anyrate with the tenets of that party, but he fastens on their immoral tendencies like Judas, whereas the first epistle of John deals more definitely with the error about the person of Christ, an aberration which Judas merely notes in passing.

It would be interesting to know if, in ver. 11, Judas had in mind the extremists who maintained that Cain, the Sodomites, and Korah were maligned victims of the creator-god, and therefore heroes ! These extremists belonged to the party named or nicknamed Serpent-worshippers (Ophites), since they viewed man's fall as his real emancipation, thanks to the serpent, from the tyranny of the creator-god. In any case, all such views about God, which separated creation from redemption, were to Judas an infringement of the prerogatives of the Christian deity. It is not against pagan polytheism, nor is it a merely liturgical flourish, when he lifts his doxology **to the only God, our saviour.** There is but one God in the universe, good and just, and Jesus Christ is **our sole liege and Lord,** by whom He saves us, keeping us **unblemished.** Yet Judas is absorbed, not in the speculative error about God's nature, but in the immoral practices which ooze out of it. Mr. Gladstone once wrote to the Duchess of Sutherland, ' There is one proposition which the experience of life burns into my soul ; it is this, that man should beware of letting his religion spoil his morality. In a thousand ways, some great, some small, but all subtle, we are daily tempted to that great sin.' There is much about this tract of Judas which is remote and obscure, but it clearly shows an early Christian teacher passionately warning people inside the Christian church against religious theories that spoil morality.

' I read my Bible,' says the mother of Felix Holt, in George Eliot's romance, ' and I know in Jude where it's been stained with the dried tulip-leaves this many a year, as you're told not to rail at your betters if he was the devil himself.' Most people know the epistle of Judas from the same passage about the railing accusation against the devil, or from the passage at the close about 'building ourselves up in the love of God.' The rest of the writing has little permanent interest or value. It is full of denunciations which sound to a modern more forcible than profitable. Judas was evidently indignant and alarmed about some development in the religious world of his day, but who he was and what he was attacking, we neither know nor greatly care to inquire. 'To a modern reader,' as its ablest English editor, Professor J. B. Mayor, observes, 'it is curious rather than edifying, with the exception of the beginning and the end.' But it must have impressed the church deeply in these early days. The first trace of it is either in the *Martyrdom of Polykarp* (see on 2, 25)—at Smyrna the message would be welcome !—or in the second epistle of Peter, whose author thought so highly of it that he made copious use of it in his treatise. By the end of the second century it was widely known and read at worship, in spite of its brevity. Alexandria, Carthage, and Rome esteemed it as scripture. This is hardly surprising, when we remember that libertinism and gnostic errors were surging through the churches during that period. No wonder an early, pungent warning like the tract of Judas, coming from the border of the apostolic days, was appreciated and circulated !

The feature that compromised it in some quarters before long was its use of the book of Enoch and of legends like that about the dispute between the devil and Moses. There were simple Christians like Mrs. Holt who read such passages without taking offence at them. But the day came—even in the second century it was dawning—when a strict, narrow view of inspiration resented any imprimatur being given to the book of Enoch as inspired, and the tract of Judas was on that account either read with hesitation or excluded from some lists of the N.T. canonical writings. For the vogue of apocalypses like the *Assumption of Moses* and the book of Enoch was waning. To the primitive church these had come as prophetic contributions from the ancient world.

In the first epistle of Peter, as we have seen, the collection of apocalyptic tractates called the book of Enoch is familiar to Peter and his circle, and Judas definitely cites it as inspired. Any modern reader who looks into it will marvel at the reputation it once enjoyed in these enthusiastic Christian communities. Unless he has been in touch with simple, uneducated pietists of a prophetic cast, he may even fail to understand why such apocalypses ever held the mind and heart of the church. ' In the apocalyptic and eschatological literature of the time, the world was to come to an end. But what really did come to an end,' says Professor Vladimir Simkhovitch, ' in that literature was the last shred of thinking capacity and common sense.' This is far too severe. Still, by the end of the second century Christians were losing interest in the immediate end of the world and in the hectic prophecies that predicted it ; they began to ask inconvenient questions even about the book of Enoch. How did it survive the Flood ? Once this decline of sympathy with the naïve belief in Enoch set in, the tract came under suspicion. ' Because Judas draws a testimony from the apocryphal book of Enoch, his epistle is rejected by very many,' says Jerome in the fourth century ; but by the end of that century it was nevertheless finally canonized. Indeed it is fully owned as scripture in the so-called Muratorian Canon of the N.T., a second-century list of N.T. books. The Muratorian Canon came from the Egyptian church, and it was there that the tract found its earliest admirers, in Origen and Clement ; the latter wrote comments on it. Its affinities with the *Didaché*, perhaps another Egyptian book, further confirm the hypothesis that the tract was of Egyptian origin. It was in Egypt that the first weeds of the sinister Carpocratian heresy shot up ; we are not far wrong in supposing that Judas was some teacher or prophet of the Egyptian church, that is, in all likelihood, of the Alexandrian.

No tradition, however, has come down to us about its origin. Like the epistle of James, another Egyptian church encyclical, while it reflects some personal experience and local observation, it is a homily or pastoral which the writer designs for more than his immediate circle. As a teacher of the church, he writes *urbi et orbi*, in a Christian sense. It was the weight of his tract, for all its apparently fugitive character, that carried it so far, in the second century. Judas, like James, had the immense spiritual prestige of a teacher, and the intrinsic merits of his tract, so timely and pungent, were backed by the spiritual authority of his vocation. No wonder that Tertullian and others were calling him an apostle by the end of the century. But Judas was no apostle. So much we know, though little more. **Judas** was not an uncommon name among Hebrew Christians, and **Judas the brother of James** may quite conceivably be some Judas otherwise unknown to fame. There was a Judas in the reign of Hadrian who was bishop of the Jerusalem church, for example, though this is not likely to be our author. Or, we may ask, was the original title merely **Judas a servant of Jesus Christ,** and did some one insert **and a brother of James,** to guarantee, as it were, the credentials of the writer by connecting his person with the first head of the Jerusalem church, whose antipathies to pagan antinomianism were well known ?   Or is the entire title pseudonymous ?

This throws us back upon the fact that among the brothers of Jesus were two called **James** and **Judas,** who would be born about the beginning of the century.   The former we know.   The latter is unknown to tradition, except in connexion with a tale of his grandsons, who were haled before the suspicious emperor Domitian, because they belonged to the Davidic lineage and were supposed to have hopes of a messianic empire.   They were horny-handed peasants, who had no difficulty in proving their innocence of any revolutionary designs.   Now, as this interview took place after Judas was dead, he must have written his tract by about A.D. 90 at the latest.   There is nothing in the references to the errorists which quite shuts out this as a possibility.   Those who prefer to think that in the second century some anonymous writer composed the manifesto under the pseudonym of **Judas a brother of James** have to explain how so unimportant a figure was likely to have been chosen to voice the warning.

The difficulty on either of these hypotheses is to understand why he called himself or was called **a servant of Jesus Christ,** instead of **a brother.**   This was felt early, and answered by Clement of Alexandria, who thought it was due to reverence and humility.   This is ingenious, but is it necessary ?   Some Judas who had a brother called James may well have written the manifesto.   And this is the more likely when the James who wrote the canonical epistle is seen to have had no connexion with the strict Jewish Christian head of the Jerusalem church. So far from claiming to be an apostle, Judas bids his readers recall how the apostles of our Lord Jesus Christ had predicted this latter-day movement of mischief. He looks back on the apostolic age. But probably all the apostles were dead by about 90. On the other hand, his tone of surprise at the news or sight of the errorists would indicate that the phenomenon was new, or that it had but recently been brought under his notice. He starts back from it in horror, shocked by its appearance and inroads, even while he insists that it is an innovation which had been foreseen beforehand by the apostles. His very allusion to the apostles is an indication that he wrote comparatively early in the post-apostolic age, for he does not call the loyal Christians to rally round the ministry of bishops and presbyters as preserving true doctrine. Ignatius does this in the first quarter of the second century, and against gnostic perversions of the gospel it became increasingly a natural and needful safeguard. For Judas it is enough as yet to uphold the apostolic tradition as such. Remember the words of the apostles, he urges; he does not say, hold by their true successors in authority over the church. All this renders it rather unlikely that the pastoral is much later, if later at all, than the close of the first century, when already, as we know from the book of Revelation, some forms of this heresy were rampant in the churches of Asia Minor.

Whatever view be held of its authorship, it was either written or meant to be taken as having been written at the close of the apostolic period as a sort of fiery cross sent through the churches to rally the faithful against a new insidious foe. The danger against which it sought to forewarn Christendom has altered its form, but it is always present, and the burden of the letter retains its significance. For antinomianism, like gnosticism in general, is by no manner of means a far-off unhappy tendency in the religious world, whose interest for ourselves is purely historical or antiquarian.

THE address or salutation (1–2) is modelled on lines already indicated by letter-writers like Paul and Peter.

1 Judas, a servant of Jesus Christ and a brother of James, to those who have been called, who are beloved by God
2 the Father and kept by Jesus Christ : mercy, peace and love be multiplied to you.

1   A servant means one who is at the disposal of Jesus Christ for service in his cause, here for the special service of warning and counselling fellow-Christians. A brother of James (see Introduction) is a unique addition ; no other N.T. writer mentions his family in this way. He writes to those who have been called, and who have accepted the divine call. But they are not left to their own resources ; they are beloved by God the Father (literally ' in God the Father,' a Greek phrase which means dear to Him or loved by Him) and kept safe (same word as in Revelation iii. 10) by Jesus Christ. In the original called comes last in the clause, so that the three following words answer in reverse order to the descrip-
2 tion of the Christian position ; mercy underlies God's calling of those who owe everything to His undeserved pity (see on 1 Peter i. 3), those who are preserved by Jesus Christ may enjoy peace of mind, and God's beloved may count upon fresh experiences of His love. Multiplied is explained on 1 Peter i. 2. The phrase reappears in the second-century

Martyrdom of Polykarp, where the Smyrniote church prays:
' Mercy, peace, and love be multiplied.'

Now for the occasion of the letter (3-4).

> Beloved, my whole concern was to write to you on the subject 3
> of our common salvation, but I am forced to write you
> an appeal to defend the faith which has once for all been
> committed to the saints ; for certain persons have slipped 4
> in by stealth (their doom has been predicted long ago),
> impious creatures who pervert the grace of our God into
> immorality and disown our sole liege and Lord, Jesus
> Christ.

Beloved (for I love you too ; so in 17, 20), I fully intended 3
to write a treatise on our common salvation (shared by all
true Christians). The present letter is an urgent special
appeal to the readers to defend the faith by adhering to it
(see 17-23). For while the faith has been finally and fully
entrusted to the saints (i.e. to those called and set apart by
God for Himself), a novel abuse of it has been surreptitiously
introduced by certain persons (the Greek has the same 4
scornful tinge as in Galatians i. 7).

This is the danger which has roused Judas to put his
friends upon their guard. The peril is not caused by any
persecution stirred by Jews or by the Roman Empire. Neither
is it an attack upon the principles of Christianity by some
outside critic. It is an insidious distortion of Christianity
from within, due to the influence of some who claimed to be
members of the church. Judas denies their claim. They
have slipped into the church somehow; instead of being
called by God, they are doomed. Their ultimate doom has
been predicted long ago (the thought of 1 Peter ii. 8). But

meanwhile they are working mischief, these **impious creatures,** by their practices and their principles ; they make the freedom of a Christian man a pretext for loose living, and they compromise the full divinity of Christ. The perversion of **our** (He is not their) **God's grace into immorality** means that a forgiven, spiritual person is above the moral law, free to indulge the impulses and instincts of life, since nothing done in the flesh can stain the inner spirit. The only difficulty here lies in identifying the particular form of this error to which Judas is alluding (see Introduction).

The other charge is less clear. Jesus had spoken of those who might **deny** him before men, but this meant Christians who disowned their Lord under the stress of persecution. It was also possible to speak of Christians denying **their** God by misconduct which contradicted the truth of his religion (so Titus i. 16). But in his favourite book of Enoch (xxxviii. 2, etc.) the denial of God had the specially ominous sense of disavowing Him openly for sinister ends ; it was the dark antithesis to true belief. So Judas uses it here of errorists who took some view of the person of Christ which he regarded as infringing its fullness, as, e.g., when some held that **Christ** meant a heavenly aeon or spirit which only descended upon the human **Jesus** at the baptism and withdrew from him before the crucifixion. This view was the result of a dualism which regarded the divine nature as too pure to be directly connected with anything so vital to the flesh as birth and the suffering of death. It was sincerely designed to pay honour to the divine Christ, but Judas sharply characterizes it as a repudiation of him altogether. He never alludes to this again ; other aspects of the errorists occupy his attention in the rest of the letter. Whatever their tenets about Christ were, however, he regarded them as implicitly disowning our sole liege (generally used elsewhere of God) and Lord, Jesus Christ.

Remember the terrible warnings against such a sinful course in the past history of the People of God (5-7).

Now I want to remind you of what you are perfectly aware, 5 that though the Lord once brought the People safe out of Egypt, he subsequently destroyed the unbelieving, while the angels who abandoned their own domain, 6 instead of preserving their proper rank, are reserved by him within the nether gloom, in chains eternal, for the doom of the great Day—just as Sodom and Gomorra 7 and the adjacent cities, which similarly glutted themselves with vice and sensual perversity, are exhibited as a warning of the everlasting fire they are sentenced to suffer.

A courteous reminder of what they had heard from scrip- 5 tures like the Pentateuch and the book of Enoch, read aloud in church-worship. The present situation throws light on these old lessons, so familiar and so sombre. First there is the doom that befell the unbelieving Israelites who proved sceptical when the promised land was set before them—an incident which had powerfully impressed Christian (1 Corinthians x. 5 ; Hebrews iv. 7 f.) and Jewish piety as an outstanding example of unbelief and lapsing.

There may be a warning here for the errorists, some of whom thought that their baptized adherents were immune from any risk or danger, in virtue of their profession of faith. But the direct warning is for the readers ; people may once be saved and yet fall away subsequently into an unbelief which ruins them, as will be the case with you, if you listen to these insidious creatures. ' Let therefore none presume upon past mercies, as if he were now out of danger ' (Wesley). This is hinted, but no more than hinted. It is not till the close of the tract that Judas urges (ver. 20) the truth that any sense of security for Christians involves a serious moral and spiritual discipline.

At present he hastens to recall a second, equally notorious instance of punishment for disobedience ; it is the fall of 6 the angels who had abandoned their own domain in heaven, instead of preserving (literally, *keeping*) their proper rank. This is the famous legend of the later Judaism, based upon Genesis vi. 1 f., and popularized for Judas and his friends as for Peter (see on 1 Peter iii. 19) by the apocalypse of Enoch, which tells how the angels or 'sons of God' conceived a passion for the daughters of men and conspired to break away from their heavenly domain. Though spiritual beings, with their domain (Enoch xv. 7) above, they abandoned (Enoch xii. 4) high heaven. Judas recollects the very language of Enoch also in depicting their punishment. They are reserved (literally *kept*—a grim play on the word) by God for the doom of the great Day of the last judgment (a phrase used in Revelation xvi. 10), imprisoned within the nether gloom, in chains eternal. ' The great Day of judgment' occurs in another connection in Enoch (Greek text of xxii. 11). but the tragic tale of the rebellious angels yields the main points of the allusion here ; thus God orders them to be bound fast ' in the valleys of the earth till the day of their judgment ' (x. 12), and in liv. 4 f. huge iron chains are forged to fetter them till that great Day of final doom when they are to be ' cast into the burning furnace.'

A ghastly human parallel to the sin and punishment of the **7** apostate angels is now cited, in the O.T. tale of **Sodom and Gomorra and the adjacent cities** (Zoar, Admah, and Zeboim, according to the O.T.). Their inhabitants had been guilty not only of **vice** like the fallen angels who had lusted after women, but of sodomy, **sensual perversity** (Genesis xix. 5). And look at their punishment ! The land is still smoking with the subterranean fire in which they burn till they are flung finally into **the everlasting fire they are sentenced to suffer** like the fallen angels (see above) at the last day. A solemn **warning** to all !

According to Enoch (lxvii. 12), the punishment of the fallen angels is ' a testimony for the kings and the mighty who possess the earth,' but Judas does not limit the range of the warning. Under the Gehenna ravine, including the site of the cities of the Dead Sea, a subterranean fire was supposed to burn, and the volcanic phenomena proved to the religious mind the lasting punishment of the district. ' The land still smells of fire,' Tertullian writes (*Apolog.*, xl.), ' and any fruit borne by the local trees can only be looked at ; once touched, it crumbles into ashes.' Such was the Jewish belief, as Josephus witnesses in his *Wars* (iv. 8, 4) : ' The land was burned by lightning for the impiety of its inhabitants. Still there are vestiges of that fire, and the traces of five cities are still to be seen.' This Palestinian belief underlies the remark about the cities being **exhibited as a warning of the everlasting fire.** It is due to the fact (see on 2 Peter ii. 6) that ' in this awful hollow, this bit of the infernal regions come up to the surface, this hell with the sun shining into it, primitive man laid the scene of God's most terrible judgment on human sin. The glare of Sodom and Gomorrha is flung down the whole length of Scripture history. It is the popular and standard judgment of sin ' (G. A. Smith, *Historical Geography of Holy Land,* p. 504).

The gross irreverence of these religious visionaries at the present day (8–10).

8 Despite it all, these visionaries pollute their flesh, scorn the
9   Powers celestial, and scoff at the angelic Glories. Now
    the very archangel Michael, when he disputed the body of
    Moses with Satan, did not dare to condemn him with
10   scoffs ; what he said was, *The Lord rebuke you!* But
    these people scoff at anything they do not understand ;
    and whatever they do understand, like irrational creatures,
    by mere instinct, that proves their ruin.

These pseudo-prophets claimed to have revelations and visions (of what they were allowed or ordered to do or to ask), i.e. to be specially inspired, but this merely meant loose living and disrespect for angels, the two sins of which Sodom and Gomorra had been guilty. The close connexion of sex and religion produced moral aberrations which Judas calls a
8 pollution of the flesh ; the primitive love-feasts (ver. 12), where men and women met in exalted fervour, gave opportunities for indulging such passions. So-called ' spiritual ' men might urge and did urge that the ordinary restraints of the sexes were abolished by the new freedom of the Spirit, and that the impulse to promiscuous sexual intercourse was a genuine expression of the love-spirit in the community. Religious communism for some enthusiasts meant free love as well as no property.

Disrespect for angels is less intelligible ; in the primitive church it was usually angel-worship which was the danger. *Kuriotes* (a generic singular) here, as in Ephesians i. 21 and Colossians i. 16 (where it is rendered *angelic Lords*), denotes a class of higher angels, who are also termed **Glories ;** but we can only guess how the errorists depreciated the angelic hierarchy in their theories or practice. Possibly they were precursors of the later sects, who taught that Christians must follow Christ in despising and repudiating the angels who had made the created world with its passions ; the human soul in returning to its spiritual orbit scorns these inferior angels and has also the right to regard human actions in the present order as morally indifferent (see Introduction). At anyrate, it is the open contempt for angels which excites the anger of Judas, who proceeds to argue that these errorists might well learn a lesson from **the archangel Michael.** He 9 alludes to the legend told in a Jewish apocalypse called the *Assumption of Moses* ; when God commissioned Michael with his angels to bury the **body of Moses,** after his soul had been taken to heaven, the devil appeared to claim the body as a material object belonging to his sphere as the Lord of matter ; whereupon Michael mildly replied (in the words of Zechariah iii. 2, the rebuke of the angel to Satan), **The Lord rebuke you !** No unmannerly scoffing here, even from an archangel to the devil ! **But these people dare to scoff at anything they do not** 10 **understand** (i.e. at the celestial hierarchy). It is a side-stroke at the pretensions of these votaries to superior insight into the mysteries of creation and the moral order, and also a reminder that they might well learn respect and reverence from the angels whom they affected to contemn. If the glorious archangel would not revile even the devil for his insolence, who are these low-minded creatures to disparage the holy angels by whom, under God, the law was given and the universe ruled as well as made?

The closing words are stern, but no sterner than the language often used by men like Luther or Wesley who had to encounter such antinomian perversions among their followers. Even the gentle Ruysbroeck, despairing of the fanatical mystics in the thirteenth and fourteenth centuries who advocated and practised libertinism, was moved to declare, ' They perish like mad dogs.' These mediaeval votaries of the Free Spirit defended their gratification of any appetite on the speculative ground that such desires were all part of the one divine Matter. Their precursors in the days of Judas started from a less pantheistic view, but some of their followers at anyrate were prepared to draw the same practical conclusion, and Judas roughly dubs them brutes (**irrational creatures**) ; they have only the animal instinct for physical self-gratification, and that proves their undoing at the end.

Note on the ' Assumption of Moses.'—This was an apocalypse written about the beginning of the century, in which the dying Moses predicted the future of his nation and in which his death was described (though this closing part has been mutilated). It specially appealed to Judas for two reasons. (i) It contained assertions of the creation of angels and of the world by God. Thus a quotation has been preserved giving the original finish to Michael's rebuke ; he said to the devil, ' For from His holy Spirit we were all created,' and also, ' From before God went forth His Spirit and the world was created.' No lower origin for angels or for the universe, as these errorists alleged ! (ii) It contained also apt words of protest against secular religion and selfishness, as Judas recalls in ver. 16.

A passionate denunciation of their practices (11-13).

Woe to them ! they go the road of Cain, rush into Balaam's 11
error for what it brings them, and perish in Korah's
rebellion. These people are stains on your love-feasts ; 12
they have no qualms about carousing in your midst, *they*
look after none but themselves—rainless clouds, swept
along by the wind, trees in autumn without fruit, doubly 13
dead and so uprooted, wild waves foaming out their own
shame, wandering stars for whom the nether gloom of
darkness has been reserved eternally.

Like other N.T. writers, he brands the errorists by com- 11
paring them to some notorious O.T. characters. **Balaam's**
error is clear ; Balaam was the prototype of false teachers
who inculcated lax principles of morality (this is the point of
the comparison in Revelation ii. 14) and made a good thing
out of their pseudo-religion, as did these errorists and others
(1 Timothy vi. 5—the principle of these unprincipled creatures
being that ' religion is a paying concern '). Balaam also had
dreams and visions, and he had tried to defy angelic authority.
The sinister reputation he had acquired in the later Judaism
lies behind this reference of Judas ; ambition and haughtiness
are his characteristics in the *Pirke Aboth* (v. 29), and this
recurs below in ver. 16 (their talk is arrogant).

Korah is not mentioned elsewhere in the N.T., but he was
the typical rebel against divine authority in the church ;
these highflying teachers of the inner Light who claimed that
their revelations were above criticism, naturally disclaimed
the right of anyone to guide or rule them, and again resented
the opposition of the church-leaders to their views (which is
one of the points of murmurers in ver. 16). Judas predicts

their ruin at the hands of God as the result of their rebellious, insubordinate attitude.

The **road of Cain** sounds less relevant. In Jewish tradition he had become the type of self-seeking men as well as of sceptics who refused to believe in any moral retribution or in the after-life. The latter does not fit these errorists exactly, though some denied that any bodily excesses could be punished in their case after death ; the former trait of unbrotherly egoism may be what Judas means, in the next verse, by
12 quoting from Ezekiel xxxiv. 8, **they look after none but themselves.** Literally this is, ' they shepherd [indulge] themselves alone,' referring to their greedy conduct at the love-feasts (like the people whom Paul had denounced at Corinth in 1 Corinthians xi. 20–22) ; such grasping behaviour might be termed the Cain-spirit, especially if it carried the deeper suggestion of murdering the souls of men by their conduct, and thereby ruining themselves—which would be the result of taking the road of Cain, according to Wisdom x. 3, where Cain, ' falling away from God's wisdom in his anger, perished himself by his fratricidal passion.'

The **love-feasts** were charity suppers in the primitive church, where the members gathered for a common meal to express their fellowship as a household of the faith. The food seems to have been provided out of the church funds or by the wealthier members. But what happened at Corinth evidently happened elsewhere ; selfishness and bad behaviour spoiled the simple meal. Instead of sharing alike, some snatched at the food before others arrived (i.e. slaves or humble tradesmen who could not attend till the day's work was done). So ' one goes hungry while another gets drunk.' The pushing and grasping members took advantage of others.

Judas is angry not only at these errorists daring to attend the love-feasts, but at their callous, cavalier conduct there. They were spots and blots on the proceedings anyhow. For **spots** is a better rendering of the Greek term *spilades* here than ' squalls ' or ' sunken rocks.' They were out of keeping with true Christians in a church meeting. But, worse than that, **they have no qualms about carousing in your midst,** bold creatures that they are, attending to no one but themselves— a flagrant violation of what a love-feast meant !

Sky, land, and sea are then ransacked for illustrations of their character. No refreshment of the soul comes from these **rainless clouds, swept along by the wind** of impulse ; they are **like trees in** the late **autumn** (the season when fruit was expected) that are **without fruit.** Such men, Judas adds, are 13 **doubly dead** (i.e. dead in sin before they were baptized and dead through their subsequent misdoings) **and so uprooted** finally (see on ver. 10). They make a great splash and noise in the church, with their **arrogant talk** (ver. 16), but it only brings out **their own shame,** exposing their frothy, restless and discreditable aims. Finally, there is no light or guidance to be derived from such **wandering stars,** erratic comets or shooting meteors, who are doomed to a dark fate (see ver. 6). The notion of stars being punished is a reminiscence of the book of Enoch (xviii., xx., etc.), where **the nether gloom is** the punishment of stars (i.e. angels) who have deserted their proper orbit **and** broken away from the regulations of the Lord.

But Judas does more than recall Enoch ; he cites the book triumphantly as an inspired prophecy of these loud, licentious mischief-makers, whose **doom had been predicted long ago** (ver. 4) in its message. Here is the actual prediction (14-16) :

14 It was of these, too, that Enoch the seventh from Adam
prophesied, when he said,

Behold the Lord comes with myriads of his holy ones,

15 *to execute judgment upon all,*
and to convict all the impious
of all the impious deeds they have committed,
and of all the harsh things said against him by impious sinners.

16 For these people are murmurers, grumbling at their own
lot in life—they fall in with their own passions, their talk
is arrogant, they pay court to men to benefit themselves.

14 In the book of Enoch (lx. 8), Enoch is described as the
15 seventh from Adam. The quotation is from a prediction
(i. 9) of God's intervention against impious members of the
People ; it is free, and the words about the harsh things said
against God are taken from a later passage (xxvii. 2). The
holy ones are angels, for the author of Enoch was thinking
of Deuteronomy xxxiii. 2, where God's coming is with ' ten
thousands of his holy ones.' Even in applying the passage
to the errorists of his day Judas uses language already familiar
to his readers in the *Assumption of Moses*, where (v. 5, vii, 7, 9)
16 the vicious religionists are called grumblers, whose talk is
arrogant, and who pay court to well-to-do or influential people.
No other N.T. writer uses the word for murmurers. It refers
to the discontented spirit which, according to Judas, led
them to object to angels (ver. 8), and also, like Korah (ver. 11),
to chafe under the refusal of the church authorities to recognize
their pretensions. Probably this was one expression of their
grumbling at their own lot in life ; they were recalcitrant to
men as well as insolent to God.

Judas views their whole religious position as a restless,

arbitrary defiance of the divine order in the universe and in
the church. Their one guide was their own passions ; no
other power could sway their self-indulgent lives. Arrogant
enough in their criticisms of providence, they were also
toadies, courting important or wealthy Christians (the charge
hinted in ver. 11) for personal ends. This last charge is
added to the general denunciation drawn from the heated
oracles of Enoch. It is curious that George Fox found a
similar trait in the English Ranters of his day (' these lewd
persons and their wicked actions '), who were antinomians
openly. ' It was the manner of the Ranters,' he notes in
his Journal (1654), ' to be extreme in their compliments ' to
anyone in high position or authority. These highly superior
' elect ' apparently had an eye to the main chance, in a
variety of ways.

Judas now reminds his readers that the Christian apostles
as well as Enoch had foretold the rise of such errorists (17–19).

Now, beloved, you must remember the words of the apostles 17
of our Lord Jesus Christ : they told you beforehand, 18
' At the end of things there will be mockers who go by
their own impious passions.' These are the people who 19
set up divisions and distinctions, sensuous creatures,
destitute of the Spirit.

For true members of the church the apostles are authorita- 17
tive. Either this quotation is from some writing which has 18
not survived (see on 2 Peter iii. 3), or it is a summary of
traditional warnings like 1 Timothy iv. 1 f., that the imminent
end of things would be heralded by the rise of scoffing, loose-
living religionists within the churches, who derided the stricter
moral code of the apostolic faith. Here the allusion is to

19 the precursors of the gnostics, who divided mankind into three classes, (*a*) the ' spiritual,' who, as being possessed of the Spirit, were sure of salvation, (*b*) the sensuous, or ordinary persons in possession of the *psyche* merely, who might or might not be saved according as they used their freewill, and (*c*) the material or worldly class, who were incapable of salvation. The highflying errorists regarded themselves as belonging to the first class, and generally derided the ordinary church-believer as belonging to the second. ' They hold,' says Irenaeus indignantly (i. 6, 2–3), ' that good behaviour is necessary for us members of the church (being merely sensuous), since otherwise we cannot be saved ; they themselves will be saved, however they behave, because they are by nature spiritual.' So Judas attacks these errorists for dividing men up into classes determined by God, and throws their language back upon themselves ; ' they are the sensuous,' using the term in a derogatory sense (as in James iii. 15), almost equivalent to ' sensual.' They claimed that their possession of the Spirit exempted them from the ordinary restrictions of morality ; the pure inner spirit could not be stained by the passions of the flesh, any more than gold by mud ! Judas repudiates the notion that any enlightenment gave the right to follow the impulses of nature unchecked, and denies outright their claim to a monopoly of the Spirit ; they are destitute of the Spirit, for all their arrogant pretensions to the higher life !

Mockers denotes their contemptuous rejection of tne moral laws of God ; they would also show insolent airs of superiority towards Christians who still believed that the spiritual life was bound by ethical principles. Bunyan, in *Grace Abounding* (44, 45), tells how the seventeenth-century sect of the Ranters,

who claimed similar freedom from moral laws, derided the
stricter Christians. ' These would condemn me as legal and
dark, pretending that they only had attained perfection that
could do what they would, and not sin.' One of them ' gave
himself up to all manner of filthiness, especially uncleanness
. . . and would laugh at all exhortations to sobriety. When
I laboured to rebuke his wickedness, he would laugh the
more.'

Judas now turns (20-23) to the positive duty of church
members, explaining how they must in their lives **defend the
faith** (ver. 4), which these errorists impugned by such loose
principles and practices.

> But do you, beloved, **build up yourselves on your most holy** 20
> **faith** and **pray in the holy Spirit**, so **keeping yourselves** 21
> **within the love of God** and **waiting for the mercy of our**
> **Lord Jesus Christ** that ends in life eternal. *Snatch some* 22
> *from the fire,* and **have mercy on the waverers**, trembling 23
> as you touch them, with loathing for *the garment* which
> the flesh has *stained*.

The **faith** is the faith which has been once for all com- 20
mitted to the saints (ver. 3), i.e. the body of Christian belief,
the apostolic confession of faith ; it is **most holy** as opposed
to the demoralizing creed of the errorists. Instead of abandon-
ing it for any so-called higher ' spiritual ' life of enlightenment,
you must **build up yourselves** on this common basis ; the
fabric of the church depends upon it for consolidation. Also
the real experience and possession of the **holy Spirit** inspires
prayer, not any proud sense of superiority to others or any
false independence towards God. Prayer is love in need
appealing to Love in power, and the upbuilding of the church

depends upon this living intercourse between God and His People.

Christians are **beloved by God** (ver. 1), but this experience is a reality as they fulfil the conditions and so keep them-
21 selves **within** God's love, which has its own terms of communion. This standing alone justifies a quiet hope of **the mercy of our Lord Jesus Christ** (see 1–2). Such an expectation is for those only who know they do not deserve life eternal, and who yet have endeavoured to meet the moral and spiritual demands essential to it in the faith of Christ. **The Lord is coming** (vers. 14, 15) for judgment on the impious. Only in the humble, prayerful, dutiful fellowship of the church is any hopeful outlook on that final scrutiny possible.

22 This positive sentence is followed by a sentence on the duty of counteracting the propaganda of the errorists. They themselves may be beyond reach, but some of their deluded followers may and ought to be rescued. 'When the power of reclaiming the lost dies out of the Church,' said Sir John Seeley, 'it ceases to be the Church.' Judas recognizes this impulse and power as vital to a genuine Christianity; the Church is not to enjoy itself in the thought of its own privileges, but to stretch out its hands to those who are caught in the pernicious teaching which is abroad. The original text has been preserved by Clement of Alexandria and Jerome as well as in the Philoxenian Syriac version; afterwards it was expanded into the later text in one form or another.

Snatch some from the fire is another (see on ver. 9) reminiscence of Zechariah iii. (ver. 2); rescue forcibly some weaker natures who can be pulled out of **the fire** of immoral tempta-
23 tions set ablaze by these libertine religionists. Others are

hesitating, not yet wholly committed to the false teaching ; instead of scolding them, **have mercy on waverers** ; deal with them in a spirit of pity ; have mercy on them as you hope for mercy yourselves from Christ.

Only, such rescue efforts have their dangers. There have been sad cases of people engaged in rescue work who have been actually drawn into the very sins which they were endeavouring to defeat ; in trying to lift others, they have been pulled down and stained in the mud (see on James i. 27). So do your work among these misguided people, **trembling as you touch them,** not allowing pity for the sinner to make the sin seem less heinous, but **loathing** *the garment* **which the flesh has** *stained*—another reminiscence of the story in Zechariah (iii. 4). Foul traces of sin must not be permitted to fascinate the mind of the Christian who has to deal with them in rescue work ; to avoid the possibility of being tainted by contact with them, you must maintain an instinctive aversion to them. This was a favourite text of Oliver Cromwell's. When he quoted it to the New Parliament of 1654, he observed that Judas uttered the counsel, ' Save some with fear, pulling them out of the fire,' when he ' reckoned up those horrible things done haply by some upon mistakes.'

The warning against contamination is absent from the similar injunction in the *Didaché* (ii. 7 : ' You shall hate no man, but some you must reprove, for some you must pray, and some you must love more than your very life '), but then the *Didaché* contemplated a much less serious position of affairs.

The pastoral closes with a doxology (24, 25), arising out of what has just been said. The danger of making a slip and falling away from the faith, in the effort to help others, as well as in the general practice of personal religion, leads Judas to end as he began by exalting the power of God.

24 Now to him who is able to keep you from slipping and to make you stand unblemished and exultant before his
25 glory—to the only God, our saviour through Jesus Christ our Lord, be glory, majesty, dominion, and authority, before all time and now and for all time : Amen.

24   This is the third doxology in the N.T. which opens to him who is able ; the others are in Romans xvi. 25 and Ephesians iii. 20. Unblemished (from such stains as are mentioned in ver. 23) is much, but exultant is more—exultant because they are unblemished, and exulting in the power and goodness of the God who has brought them through the strain and stains of this world.   To stand before his glory alludes to the final scrutiny at which the divine mercy (21) issues in life eternal.   The term (free) from slipping (never elsewhere in the N.T.) occurs in 3 Maccabees vi. 39 (' on them did the Lord of all manifest his mercy, delivering them one and all
25 free from slipping.'   God is termed the only God, our saviour through Jesus Christ our Lord, in opposition to the teaching of the errorists (see Introduction) ; the one (ver. 4) effective saving power in this world of corruption works through Jesus Christ as the Church confesses him.   Here at the end as at the beginning (ver. 2) the pastoral is echoed in the *Martyrdom of Polykarp* (xx.), written from the church of Smyrna, where the doxology runs : ' Now to him who is able to bring us in his bounteous grace to his heavenly realm by his only-begotten Child Jesus Christ, be glory, honour, dominion, and majesty for ever.'

246

INDEX

ABRAHAM, 42–4, 60
Advent. *See* Return (of Christ)
Adversity, 8, 13
Angels, 102, 195, 218, 220, 232–5, 240
Anger, 23–5
Antinomianism, 173, 195, 199 f., 216–18, 225, 227, 236
Apocalypse of Peter, 30, 186, 191
Apostle(s), 89, 202, 226
Apostolic Constitutions, 171
Apuleius, 27
Ascension (of Christ), 144, 187
Ascension of Isaiah, 144
Assumption of Moses, 197, 223, 235 f., 240
Aurelius, Marcus, 18, 45, 54, 110, 120, 166, 174 f.

BABYLON, 170
Bagehot, Walter, 47
Baptism, 140–3, 182 f.
Barnabas, 29
Baxter, Richard, 195 f.
Belief. *See* Faith
Blood, 91 f.
Blood (of Christ), 106
Book of Ahikar, 200
Brace up, to, 103 f.
Bunyan, 195, 215, 242 f.
Burke, 51

CERINTHUS, 219
Character, 8–10, 12, 39 f.
Chastity, 130 f., 133, 148
Christ, as Divine, 6, 177, 179 f., 186, 230 f.
  as Example, 126–8, 139, 147, 182
  as Glory, 31 f.
  as Guardian, 128, 144
  as Just One, 140
  as Judge, 150
  as Lord, 137 f.
  as Messiah, 100 f., 116

Christ, as Redeemer, 107
  as Saviour, 177, 212
  as Shepherd, 128, 162–5
  as Stone, 114–17
  His Pre-existence, 107 f., 145
  His Sinlessness, 107
  His Suffering, 146 f., 156, 161 f.
Church, 7, 9, 14, 90, 119 f., 128, 158
Cicero, 169
2 *Clement*, 179, 191, 204
Clement of Alexandria, 171, 219 f., 224 f.
Clement of Rome, 1, 42 f., 45, 64 f., 80, 87, 165, 193–5, 204
Cobden, 47
Confession (of Sin), 80
Conflicts, 56–8
Conscience, 16, 143 f., 147, 210
Consecration, 90 f., 115
Covetousness, 57 f.
Cramer, 144 f.
Cross of Christ, 117, 127 f.

DAVIDSON, A. B., 25
Death, 19, 83, 150 f., 159
Death of Christ, 92, 106 f., 127 f., 139 f.
Deeds, 40–5, 52
Demas, 12
Descent (of Christ), 145, 151
Desire(s), 18 f., 22, 56–8
Didaché, 80, 89 f., 104, 216, 224, 245
Diognetus, Epistle to, 120
Dispersion, 6 f., 89

ELDAT and MODAT, BOOK OF, 60, 63–5
Elijah, 81 f.
Eliot, George, 221 f.
Endurance, 9, 12 f., 16 f., 73 f.
Enemies, 136 f.
Enoch, 70, 92, 94 f., 98, 101 f., 108, 111, 140–2, 144 f., 149, 151,

247